# Too Young

## TO TRAVEL ABROAD

Agnes Woolsey
Married in 1863 to
Edgar Laing Heermance (1833-1888)
Their Children
Theodore Woolsey Heermance (1872-1905
Unmarried
Laura Woolsey Heermance (1874-1966)
Unmarried
Edgar Laing Heermance (1876-1953)
Married 1907 to
Nora Kate Livingston (1882-1954)

# Too Young

## TO TRAVEL ABROAD

### Journal of a Year
### of European Travel
### in 1856–7

*Illustrated*

*Agnes Woolsey*

*Introduction by*
*Louise Heermance Tallman*

Peter E. Randall Publisher
Portsmouth, New Hampshire
1995

© 1995 by Louise Heermance Tallman
Printed in the United States of America

Design by Tom Allen

Peter E. Randall Publisher
Box 4726
Portsmouth, NH 03802

Library of Congress Cataloging-in-Publication Data

Woolsey, Agnes, 1838-1915.
    Too young to travel abroad : journal of a year of European travel in 1856-7
: illustrated / Agnes Woolsey ; introduction by Louise Heermance Tallman.
    p- cm.
Previously published: Journal of a year of European travel in 1856-7. 2nd ed.
New Haven, 1882.
    Includes index.
Summary: The eighteen-year-old author chronicles her experiences visiting
antiquities, museums, and artists during the year she spent traveling on a
European Grand Tour.
    ISBN O-914339-53-2 (alk. paper)
1. Europe--Description and travel. 2. Woolsey, Agnes, 1838-1915-Journeys--
Europe. [1. Europe--Description and travel. 2. Woolsey, Agnes, 1838-l915. 3.
Diaries.] Title. II. Series; Woolsey, Agnes, 1838-1915. Journal of a year of
European travel in 1856-7.
D919.W88 1995
914'.04285--dc2O                                                95-36017
                                                                    CIP
                                                                    AC

# Contents

# The Travel Party

Agnes Woolsey
1838-1915

Mary Salisbury
1837-1875

"Auntie"
Abigail Phillips Salisbury
1814-1969

"Uncle"
Edward Elbridge Salisbury
1814-1901

# Introduction

In 1966 I discovered this manuscript in New Haven at the home of my aunt, Miss Laura Woolsey Heermance. This is the writing of a eighteen year old girl. Since I never had the chance to meet my grandmother Agnes, it was a real satisfaction to make her acquaintance through this journal she had written.

Agnes had been invited by her uncle Edward to join a year of travel with his wife and daughter Mary. Edward Elbridge Salisbury had served as Professor of Semitic Languages at Yale "without the expectation of pecuniary remuneration." In 1856 he resigned this post, as a qualified replacement had been found. When Agnes' father, Yale President Theodore Dwight Woolsey, learned of the travel proposal, he wrote to her from a Vermont vacation spot. He urged her to decline the invitation, saying that she was too young to appreciate what she would see. The following is part of the letter to Agnes from her father dated Aug. 21, 1856:

> I must now say a few words, my dear daughter, on the subject of your going abroad. I knew nothing of the project until near the time when I went from Kent, when your uncle first broke it to me. I don't feel that mere pleasure ought to be regarded by you as a sufficient motive; the question is what will be for your good. On that point I would say that you are quite too young to travel abroad, and if you should rest and study, you will study to disadvantage, except so far as the acquisition of the French spoken language is concerned. You cannot yet judge works of art, you know little of the modern history and little of the institutions of the countries you would see, and your mind needs the improvement of further discipline and study before you can see more than the outside of things. I think then, my very dear Child, I am consulting for your interest, when I advise and wish that you should not embrace this opportunity of seeing with your eyes those countries, of which you have heard so much. I think also that if your uncle, aunt and cousin go, your grandmother has some claim on you. She would not urge this. But you, under the circumstances, ought to stay and do what you can to take care of her in her increasing feebleness. I wish you to keep the latter part of this letter to yourself, and should be glad to hear from you soon. Remember me to Laura, Mattie and Helen, to Mary (Tomlinson) and the baby. Give

my love to Grandmama, and to the rest. I have written to uncle by this mail. There are as yet no good peaches here. If I can find some I will send them up by Express soon.

    Your affectionate father
    Theodore D. Woolsey

This letter would have been the supreme challenge. Did her father really think he could keep her from going abroad? We do not know what special promises may have been made. All we have is the record of a year of travel that was far more than mere pleasure. I feel that she tried very hard to prove that she had the maturity to appreciate what she saw. The year was certainly a real education. Uncle, as a seasoned traveler, was a superb guide.

Art works were a special focus on this trip. Not only does Agnes list the items seen, but often describes them with her opinions. The studios of American and European artists were visited. One could wish for more detail about these. There are notes on the history of the towns visited. Some references are made to current political figures such as Queen Victoria of England. Agnes noted that the author Thackeray made an unsuccessful attempt to enter politics. Through Great Britain, there are many literary associations.

Several years after her trip, Agnes copied the day-by-day notes into the neat notebooks as found. Pictures collected on the trip were pasted onto the pages. Thus the illustrations in this book are those collected by Agnes herself. I was sufficiently impressed with the wealth of material in the journal, that I embarked on making a typed transcript of the text. This was a project that stretched over two years. Often the fine, faded handwriting required a magnifying glass to decipher. In editing the text, changes have been kept to a minimum, mostly adjustments to spelling or punctuation.

The style of writing is very precise, typical of the Victorian ear. I had the feeling that Agnes would have had the best education of the times. The *New Haven City Directory* for 1856 lists no less than nine "Young Ladies' Seminaries." Letters discovered from Laura, younger sister of Agnes, express the intensity of school studies. A good variety of subjects were taught. A written composition was required each week. Besides keeping up journal entries for a year, Agnes wrote long letters home. These are preserved in the Manuscript Section of Yale Library. The Woolsey girls were great readers. Laura writes from New Haven of reading *Dred*, a new book by Harriet Beecher Stowe. The author was in Europe early 1857. Mrs. Stowe and her sister Mary were with the travel party on two occasions in Rome.

Through the nineteenth century many travel books were published, generally written by adults. Most of these are now regulated to the shelves of historical libraries. This text offers a fresh look at travel mid-century, from a youthful point of view. It is my hope that the book will prove to be of general interest to many readers.

Louise Heermance Tallman
Granddaughter of Agnes Woolsey

Hast thou a charm to stay the morning-star,
In his steep course? So long he seems to pause
On thy bald awful head, O sovran Blanc!
The Arve and Arveiron at thy base
Rave ceaselessly; but thou, most awful Form!
Risest from forth thy silent sea of pines,
How silently! Around thee and above
Deep is the air, and dark, substantial, black.

Chamonix

An ebon mass: meethinks thou piercest it,
As with a wedge! But when I look again,
It is thine own calm home, thy crystal shrine,
Thy habitation from eternity!
O dread and silent mount! I gazed upon thee,
Till thou, still present to the bodily sense,
Didst vanish from my thought: entranced in prayer
I worshipped the Invisible alone.

Samuel Taylor Coleridge

# Journal of a year of European travel in 1856-7

*illustrated*

## By Agnes Woolsey

*New Haven*

*2nd edition*

*1862*

*Agnes Woolsey*
*at the time of her European travels*

*Monday, Oct. 13th 1856, Adelphi House, Liverpool, England.*

This is my first day in England. We arrived this morning at about half past ten in the Cunard Steamer *Asia*. But to go back to the commencement of our voyage. We left New York on Wednesday the 1st of October, a bright and beautiful day. It was not long before we felt the first effects of sea motion, and we soon threw ourselves upon our berths in utter wretchedness. For three or four days more we had pleasant weather, until Sunday, when being off Newfoundland it became damp and cloudy and continued so all the rest of the voyage. We landed at the Landon Dock, a tender came to take off the Royal Mail, and then the custom house officers arrived to examine our luggage and finding nothing dutiable permitted us to land. Terra firma and soft beds are indeed delicious. We took breakfast in the English fashion and have already tried the two national dishes shrimps, and soles both of which I like very much. It is hard to realize where I am, there is so much similarity between this and our own land, and yet many differences. Our heads are still dizzy from the constant rolling motion we have had for nearly two weeks. We have much cause of gratitude for being brought safely across the great and wide sea, preserved from every danger.

*Tuesday, Oct. 14th, Liverpool.*

We have been to see the city today and the objects of interest which it contains, which are not so very numerous. We drove to the St. James' Cemetery and went in to look at it. It was formerly a quarry whence stone was obtained for the docks, and as so deep an excavation would be rather unsightly in such a city as this, the present use was made of it. A walk slopes down, partly through solid rock, to the bottom which is covered with graves. The perpendicular walls which surround the place are mostly covered with the English ivy and growing most luxuriantly and throughout the grounds are little clumps of shrubbery tastefully set out. The principal monument is one to Mr. Huskisson killed by the engine, at the celebration of the completion of the London and Manchester rail, one of the first laid and at which the Duke of Wellington was present. Of

St. George's Hall we saw only the exterior, it is a very large and fine building for concerts, etc. In front of the Exchange is a statue of Lord Nelson seated, an angel holds four crowns above his head. Death and Victory are by his side, at the four corners sit chained Africans and bas reliefs upon the monument represent his victories. It is in bronze or some other dark material.

Driving somewhat out of the city we came to Prince's Park. A terrace of fine houses overlooks these grounds, and through them winds an artificial river with green grass sloping down to the water's edge and trees and shrubs arranged in small enclosures which seems to be a common method. Many of the buildings are composed of Portland stone, the rest of dingy brick, variegated in color like mosaic. I have not seen a wooden house since I have been here. We have met friends in this house which is very delightful. They are Prof. Morse his wife Louisa and Miss Lyman the deaf mute, who are all to sail tomorrow in the *Atlantic*. Mr. and Mrs. and Helen Waterston whom we shall probably meet somewhere again as they intend to be abroad some time longer. We go up to London tomorrow having in a great measure recovered our senses after our sea voyage.

*Wednesday, Oct. 15th 1856, Thomson's Hotel, Berkley Square, London.*

We left Liverpool at half past eleven and traveled the distance of 212 miles in about eight hours, reaching London at eight. The rail cars are very different from ours. It is like a stage coach with six armed seats three facing three. The conductor called a guard locks the door of each car, both to keep the passengers in and prevent others from intruding. The seats are very comfortable and lamps are kept lighted to give light through the numerous tunnels with which some of the roads abound. The train we took, was not the swiftest one, which I believe, travels at the rate of fifty six miles an hour. The banks on either side of the track, were turfed and had often a hawthorn hedge at the top. I was delighted with the country, through which we passed; very few fences are to be seen hedges or rows of trees, mark the boundaries of the fields. We saw a great number of sheep, looking as plump and well fed as can be imagined, and so they ought, for they have the most exquisite green fields to feed in a perfect emerald green.

At Stafford we saw the first ruin of a castle that I have ever seen. It stood on a hill at some distance off and consisted of two rather low towers, with a communication between. Other ancient buildings appeared in various places, but we had no guide to tell their story. Several little churches pleased me very much, so picturesque were they covered with rich ivy. We experienced English weather, for we had showers a great part of the way. We passed through Litchfield where Dr. Johnson was born, and Rugby, where is the school founded in the reign of Elizabeth, and of which Dr. Arnold was the celebrated master. We are in the west end of London looking out upon an oblong enclosure called Berkley Square and it is very quiet for London.

*Thursday, Oct. 16th.*

A rainy day. The weather is said to be unusually rainy this autumn even for England or I should say London. Braving the rain however Mary and I took a little walk this morning into Regent St., to make one or two purchases. Antonio accompanied us, he is the courier whom Uncle engaged in Liverpool. He is a native of Malta though half Italian his last name is Saliba and he is a fine courier. This afternoon we drove out to 24 Gower St. to visit Dr. and Mrs. Boot. We saw the latter, who was very pleasant. She was delighted to see Auntie again. Then to the bazaar in Soho Square, where we were almost bewildered by the various beautiful things we saw, a perfect labyrinth of tables covered with every imaginable fancy articles. One thing that struck our taste was a leather basket, with implements for sewing arranged on the cover and around the sides, also writing materials envelopes etc., a box to hold sandwiches, a cup and a little flask for wine or water in traveling, with an open space for work or anything else. The whole could be easily carried on the arm. When we came home, we found Mr. Sidney Morse here.

*Friday, Oct. 17th.*

We have had a most interesting day rich in historical associations, and scenes of interest, which I will do my best to give the history of. We preferred today to take an outside view of the various buildings, and at another time to examine the interior, more particularly. We passed in the first place the city residence of the Marquis of Lansdowne one of the wealthiest peers in the realm, it was a large massy structure but somewhat dingy. Then entering Picadilly saw the Duke of Devonshire's house of brick and rather old looking. The mansion of Lord Palmerston, nothing very striking. Then came to the palace of the Duke of Wellington called Apsley House. It is close to the entrance of Hyde Park, a most elegant pile, where the iron duke died, and where the present one now resides. Opposite the entrance of the park (called Hyde Park corner) is a monument to his memory, an equestrian statue. Entering the Park by a splendid gateway, we passed on our right, a statue of Achilles holding in his arm a shield and pointing toward France, emblematical of the victories of Wellington, and presented to him by the ladies of England it was cast from cannon taken at the battles of Vittoria, Toulouse, Waterloo and Salamanca. A drive through Hyde Park is perfectly delightful, in the season which is summer it is the fashionable drive for nobility and gentry. The present is the dull season so that there are few, besides children playing about. The Serpentine River with it's pleasure boats is a beautiful piece of water, and the opposite shore is almost a fairy land with its smooth sloping green lawn, and clumps of splendid oaks. At one point we had a distant view of Kensington Palace, the gardens were hid by trees. Another gateway was brought from Buckingham Palace, called the Cumberland Gate, and is built of white marble. The park contains 388 acres and is called one of the lungs of London.

Leaving Hyde Park we drove in the direction of St. James' Park which was first formed and walled in by Henry VIII. Buckingham Palace, which is Queen Victoria's residence faces it. This is a very showy splendid building, extending the length of the square. The queen is not there now, so we shall probably visit the interior. The grenadiers who patrol in front are quite imposing with their fur helmets and scarlet coats. We passed the Duchess of Sutherland's palace, and that of the Duke of Bridgewater by whose direction the treatises bearing his name were written. The latter faced the street called Pall Mall; and also St. James Palace, a most interesting spot, it is built of brick, and has a very ancient appearance. Charles I lived here, and passed thence with Bishop Juxon through the park, to be executed at Whitehall. Marlborough House is near, facing also Pall Mall and having St. James' Park on its rear. Marlborough House where the Duke of Marlborough lived and where now the Prince of Wales resides, is made of the brown Portland stone, of which so many of the houses and palaces in London are built and is smoky with age. Continuing through Pall Mall we reached the column of the Duke of York, second son of George III and uncle of Victoria. At the top is his statue, which faces St. James' Park. Trafalgar Square came next in our route, it has in the centre a monument to Nelson and near by a statue of Charles I, in the spot where Charing Cross stood, built in honor of Eleanor queen of Ed. I and pulled down by Puritans. Northumberland Palace faces the "Strand" in view of the Square. It was built by Henry Howard, son of the Earl of Surrey the poet. He left it to Thomas

Howard Earl of Suffolk, father of Frances Countess of Essex and Somerset who lived there with her husband. Upon the roof are lions the Percy's emblem; only a part of the ancient building remains. We drove past the Admiralty, Horse Guards, and Treasury all fine buildings. Then on the left Whitehall, only the banqueting hall remains, built by Inigo Jones in 1619-1622, now the Chapel Royal. It was first used by Henry VIII and continued a royal residence till the time of Wm. III. On a scaffold behind the palace, Charles I was executed.

Next in order came Westminster Abbey and here description fails me, it must be seen, to be known. It was founded by Sebert king of the West Saxons, enlarged by Edgar and Edward the Confessor and rebuilt nearly as at present by Henry III and his son Edward the Ist. From Edward the Confessor to Victoria all the kings and queens have been crowned here. We left the interior for another time. The Houses of Parliament are upon the other side of the street. They are the largest buildings ever erected continuously in Europe and the largest Gothic edifice in the world. They perfectly overpowered me with their magnificence. It has taken sixteen years to build them, and a considerable part still remains incomplete. The architect is Sir Charles Barry. We crossed the Thames at Westminster Bridge. A new bridge is planned in the same style as the Parliament Houses. We continued on the Surrey side of London, through a place where several streets met, and the Elephant and Castle Inn stands, and then crossed the new London Bridge. The Tower of London was in sight looking down the river. At East Cheap was a statue of King Wm. IV on the spot where stood the Boar's Head Tavern famous as the scene of Falstaff's carousals with Prince Hal. We saw St. Paul's Cathedral built by Sir Christopher Wren in 1675. It is a fine though dingy structure, in front is a statue of Queen Anne. We passed the Post Office and then Newgate Prison. It has iron chains hanging emblematically over the doors, and seems strength itself. Smithfield now used as a cattle market but formerly martyrs were burnt next occupied our eyes and thoughts. Wat Tyler was killed here, and here were held the Batholemew Fairs. Near the Old Baily we got out of the carriage and walked down a lane leading to a spirit shop, to see a part of the old Roman wall of London. It appeared indeed very ancient, and interested us much, it formed part of a building and was ten or twelve feet high. Then we went to Lincoln's Inn Fields the haunt of lawyers and Cromwell was often here. It is a large pile of brick buildings and quite handsome. In the centre of the square Lord Russel was executed. We went next to Convent Garden Market the finest in London, near by is St. Paul's Church built by Inigo Jones. Upon Fish Hill we saw a monument to commemorate the great fire of London, designed by Sir C. Wren in 1666. Besides these things we saw the Exchange, the Bank, various fine club houses, asylums, hospitals, and famous streets. Then we returned to our Hotel.

In the afternoon we spent two hours at the British Museum but that we shall visit again, once is nothing in such a maze of wonders. I omitted to mention having seen in the morning, Exeter Hall a building where religious meetings are held, it is in the Strand. We passed through Temple Bar also. This which divides the old and new city is a gateway or arch of Portland stone built by Wren in 1670. It is never closed except when a sovereign is to enter the old city for the first time. A herald then knocks and after a parley, the gates are opened and the keys delivered to the sovereign by the Lord Mayor. It divides the Strand from Fleet St. The National Gallery we passed by it faces Trafalgar Square.

*Saturday, Oct. 18th.*

Went this morning through Covent Garden Market. It exhibits every variety of vegetables, fruit and flowers. The latter were beautiful. I bought a sweet nosegay of purple violets which at this season are quite remarkable. Peaches we saw and blackberries, plums, pears, and pomegranates and grapes. In the afternoon having before obtained a permit, we started off to view the interior of the New Houses of Parliament or Palace of Westminster as it is called. It is still in process of erection by Sir C. Barry on the site of the old one burnt down. It was commenced in 1840 and will still require several years to finish it. We entered by the Victoria Tower the largest square tower of that height I believe in the world. Here the queen enters and drives to the Royal Staircase when she goes on business to the House. The entrance arch is 65 feet high and its vault beautifully groined. After traversing the Royal Court, and various passages, the House of Peers broke upon us, in its gorgeous magnificence. Gilt and carved oak are tastefully and elegantly mingled, and the stained glass windows represent the kings and queens of England from Wm. the Conqueror to Wm. IV. The coats of arms of the kings and chancellors surround the chamber, beneath a light and beautiful gallery. The Throne with a splendid canopy and stool is at one end of the room and on each side seats for the Prince of Wales and Prince Albert. Above the throne are three frescoes, viz. Ed. III conferring the order of the garter upon the Black Prince; the baptism of Ethelbert; and Henry V submitting to Judge Gascoine after one of his youthful frolics. At the opposite end are frescoes of the Spirit of Religion, Law and Chivalry. In the centre of the room is the red wool-sack on which the Chancellor sits and seats for the peers. It is intended to be one of the most magnificent halls in the world; and certainly has claims to the distinction.

Passing thence through the Central Tower exquisitely groined, but not supported by pillars, we came to the House of Commons. This of course is not so splendid as that of the Peers but still there is a chasteness and subdued appearance which is very beautiful indeed. Strangers are admitted to hear the debate with an order from a member, and a gallery with a grating in front is intended for ladies. Leaving this and returning through the Central Tower again, we entered St. Stephen's Hall, where the chapel of the Old Palace stood. Along each side, stand upon pedestals statues of the men most distinguished for eloquence as Hampden, Walpole, Mansfield, Clarendon, Falkland, Selden, etc. This Hall leads into Westminster Hall, which is the old Parliament Hall, and exceedingly interesting, both from its associations, and the structure of the hall itself. The lower part has been lately altered, but the roof is the same one erected by Richard II and his favorite device of a white hart is seen in the molding. Wm. Ruful built the first hall on this spot, before Richard erected the present one. The roof is of hammer beams as they are called and carved with angels projecting outward, and it is most skillfully sustained without pillars. The early Parliaments were held here, and the very first, was to depose Richard II. The banners of Naseby were hung here, where Charles I was tried. Cromwell was inaugurated, and after his death, his head was stuck upon a pole in this hall. Sir Thomas Moore and the Protector Sommerset were doomed, Earl and Countess of Sommerset tried for Sir T. Overbury's murder and Strafford condemned here. Here also the seven bishops were acquitted in James II reign. And Lord Byron tried for killing Mr. Chaworth. Lord Melville's was the last public trial. And the last coronation dinner that of George IV. Some improvements are contemplated, but the roof will not be touched it is perfectly sound. It is the largest apartment unsupported by pillars in the world. We came out by St. Stephen's Porch and rode home through Long Acre a street in which Cromwell lived.

*Sunday, Oct. 19th.*

Went in the morning to hear Dr. Alexander Hamilton author of *Life in Earnest, Mount of Olives* etc. He preaches in a church on Regent

Square. The subject was Ishmael. I was very much interested in it, he has a good deal of the Scotch brogue and is sometimes a little difficult to understand. I had never seen so peculiar a church. The pulpit is on a level with the galleries, and is only large enough for one person. In a lower seat the Precentor sits to lead the singing. An afternoon service is not common in London so we went at half past six to hear the Hon. Rev. Baptist Noel. He left the Established Church on account of his convictions, and has become a Baptist minister, and preaches in a plain church to a plain congregation. I liked his discourse very much.

*Monday, Oct. 20th.*

This day was devoted to the Crystal Palace at Sydenham. We reached the place in an hour and a quarter starting at ten. The palace is much the same as the original one on Hyde Park, only considerably larger and a beautiful park is connected with it. In order to use our strength when it was most needed we explored the grounds first. The land slopes and advantage is taken of this, to form terraces, with stone arcades surrounding each. The upper one was ornamented with allegorical representations of the various large cities of the world in bronze. Flights of steps lead down to the next terrace, where were ponds edged with stone carved and angular, with fountains in the centre, and allegorical representations of the Thames, the Nile, and other rivers. Descending this terrace you reach the central fountains. We afterwards saw these playing and they were very beautiful as well as curious. They threw up jets in various shapes, some to the height of seventy feet. From the edge of some rose a kind of hedge of water, others came up in the form of baskets and many other devices. At no great distance from these were what appeared summer houses of colored iron work, rising from a basin of water. They also are fountains, the water rises up through the pillars to the centre of the roof, pours out from a figure at the top, and sheets of water flow over the whole, enveloping it with spray and flowing thence down a flight of steps, forms a pretty cascade. The effect must be exquisite but it only plays on grand occasions.

Wandering on wherever it looked most inviting we came upon a geological representation. From a rustic bridge you see several strata of rocks in layers, the carboniferous and limestone below it, and a fault was exhibited, where an under force had thrust up a portion of a lower strata so that it was in a different line from the rest. On the other side were huge representations, made of rock and stucco, of the animals of the secondary period, chalk, oolite, lias, and new red sandstone. Here was the Plesiosaurus the Icthiosaurus, the Iguanadon and various other sauri all arranged upon an island with their open mouths, ready to devour as it seemed, whatever should fall in their way. I had seen pictures and skeletons of these, but nothing so near the veritable animals, and shall probably never see anything nearer. The first part of the gardens was Italian in its arrangements and architecture and the most remote purely English, with its trees and flowers arranged in groups and clumps. The flowers were very beautiful for this season especially the rhododendrons. In the Italian part, were statues placed at every corner, copies from the most celebrated masters. There was the Apollo Belvedere Canova's Graces, Thorwaldsen's Mercury, and hundreds more that I know not. It was a perfect fairy scene, much like what I had heard described but hardly imagined real. The air was fresh and clear, the birds sang, and nature and art united to form a charming picture.

The interior of the palace was perfectly bewildering in its multitudes of objects, we knew not where to go or what to look at first. Five stories rose one above the other, that is four galleries above the lower floor, and surrounding the four sides. In the centre and scattered among trees and vines, were statuary in plaster or marble. Copies were there of Castor and Pollux from Monte Cavallo in Rome, and of the Toro Farnese. In large basins of water, from which fountains threw up their jets, grew rare water plants, the Victoria regia, the blue lily of the Nile and many others. The fig, the palmetto, and the century plant were to be seen growing in other places. What most delighted me were the courts of the Alhambra and Pompeii. These were arranged to be as nearly as possible models of the antique. The first was the Alhambra, on a somewhat smaller scale from the original but copied exactly. We entered by the court of lions. These animals sustain a marble fountain in a basin of the same and around it is in the original, an Arabic poem, of which, two lines are

_O you who behold these lions crouching fear not._
_Life is wanting to enable them to show their fury._

Passing thence through the Hall of Justice you reach the Hall of the Abencerrages. The ceilings and walls are covered everywhere with beautiful and gorgeous arabesques, while an inscription runs round the rooms in Arabic. The pavements are mosaic with some kind of character in it. A stalactite roof ornaments the Abencerrage's Hall of a pink and purplish color and the colors everywhere are most brilliant. Divans are placed upon the pavement and if the fountain had played and thrown up its crystal streams and soft music wafted through the air, with rich perfumes, I should verily have imagined myself transported to the ancient palace of Granada and its days of splendor returned. The House of Sallust at Pompeii was beautifully represented. *Cave Canem* was seen in mosaic at the entrance. We entered the atrium the roof of which was open to the air, and in the centre was a marble basin for water. Around this were the cubiculi and further on the Triclinium or drawing room, with statuettes and vases placed upon marble tables. Beyond was the Kystus or flower garden, and the Tablinii summer and winter dining rooms. A bath was to be seen, and more cubiculi, a banquet room, and niches too for the Penates, all perfect and beautiful. The walls were adorned with the frescoes found in this house, and the floor with many colored mosaics. It was a great enjoyment to see such a place, and to see afterwards the original will be still more interesting.

There was an Assyrian court too, with its great bulls and winged creatures, and an Egyptian and Byzantine one, all beautiful, interesting and instructive. There was much very much that we could not see, but we hope to revisit the palace and see more. Various manufactures are exhibited, most exquisite Bohemian and silver ware, and other more common objects, for sale, or merely for exhibition. This immense structure was first designed by Sir Joseph Paxton, and he had a large share in the rebuilding if it at Sydenham. It is not a government affair, a few private individuals manage the whole. They sent to Europe for copies of statuary and were mostly successful, though in some instances they were refused the privilege. At one time 6400 workmen from different countries were working together in perfect harmony. We wandered round in a maze of wonder and admiration, losing our way, and confused still more at every turn; till catching sight of some central object, we could at last define our true position. When this was the case, is it strange that we could not easily describe such a scene?

*Tuesday, Oct. 21st.*

We went today to the Zoological Gardens bordering upon Regent's Park, and saw a great many new and wonderful animals of which I will mention the most remarkable. I saw a rhinoceros, his skin is hard like a coat of mail almost, and a hippopotamus or "sea horse" as his name implies he swam about in a pool of water as he is in the habit of doing in rivers and lakes. There were several beautiful giraffes with spotted skins.

Dromedaries much resembling camels, and antelopes with long horns, turned backwards over their heads. There were lions and lionesses, tigers, hyenas and the huge white polar bear found in Arctic expeditions. Zebras, a reindeer, deer of various sorts, a lama, a sacred Ibis from Egypt, and ostriches, one of which was covered with beautiful black glossy feathers. Among smaller animals were, a beaver, a porcupine, a kangaroo, a bittern a most melancholy looking bird, and a cormorant, eagles, vultures, a flamingo, herons, and pelicans; these were most greedy creatures a basketful of fish that was thrown in to them was devoured in an amazingly short time. Peruvian sheep, a sloth and a sloth bear, an American tapir, and an armadillo. Storks also, owls which could scarcely keep their eyes open, in the glaring light of day, parrots, paraquets, beautiful pigeons, Sandwich Island geese, and various reptiles, among others, an anaconda, a rattlesnake, a chameleon, adders and what interested me perhaps more than all, a room with glass cases in which were living Polyps, axtinia of beautiful colors, moving their delicate tentacula and star shaped polyps. Living oysters, and fishes of many kinds, swimming in the glass cases, also water spiders and turtles. It must be an immense labor to take care of and feed all the animals.

*Wednesday, Oct. 22nd.*

We visited today the Bank of England, a very large building covering irregularly four acres. We went over the most interesting parts, into the vaults where the bags are kept and to the treasury, where we each took in our hands bank notes to the value of 5,000,000 dollars. We were shown the weighing room, the counting room and where the notes are printed, and books made for the use of the bank, all the parts of which are made in the building except the making of the paper. Employment is given to about 500 people men women and boys. The latter receive generally a shilling a day out of which they have to provide meals and lodging.

Thence we drove to the Tower of London a place of the most absorbing yet painful interest. We saw the Traitors gate from which a boat is necessary to cross a ditch of water to the Tower Yard. We went first to the Armoury in the White Tower built by Wm. the Conqueror and saw many figures on horseback, clothed in the actual armour, worn by the kings of England. Knights' armour of the time of Ed. IV and Henry VI and VII. The armour of Henry VIII, that of Charles Brandon, Frances Hastings, Earl of Huntingdon, Robert Dudley earl of Leicester with the bear and ragged staff and his initials R.D. That of Devereux Earl of Essex, James I, Thomas Howard earl of Arundel beheaded for aspiring to marry Mary Queen of Scots. George Villiars Duke of Buckingham, Wentworth earl of Strafford, George Monk, and James II. Henry son of James I and his brother Charles I are represented clothed in their armour when boys. A crusader in the time of Henry III. Stephen's armour and Edward the I's. Weapons used at the battle of Hastings and those in the Wars of the Roses. A gun carriage made from the wood of the *Royal George* lost in 1782 off Spilthead. We saw also the cloak on which Gen. Wolfe died before Quebec, the mask of Henry VIII's fool Will Somers and an executioner's mask. Chinese and Turkish armour, steel cross bows taken from the French at Cressy. We saw the axe used, as they said, in beheading Anne Boleyn, and the block on which Balmerino Kilmarnock, and Lovat were executed, on Tower Hill in 1746, with marks of the axe upon it.

From these rooms we were shown by the guide into Sir Walter Raleigh's cell; he was imprisoned and executed, on suspicion of joining the plan, to raise Arabella Stuart to the throne. It is a good sized cell but the place where he was locked up at night, is dark and small. We saw in the outer cell a figure of Queen Elizabeth with an imitation of her richly adorned dress. Here too we saw the thumb screw called the Scavenger's Daughter and a Spanish collar, horrible instruments of torture used in ancient times. The Beauchamp Tower had been used as a prison for many people. In the lowest story the Dudleys had been confined and we saw an inscription on the wall ROBERT DUDLEY. Some of this family were executed, the rest were spared. Ascending a staircase, along which prisoners had written their names, for with proper security they were sometimes allowed to walk about, we came to a room whose walls were quite covered with devices, names, and inscriptions, some of which we could decipher. One I found by Thomas Rooper 1570. "Per passage pénible passons ä port plaisant." Another "Mala conscientia facit ut tuta timeantur." G. Gyfford 1586 charged I believe with having attempted to poison Queen Elizabeth, and another by the same person "Dolor patientia vincitur." An oak tree with acorns and R.D. is supposed to be Leicester's. The name Peveril is found in several place, one is "Adoramus te" "Thomas Peveril 1571" Sir W. Scott makes his Peveril and Niegel to be imprisoned in the tower. As a special favor our guide, who was an old soldier and dressed in the style of Henry VIII, conducted us up still another staircase to his own room where he said Anne Boleyn and Lady Jane Grey had both been imprisoned. Probably the former was, but the Brick Tower is asserted to be the place where Lady Jane resided, and whence she was led to execution, but it is not possible to fix such things. A spot in the Yard is pointed out as the place of execution of Anne Boleyn. In this same Beauchamp Tower is the inscription "Egremond Radclyffe 1576 Pour Parvenir." only son of the Earl of Sussex, he rebelled against Queen Elizabeth. We saw but did not enter the Chapel of St. Peter erected in the time of Ed. I one story only is left of the old building and its floor is covered with boxes of records. In the Boyer Tower the Duke of Clarence was drowned in a bath of wine, by order of his brother Ed. IV. Tower Hill or rather its position is seen from upper windows. We went into the dungeon of the Tower where was the cell of Sir Thomas Moore and the rooms of torture, at the entrance of which was a niche, where a person stood concealed, and reported any words that the prisoner might let fall during torture. Beyond was the poisoning room, where heaps of bones were found, of unhappy victims, one of whom was Sir Thomas Overbury. In the tower the Countess of Somersett and her husband were imprisoned on account of his murder. I have not yet spoken of the Crown Jewels, they are exhibited in a glass case by a woman who has learnt her lesson like a parrot. In the centre is Victoria's crown, diamonds and precious stones shine resplendent and in front is a ruby worn by the Black Prince, the crown the Prince of Wales is to wear when older was also seen. Anne Boleyn's crown and that of James II's wife. We saw the Cohinoor diamonds, the largest in Europe, taken from the Sultan of Egypt. The state salt cellar in the form of the White Tower. The golden baptismal font for the royal children, scepters, bracelets, and Blue Sea Diamond and the communion service for state occasions.

Having passed through these interesting rooms we left wishing that a little more time could have been allowed us to examine at our leisure. We then visited St. Paul's Cathedral where are monuments to the most illustrious men of modern times and the graves of many. We went into the Choir and attended the service there, which was quite new to me. The chanting by boys dressed in white gowns, was quite beautiful, some of them had very sweet voices. The chapel or choir was ornamented with massive wood work and was but a small part of the whole church. The church is in the form of a Latin cross. We saw in a crypt below, by dim light, the tomb of Lord Nelson and that of Wellington not yet finished. There was a monument to Nelson above in the cathedral. We saw the grave of Wren the architect, of Benjamin West the American Painter,

Turner's grave who died in 1851, Sir Joshua Reynolds, and that of Sir Thomas Lawrence. We were shown some effigies the only remains of the old Church of St. Paul which stood on the same ground. It was a fearful gloomy place down in the crypt. In the upper part was a Sir J. Reynolds of Dr. Johnson and Lord Bacon. A monument to Lord Cornwallis, another to Admiral Howe and to General Abercrombie and an inscription to Brock. Statues of the Earl St. Vincent, Sir Astley Cooper the physician and Sir Wm. Jones, the Orientalist. A monument to Sir John Moore one to Admiral Rodney and another to Pictou and Ponsonby who fell at Waterloo. We came home well tired with our day's sights. I omitted to bring in, in the right place. the following which is a copy from the warder's copy of the original paper found in Sir Walter Raleigh's room on which he had written these lines:

> *E'en such is time, that takes on trust,*
> *Our youth. our joys, our all we have*
> *And pays us but with age and dust.*
> *Who in the dark and silent grave,*
> *Shuts up the story of our days.*
> *But from this earth, this grave, this dust,*
> *My God shall raise me up I trust.*

*Thursday, Oct. 23rd 1856.*

Visited Westminster. We entered at the Poet's corner it is full of interest. We saw Spencer's tomb, the inscription is "Here lies, expecting the second coming of our Saviour Jesus Christ, the body of Edmund Spencer, the Prince of Poets in his time, whose divine spirit needs no other witness than the works which he left behind him." died 1598. (I have just been interrupted by the call of Mr. Waddington, Pastor of the "Pilgrims Church" in London, the descendant of the first church of the Pilgrims in England. This congregation is about to build a new church of the same name, where the records and letters of the pilgrims are to be kept, part of the money is to be contributed by Americans.) Above is an inscription to Butler author of *Hudibras*. One to Ben Johnson is,

> *O rare Ben Johnson, what a turncoat grown,*
> *Thou ne'er was such till thou wast carved in stone.*
> > *Died 1637.*

On the other side is Milton's monument, and below that one to Gray, it is a Lyric Muse holding his medallion likeness, and pointing up to Milton with the words,

> *No more the Grecian Muse unrivalled reigns*
> *To Britain let the nations homage pay;*
> *She felt a Homer's fire in Milton's strain*
> *A Pindar's rapture in the lyre of Gray. Died 1771.*

Prior is buried here, and Gay, who wrote his own epitaph

> *Life is a jest and all things show it*
> *I thought so once, but now I know it. Died 1732.*

There is a monument to Oliver Goldsmith 1774. Dr. Johnson, David Garrick, Sheridan, and Campbell lie buried here under the pavement. Campbell has a monument 1684. Thompson and Southey, Poet Laureate 1843. Wm. Shakespeare, a full length statue the lines are:

> *The cloud capped towers, the gorgeous palaces,*
> *The Solomon temples, the great globe itself,*
> *Yea all which it inherits shall disolve,*
> *And like the baseless fabric of a vision*
> *Leave not a wreck behind.*
>
> *The Tempest.*

Addison, Camden, Handell, Drayton, Cowley and Dryden are all either buried, or commemorated in some way. Dr. Busby is buried here. Isaac Watts and Sir Isaac Newton have monuments. In a very ancient tomb like a sarcophagus the old poet Chaucer rests. Sebert king of the East Saxons and founder of the Abbey is buried in it. Edward the Confessor also. In his chapel are the coronation chairs, one has in the seat the old stone, from Scone on which the Scotch kings were crowned, and the other is the consort's chair. Henry VII chapel is very beautiful. He and his wife lie in sarcophagi enclosed by an iron screen, and in the nave are the banners of the Knights of Bath, who received their installations here. You enter by a portcullis ornamented with the entwined roses of York and Lancaster, and other symbols. Mary Queen of Scots lies on one side, and Mary and Elizabeth on the other. Near the Scotch queen is a small statue of the wife of Sir Robert Walpole erected by her son Horace. Gen. Monk and Lord and Lady Granville have a monument near. Most of the kings and queens of England as far back as Edward the Confessor are entombed in various chapels in the Abbey. Villiers Duke of Buckingham,

Frances daughter of Charles Brandon and mother of Lady Jane Grey, and the unfortunate Arabella Stuart are buried here. There are monuments to Pitt, Fox, and Canning and Lord Chatham who are also buried in this place. In the baptismal chapel is a statue of Wordsworth sitting on a rock, in a meditative attitude. Major Andre of revolutionary memory is buried here and has a monument and also Cecil son of Lord Burleigh and Mrs. Oldfield the actress, Sidney Earl Godolphin, and Lord Hansdon cousin to Queen Elizabeth. There is a monument to Sir Fowell Buxton and another to Wilberforce he has a pleasant face but quite aged. The Percy's vault (Northumberland) is in one of the chapels. The shape of the Abbey is the Latin cross with the addition of one end of Henry VII's chapel. It has lancet arches with civet terminations and a clerestory above the arches and below the windows. Wherever you turn great and noted names attract your eye. But we had to go under the guidance of a verger and he hurried us so through the chapel, and ran over his explanations so glibly that while we were looking at one chapel he would be off to the next and we would lose what he said about that. And then the doors were shut and we had to depart, but we hope to go again. After this we visited the Chapel Royal, which was formerly the banqueting hall of Whitehall and all that remains of that ancient palace. This Hall was the work of Inigo Jones and the frescoes upon the ceiling by Rubens, they represent scenes from the life of James I and Charles I and symbols of the state of the times. The queen herself does not attend worship here; she has a private chapel in her own palace, but there is a service here every Sabbath. French is Dean of Westminster Abbey, but he does not preach till later in the season, we hoped to have heard him.

*Friday, Oct. 24th.*

Went to visit the museum of the East India House. The hour of opening was past, but Prof. Wilson, Prof. of Sanscrit at Oxford kindly showed us the curiosities to be seen, taking us even into his private room where were the most valuable articles. There were the ornaments worn on the turban by the wealthy sheiks made of gold and set with rubies and diamonds which being badly cut had the appearance of glass. There are bracelets of pearl, etc. necklaces and a curious gold chain elaborately wrought. There was a ring with an immense sapphire in it and a model of a very large diamond, bought I believe by the Marquis of Winchester for the top of his court sword. He showed us many very ancient coins some of them gold some Grecian left by Greeks who penetrated as far as

India. We were much interested in an ornamented silver plate found at Badakschan, and which very probably had graced the side board of Alexander the Great. A gold mask taken from the mummy of an Assyrian king, Nebuchadnezzar perhaps, it was probably taken after death, when the features had shrunk. A beautifully enamelled gold plate of later times attracted us it was enamelled with birds and flowers much better than we do it in Europe or America.

The department of natural history was very fine, we saw monkeys with long white hair hanging around them, beautifully plumaged birds, among which was the Adjutant or scavenger bird, the mantis also a sacred insect. There were models of native fruit, the jack-fruit, the juju-ber, custard apple and others. There were bones of an antediluvian deer, the height of his forelegs was perhaps eight feet, and it had four horns. Model of a turtle two thirds the original size was immense. Models of Chinese villas carved out of ivory and mother of pearl, of pagodas, and the car of Juggernaut. A statue of Buddha. The state chair of Rungcet Singh. Chinese compasses and lanterns. A hoodjah or seat to be placed on an elephant with a canopy and trappings. We saw also a very perfect Roman mosaic of figures, found under ground, in front of the East India House. We returned calls at Mr. Dallas' American ambassador. In the evening called at Dr. Boots'. Received calls from Mr. and Mrs. Gellibrand and last evening from Mr. and Mrs. Ropes.

*Saturday, Oct. 25th.*

We had made our plans to go today to visit the interior of Buckingham and St. James' Palaces, but found that they were not now visible. So we decided to go to Kew to the Royal Botanical Gardens. It is about five miles from London, on the road to Kensington Turnham Green and Chiswick. The gardens are very delightful and are fine examples of English Landscape Gardening. The trees and shrubs grow perfectly and have room for full development. The dahlias are very splendid, whole beds full of all varieties of color and rather dwarfed in size. It seems to be the English way to plant flowers of a kind and color in beds by themselves and the effect is very pleasing. There were as many as twenty-two conservatories or hot-houses. Some of the varieties of pine were very beautiful, in the Norfolk Island Pine the branches were very delicate and slightly curved upwards, another almost feathery in its foliage, drooped downwards. There were palms, as the sago, the fan, the Chinese, the cocoanut, the date, the oil, and the vegetable ivory palms.

A banana tree, a coffee, and a mahogany tree, and what is very uncommon a small banyan tree with its many roots, descending from the branches. Many cacti and aloes not beautiful but curious. The cohineal, with the insect. The India rubber tree, the guava both red and white, and a plant called elephant's foot, it looked like the trunk of an old, very old tree, with the bark covering the top also, from which grew delicate little vines, which constituted the leaves of this singular plant. Some of the orchidae were exquisite, one resembled a pink iris. There were also water plants several Victoria Regia and variously colored Nympheae or water lilies, and one papyrus from Egypt quite a tall plant and growing in the water. There was one plant there of which I have lost the name, its leaves were enormous as large as the Victoria's only not growing like them upon the surface of the water. One most delicate little plant was the Lace Leaf from Madagascar exactly answering to the name. There is also a museum in the grounds where very curious vegetable productions are exhibited. There are mosses and lichens gathered in the late expeditions in search of Sir John Franklin. Specimens of what can be made from peat prepared in a certain manner, and a glass case containing leaves and flowers of many kinds, showing the fibers only and perfectly white. They were soaked first in stagnant water to allow the fleshy parts to decay, and then bleached in chloride of lime. Flowers made of small shells and colored. Paper made from the cable of the *Royal George* after being sunk. A specimen of paper made from straw, and rice paper cut from the pith of the rice plant. Nankeen cotton from Malta and specimens to show the process of making it into cloth. A model in wax of the flower of the rafflesia, an immense thing, perhaps six feet in circumference. A section of the mustard tree of Scripture, about a foot and a half in diameter large enough certainly for the birds of the air to rest upon. There was a section also of an unknown tree, polished like mahogany and about eight feet I should think in diameter. In the grounds were fine holly trees evergreens of many kinds and a Turkey oak whose acorns were singular. Rhododendrons and magnolias were in great profusion. In one of the greenhouses, was, a camphor tree and a cinnamon tree. The Deodar cedars from the Himalayan Mts. were very fine.

*Sunday, Oct. 26th.*

We went in the morning to hear Dr. Cummings of the Scotch National Church. There was a great crowd some had to stand. Communion was received after the elders had first distributed silver tokens of membership. The body of the church first received it, they then left and others took their places. A very beautiful discourse was delivered by Dr. Cummings on the VIIth chapter of Rev. 13th verse. In the afternoon we went to Westminster Abbey. The service was conducted by Mr. Wordsworth a brother of the Poet. We were late and had to take seats far off on account of the crowd so that we could not hear much. The organ sounded very finely, echoing through the vast aisles, and among the graves of the dead. It was an impressive scene. When we came out the bells chimed sweetly, and we saw the last of Westminster Abbey for the present I hope not forever.

*Monday, Oct. 27th.*

We have been again to the British Museum and spent four hours in wandering delighted through its almost numberless halls. Before we spent most of our time in the room devoted to the Elgin marbles. The frieze of the Parthenon is the chief object brought from Athens and in quite a good state of preservation where parts are wanting they are supplied by models. Today we examined first the Assyrian sculptures many are from Kourunjik. There was an obelisk of black marble covered with inscriptions from the Central Mound. The Egyptian halls were well filled. Rameses II (Sesostris) was often repeated in statues. We saw the Rosetta stone discovered by M. Bouchard and delivered to the English according to certain stipulations. It has been the key to the language of Hieroglyphics, as there are inscriptions in Greek, common Egyptian and Hieroglyphics, upon it of the same thing. It is a black stone and one of the most interesting things in the Museum. We saw what is called the sarcophagus of Cleopatra and various mummies. We saw a cylindrical history of Sennacherib, very perfect in the forms of the letters. Various bits of stone inscribed with the names of Darius, Cyrus, and other kings. Plates of bronze, bronze shields, seals and ornaments to be placed on mummies, papyrus writing. A column from Cairo in the true Egyptian style. Beautiful and numberless vases from Etruria Corfu Greece etc. The Townby sculptures Actaeon Satyrs etc. and the Lycian marbles, remains of an Ionic monument. A colossal statue having Belzoni's name written upon the pedestal. The head of a king, ten feet high to the top of the snake ornament on his hair, the whole figure must have been twenty or thirty feet. We saw Roman remains found in Britain, and British relics. Arrow heads found in the ruins of Persepolis. Copy of the Portland Vase. Chinese bottles found in Egypt. Roman fibulae found in Britain and helmet weapons etc. There was beautifully carved ivory which when found, was ready to crumble to pieces, but by a process discovered, were restored by the addition of animal matter. They were from Assyria. Stuffed birds and animals were well represented, and such a beautiful and complete collection of shells I never expect to see again. Corals, minerals, and fossils were to be seen. In short it is a perfect museum. We saw some chess men large and finely carved made from walrus tusks and found in one of the Hebrides. I feel as if I had seen but a small part of the whole it would take days to examine it well. It is free of charge and most perfectly arranged. What advantages the Londoners have for gaining knowledge! specimens of everything all ready for examination.

*Tuesday, Oct. 28th.*

I received today my fourth letter from home, they had not then received one of mine though I have written five. Uncle wrote several days ago to the Archbishop for permission to visit Lambeth Palace which he granted. Accordingly today Auntie Mary and I drove out to see it. The present Archbishop's name is Sumner and his predecessor was Howley who died about nine years ago. The family are now at Addington Park where they reside when Parliament is not in session. The building is in the form of a square, the gateway is as old as Henry VII but except the Lollards' Tower and the chapel all had been built over by Archbishop Howley. We entered first the private library, over the mantel piece hung a portrait of Archb- Warham by Holbein. Upon the sofa was a worked cushion with the Eaton arms and "floreat Etona" upon it. The Archbishop was an Etonian. There was a fine view of the garden and grounds from the windows. We went into the drawing room a fine spacious apartment but the furniture was covered, and the carpets were taken up. Here was a portrait of Bishop Newton who wrote a commentary on the prophecies. In an adjoining room was a picture representing the four fathers of the Christian Church, St. Chrysostom, St. Augustine, St. Jerome, and St. Gregory. In a sort of vestibule was a chest which had belonged to Archb- Land, of carved wood, and very heavy. We entered the chapel next. A wooden screen very richly carved, was placed there by Land, above this was a sort of gallery. Under the marble pavement Bishop Parker had been buried, but during the Commonwealth the body was removed and the chapel used as a dancing saloon.

Passing through this we came to the Post room as it was called, leading to the Lollards Tower, and where a mock trial was sometimes held.

The regular prison was up a long flight of steps, becoming more and more narrow until we came to a small unpainted room, at the very summit of the Tower. Around the walls are rings to which the poor creatures had been chained. Names and sentences were written about the walls. Here hundreds of poor victims lost their lives, some by suffocation, some by plague and in various ways. In the door (O extremity of cruelty) was a hole or trap door, through which food was sometimes shown to the poor creatures, but of which they were not allowed to partake. The Lollards were persecuted in the beginning of the 14th century for their religious opinions. Connected with the palace is a fine large library of 25,000 volumes, and manuscripts of great value. The dining room was ornamented with the portraits, of most of the Archbishops, since the reign of Mary and some before. The one we particularly noticed was Chichely, called the boy bishop, because so young, when promoted to the see, and under whom was the chief persecution of the Lollards. Among others were, Cranmer, Land, Juxon, Cardinal de la Pole, Sutton, Howley, Hooper an the present one Sumner. In another hall were Gardiner, Bishop Berkeley Herber when a boy, Catherine Parr, Henry son of James I and Sir Robert Walpole who lived in the reign of Queen Anne. Behind the Lollards Tower is a niche where once the statue of Thomas à Becket stood.

Returning from here we passed a bridal party, two carriages with four horses and postillions dressed in pink silk vests and white coats. The bride was in one carriage and the bridegroom in the other; it is the fashionable way. We went afterwards to spend an hour at Madame Tussard's wax work exhibition. Upon entering I seated myself on a settee where was a gentleman who seemed observing a group of wax figures in front of us. He turned his head as if to look at me, and it was some time before I found that he also was one of the show, it was William Cobbet. We saw the royal family of England, the late and the present emperors of Russia, the Dowager Empress, and the Emperor, and Empress of Austria. Queen Charlotte the wife of George III, and the Princess Charlotte daughter of George IV, Mary Queen of Scots, Henry VIII and his wives, Paginini an Italian violin player, Nelson Pitt, Fox, etc. Voltaire, Marie Antoinette and Louis XVI and their children. A royal cot with the infant prince and princess, Jean d' Arc, Jenny Lind in costume of *Daughter of the Regiment*. Madame Tussard herself, watching the prostrate body of Madame St. Amaranthe. Washington Wellington after death, lying in state, Cardinal Wolsey, Oliver Cromwell, Shakespeare, Prince

Menschikoff, Lord Raglan, Omar Pasha the Turkish Commander, and Napoleon in a grey suit. They were life size, and mostly dressed in clothes that the persons had themselves worn. It was most difficult to distinguish real persons from the wax. There was a room of horrors, containing celebrated murderers, thieves, etc., which we had no desire to enter. We leave tomorrow for Folkstone and thence to Paris.

*Wednesday, Oct. 29th, Folkstone.*

We left London for Folkstone at twelve, saw in the station Mrs. Richards and son fellow passengers in the *Asia*. We rode about two and a half hours and were then accommodated in the Pavilion at Folkstone, which overlooks the channel, while in the distance, to the left, are the white cliffs of Dover. The hotel is very full of permanent boarders, though the town is in itself anything but attractive. It was pleasant to get out of the fog, for when we left London, it was so thick, that we could see but little before us, and very damp.

*Thursday, Oct. 30th, Paris.*

The steamer for crossing the English Channel left at half past ten. It was small but quite comfortable. We had heard so often of the roughness of this passage and that it was worse than crossing the Atlantic, that we all feared renewing our sea-sickness. The day was very fine though there was considerable wind. But by lying down, all the way over, we passed the two hours, without much inconvenience and arrived safely on the shore of France, at Boulogne. I soon realized that I was in France for a jumble of French was immediately heard, and "Ces sont d' Angleterre" some one said as we passed. I omitted to mention that I saw in the steamboat a Mr. Fiale whom I saw last summer at the White Mts. He is going to Egypt. It seems so singular to have met him here, I little thought last August, where I should be now.

The road to Paris is very uninteresting, we pass through Amiens and Abbeville, at the former place is quite a fine cathedral of Henri IV's time. The women were working in the field with the men and with caps only upon their heads. We arrived at last though the way was long and were deposited in the Hotel Brighton Rue Rivoli. It overlooks the garden of the Tuilleries and the view is fine. The people and everything look strange to my eyes. Gen's d'armes stand at the corners of the streets or pace up and down. I have had to try my tongue, at French a little, I was understood though how correctly I spoke I cannot tell.

*Friday, Oct. 31st, Hotel Brighton, Rue Rivoli.*

Took a walk in the gardens of the Tuilleries with Uncle and Mary. We passed through these and then the place Louis XVI and so back to the Hotel, we saw the Arc de Triumphe in the distance. Saw Mrs. S. Morse and Mrs. Livingston. Attended to a coiffeur etc.

*Saturday, Nov. 1st, Paris.*

This is "All Saints' Day" and tomorrow "All Souls Day" among the Catholics, both fete days, when a work is abandoned, and all give themselves up to pleasure. M. and I went with Antonio to the Church of St. Rock, where service was to be performed, to see for ourselves this form of worship. The church was quite full when we entered. Chairs are let for two sous apiece, and these are the only seats. A funeral service had just been performed and after the black cloths had been removed the music began. We were disappointed in this, The sound was harsh and consisted of trumpets, organ and singing. As for the rest of the service I can not tell what it was each seemed to pray for himself and all rose or knelt together. Then the beadle in a cocked hat, trimmed with white feathers, and with red trousers, and epaulettes came among the people. He was followed by two men with bags to receive money for the church. The first one said he made his way about "allons entree ici ´sil vous plait". Then came a beadle up the centre aisle followed by four boys, each two bearing a tray and two flat loaves of bread surrounded by long wax tapers. This was bread, which after being blessed, was to be given to the people, if faint, by their long stay in the church. The bread was elevated, censers thrown into the air, and then we left, for the wafers were to be distributed in the communion. It looked like a mere mummery of worship; but probably many enter into it with truly religious feelings.

After a dejuner a la fourchette, we took a carriage for a drive to see the city and the people. We passed the Place de la Concorde, or Louis XVI as it was formerly called, which we had seen yesterday. In the centre is the Column of Luxor, presented by the Egyptian government to Louis Philippe. The builder was Sesostris 1550 B.C. and it is covered with inscriptions. This Place must be named in ridicule, de al Concorde, for up to 1795 2,800 persons had been guillotined here including Louis XVI, and Marie Antoinette besides Robespierre, Danton and other revolutionists. The Champs Elysées came next in our route this is a long avenue of trees which make a pleasant shade for a promenade. The Hotel d' Industrie or Crystal Palace is here at present empty. There is more stone about it than the one at Sydenham. A band of medallions encircles it, in the middle, containing the heads of artists. We came then to the Barriere de l'etiole which marks the limits of the city on that side, and where custom house officers wait to examine whoever enters. Just beyond stands the Arch de Triomphe, erected in honor of Napoleon, and begun in his time. It is modeled after the Arch of Constantine at Rome, and it is a very magnificent structure. Bas reliefs represent the victories of this hero, and emblems of strength. The names of his battles are inscribed on medallions below the cornice, and a frieze represents some scenes in his history. Soon after passing this we turned into a side street to see La Chapelle Ferdinand. Upon this spot, Ferdinand Duc d'Orleans son of Louis Philippe was killed by jumping from his carriage when the horses were running away. He was greatly beloved by the people, and it is thought that if he had lived the revolution might have been avoided. The chapel is a very small Greek cross, upon a marble pedestal lies an effigy of the Duke said to be an excellent likeness. At its head is an angel sculptured by his sister Mary of Wurtemberg, it is beautifully executed. She designed a model for the Joan d'Arc at Orleans, which was not however made use of.

*Sunday, Nov. 2nd, Paris.*

We went in the morning to the Taitbout Chapel a French Protestant church and not connected with the government. We heard M. Du Pressance but M. Fish is the regular pastor. There were no pews wooden chairs of a very common sort supplied their place. The text was "Je crois Seigneur aide moi dans mon incredulité." It was an earnest and interesting discourse. In the afternoon went to the Marboeuf church, and heard an English Episcopal service by an unknown clergyman.

*Monday, Nov. 3rd, Paris.*

Cold November weather. We were shopping the principal part of the day. It is tiresome work.

*Tuesday, Nov. 4th, Paris.*

More shopping. We have finished now for the winter at least I hope so.

*Wednesday, Nov. 5th, Paris.*

Our hearts were this day rejoiced by more letters from home. They had not received any of ours when these were written. We made some calls today, saw Mrs. S. Morse and Mrs. Livingston. Mr. Sheffield and family have gone to Germany, Mr. and Mrs. Howland and Georgie Woolsey to Italy and Mrs. Müter was not at home. Mrs. Colgate and Mary Morse called on us today and we shall probably see them in Italy. We have finished our affairs here leaving the sights for another visit, and start tomorrow for Hyéres which we shall not reach before Tuesday or Wednesday of next week. We saw in the Champs Elysées a bronze statue of Joan d' Arc to be placed at Dornbiny her birthplace.

*Thursday, Nov. 6th, Fontainbleau.*

We left Paris this morning, and on our way to the station, saw a number of interesting buildings, and localities. We passed the Hotel de Ville of revolutionary memory and the Palais Royal the palace of the Dukes of Orleans. Within this, is a court which is a favorite promenade for the citizens, and a church whose bell gave the signal for the Massacre of St. Bartholemew. The Place de la Bastille was a very interesting spot. The Old Bastille was torn down, in the revolution that brought the Orleans family to the throne; but in its place stands a bronze column, with a gilt figure of Liberty on the top, and the names of 504 of those patriots who perished at the time and the dates "27th 28th and 29th of July 1830." The column stands in a central place, where many streets meet. Near by is a small café where some of the opposers of the revolutionists were fiercely besieged.

In the depot we met Mr. and Mrs. Wheeler and their two daughters, traveling in the same direction that we are, and made their acquaintance. We knew them from the resemblance of Mrs. W. to Miss Davenport of N.H. her twin sister. The country through which we passed, was rather interesting from its peculiarities. We saw the vineyards, quite dry now, the vines were low, and looked more like small raspberry bushes, than anything else. The villages were singular, the houses irregular and with steep roofs. We crossed the Marne and the Seine and stopt a moment at Melun, taken by Henry Vth of Eng. and retained for a time by the English. We drove a mile from the railroad to the town of Fontainbleau. We sent immediately for a permit to visit the chateau, but were exceedingly disappointed, to be entirely refused admission; for the Emperor is coming in a week, to hunt in the forest and everything is in disorder. This is a very old palace, it was used by Philip Augustus, and before that by Louis VII, though more as a hunting seat, than a palace. It was more magnificently rebuilt by Frances I, and at a late period, added to, and restored by Louis Philippe. We were permitted to enter the grounds and see the outside of the buildings, they are quite picturesque in form. At the foot of the principal staircase, in one of the courts, Napoleon bade farewell to his guards previous to his departure for Elba. In the building to the right he signed his abdication, in that to the left Pope Pius VII was confined by Napoleon, when he refused to permit the Emperor, to marry again. We walked in the gardens, they are not very well kept at this season, and we could see but a part. The trees are cut in various shapes, some looked like pears, in other places were arches of trees, forming a beautiful vista. Within the palace are many interesting things but like Tantalus, they are in sight, but beyond reach. But we did not waste time in this visit to Fontainbleau; we took an open carriage and set out to view the famous forest. To quote from the guide book, "Perhaps no forest presents such a variety of picturesque views, rocks, ravines, valleys, plains, - all are found here, the woods abound in every variety of tree; the meadows lawns and cliffs present every species of plant and flower." It contains nearly 3500 acres. The day has been very cold, we saw ice an inch thick in one place, and the shade of the trees, was not as grateful as it otherwise would have been, but the sky was very clear and the sunset clouds exquisite. We had not a great while to spend before night and so visited only the principal parts in our ride. We came first to a point where eight forest roads meet; in the centre is a cross on a pile of stones, where as the story runs, Henry IV met a spectre horseman on the night before his assassination. It is a rendezvous for hunters; where many a king has started for the chase, and here in a few days the Emperor will assemble his hunting party. We next left the carriage to go on foot to see several curiosities. We passed the hermitage of Franchard who lived, it is said, in the reign of Philip Augustus. Then an oak planted by Maria Theresa, and the "Roche qui pleure" which was formerly thought to have medicinal properties, It is a little water which trickles from the rocks, and we sipped the wonderful beverage. Then after stopping at the gorge of Franchard where is a more extended view of the hills and wood we returned to the carriage. We saw many a tree which looked like a primitive inhabitant. But those that were pointed out to us were, the "Boquet du Roi" 400 years old, the tallest in the forest, with its leaves near the top. "Les Deux Fréres" very old also and much alike. We enjoyed our ride exceedingly, the avenues of trees are very beautiful and the vistas lovely. We are in a very comfortable French inn. The floors are all waxed and without carpets. We had at lunch some of the fresh grapes which were very nice, though the crop is much smaller than usual.

*Friday, Nov. 7th, Hotel du Cloche, Dijon.*

It has been a delightfully clear day, though cold. As we left Fontainbleau the market was being held in one of the streets, and we met women riding upon their donkeys, a pannier on each side, in one of which they placed their feet; they looked quite picturesque. I was quite interested in the country through which our ride today led us. The road was almost lined with vineyards, the chasselas grape which grows in these parts, is quite celebrated. We stopt at Montereau for an hour. This is the scene, of the murder, of Jeans sans Peur one of the Dukes of Burgundy, by order of the Dauphin (Charles VII) in a conference, which they held, to arrange a union of themselves, against Henry V of Eng. We then rode for some distance on the banks of the Yonne. The Seine and Yonne unite at Montereau. We passed through Sens and saw the cathedral upon a hill. It is early Gothic, or transition Norman, and resembles Canterbury, whose builder was Wm. of Sens. Here are to be seen, we read, the garments of Thomas á Becket, for he fled to this place from England. We stopt a moment at Villeneuve, and Joigny, ancient towns, also St. Florentin. About 14 miles thence is the Abbey of Pontigny, where Becket also lived, and Stephen Langton Archbishop, when banished from Eng. by King John. We are here in Dijon the capital of the Dukes of Burgundy, and there are some interesting memorials of them here, which I hope we shall see. The apartments we have were occupied 3 months ago by the Emperor, he had Uncle and Auntie's room, but in ours only the cook was accommodated, which was quite a disappointment. The former master of the hotel was an old soldier of Napoleon's and much attached to him. He used to give better wines, to those who praised his Emperor.

*Saturday, Nov. 8th, Hotel de l'univers, Lyons.*

Left Dijon at half-past twelve but had time first to take a hasty survey of the objects of interest in the place. We stopt at the cathedral of St. Benine, here were found the remains of Philip le Hardi and effigies of others. The Church of St. Jean 1466 is noted for being the place where Bossuet was baptized and near which he lived. Notre Dame partly finished in 1229 is an example of the purest Gothic style, short pillars, alternate with plain stone work. Upon one end is the clock tower, whose clock struck by two hammer men was brought from Courtrai in Flanders by Philip le Hardi in 1382. The Palais de Justice is an example of the renaissance style, or Louis XIV, with much of this work upon it. The most interesting objects were in the Museum. This room is the Guard Chamber of the ancient palace of the Dukes of Burgundy and is almost all that remains. The kingdom of Burgundy was founded about 414, and continued until some time in the 6th cent. when it was united to France. At a much later period, 1342, king John of France, granted the duchy, as it then was, to his son Philip le Hardi, who thus became the founder, of the second Burgundian line, including Frauche Comte and Artois in his rule, and entirely independent of France. We saw the effigies of Philip and his son Jean whose wife was Margaret of Bavaria. They were originally in the Chartreuse or Ducal burial place of Dijon and have at last found a resting place in their ancient hall. The figures rest upon a pedestal carved with arches and monks in various attitudes weeping. We saw a bas relief in white marble from the Sainte Chapelle, and two guilt folding chapels used by the Dukes in traveling. The caskets of some of the duchesses are to be seen made of ivory and a bag which belonged to Isabella of Portugal wife of Philip le Bou. The crosier of St. Robert first abbot of the Cistercians 1098 and a wooden cup of St. Bernard's. And portraits of the four Dukes of the second line. We saw a fine statue of Bossuet and busts of Louis XIV and Le Grand Condé for whom was laid out the park which we saw only from the outside.

We saw many vineyards on the road from Dijon towards Lyons. This is the most celebrated wine country. The Cote d' Or wines are made between Dijon and Chagny. The principal place on the route was Chalons sur Saone, where we left the Yonne and followed the Saone. About two miles hence is the Abbey of St. Marcel where Abelard died (1142) and was first interred. We passed Macon where Lamartine was born and Trevoux where the Jesuits compiled the Journal de Trevoux. The ride was rather tedious we arrived in Lyons at half past eight.

*Sunday, Nov. 9th, Lyons.*

We went to the only English church in a little narrow street full of stables etc. A little snow in the morning cold, wet, and disagreeable.

*Monday, Nov. 10th, Hotel de Bristol, Marseilles.*

We left Lyons this morning without seeing much of the city. The streets are narrow and the city is partly built on the surrounding hills. The Rhone and Saone join here. Some houses have fourteen or more stories and in these lofty abodes live the silk weavers a poor, miserable, set of people. In this country occurred their insurrection. Irenus was bishop of Lyons. He was a disciple of Polycarp, and he of John the Evangelist. We passed on our route today, Vienne, Tournon, Valence, Montelimar, Orange, Avignon, Beaucaire, Arles and St. Chamas. There is something of interest connected with most of these, but our rapid passage in the express train, did not allow us, to see much. Vienne was the capital of Burgundy in the Vth cent. There are roman remains here; an obelisk, a temple of Augustus, remains of the forum etc. Pilate is supposed to have been banished to Vienne and to have thrown himself from a tower near by, and met his end. The Hermitage wine is made near here, within a space of 300 acres. Valence is the capital of old Valentinois made a dukedom by Louis XII for the wicked Caesar Borgia. It is the place where Pius VI died, on his return from exile in France. And here Napoleon lived when a poor sub-lieutenant. At Montelimar is a castle where a powerful family lived from the time of Charlemagne. We could see that it was quite extensive, plain but strong. Almonds grow here and olives begin to be seen. Orange is the seat of the Princes of Orange and Nassau. After the death of Wm. III of Eng., it was claimed by the king of Prussia as a descendant of the house, and he exchanged it with France for other possessions. There is a Roman triumphal arch near the city. At Avignon we saw the ancient Palace of the Popes. It is a fine large building. Near here is Vaucluse where Petrarch was wont to resort. There is a fountain in a cavern and the river Sorgues flows through the valley. Laura's tomb is in a church in Avignon. She was a married lady living there, of the name of De Sade. At Beaucaire we saw a castle which had belonged to the Counts of Toulouse, and was recovered by Count Raymond VII in 1216, from Simon de Montfort. Here St. Louis is said to have heard mass before he set off for the crusades. There are but few remains. At Arles is an amphitheatre and a forum of Roman times, but we could see nothing. It is the most ancient, and was, one of the most important cities, of France.

We entered Marseilles rather early in the evening I enjoyed the ride very much. I feasted my eyes upon ruined walls and castles; almost every high hill and crag was crowned by ruins. My longings were gratified. I imagined them in their former strength and glory, and proud knights prancing up the hills, each one a lord, defying his enemies, with his strong walls. I thought too of the cruel, bloody, deeds enacted here. We had our first view of the Alps, those of Dauphiny. What rich scenes are hidden among them! It is a feast to which I look forward with delight.

*Tuesday, Nov. 11, Hotel of the Cross of Malta, Toulon.*

Glad enough were we to leave Marseilles. It is a dingy disagreeable place and our hotel was not remarkable for cleanness or any other good quality. We took the diligence as there is no railroad. We did not travel very fast, as we had but three or four horses, changed every hour, or half-hour. The road is a very fine one, even, and smooth; it winds in and out among the hills. We were very tired riding six hours cramped up as we were; but the country was very interesting, from its peculiarities. The limestone rocks were bare and ragged but the earth was covered with vineyards, one terrace above another, to the number of ten or more; these stretched up the sloping hills, and at this season, gave a reddish brown color to the whole ground. Olive trees were very abundant with their bluish leaves and full of fruit. The people were just gathering them in. They were often planted among the vines, and formed a pleasant contrast. The mulberry is a good deal cultivated here, but more especially about Lyons, almonds also are raised. The villages that we passed were poor and dirty and the inhabitants much the same.

After a ride of several hours we came upon an elevated ground, where the blue Mediterranean was to be seen. Oh! that view it was so beautiful! I hope I shall never forget it. We were on an elevated road, below us and as far as the eye could reach, stretched up the hills, the vineyards and olive yards; the roads and hills were rugged in outline and beyond was the line of the sea, enlarging at the right, into a sort of harbour, with a rocky promontory jutting out and an island at a little distance. The clouds were dark and the sea partly covered with mist but from one spot in the sky the sun shone down into the water, and a most beautiful light was thrown over the hills. And this was the Mediterranean whose waters wash so many interesting lands, and upon which, have sailed for warfare or commerce ancient and departed peoples. We rode on winding in and out through the valley until we came to the Pass of Ollioules. "bare bleached and nearly precipitous rocks hem in the passage on either side." It is three miles long. In the narrowest part, upon the summit of one steepest crags, is perched a ruined castle, which in former days guarded the pass. Through this the republicans marched after the massacres at Lyons and Marseilles, to the siege of Toulon and in this siege Napoleon first distinguished himself, in forming batteries and directing the assault.

After emerging from this pass we saw orange trees growing and laden with fruit. The dress of the peasant women is rather peculiar. They wear large straw or felt hats, and short dresses, and look queerly enough, seated on their donkeys. Cypress trees are common especially in the cemeteries and fig trees abound. We had at dinner preserved figs, almond cakes, grapes, and chestnuts as large as horse-chestnuts, all productions of the country. We were received in Toulon into very large comfortable rooms. In entering the city we crossed the moat upon a drawbridge, then entered the gates of the wall, another moat, and another gate, so that the city is strongly defended, besides forts on the bare, steep, rocky, hills, behind. Toulon is one of the chief sea-ports of France. The sailors were very noisy, singing in the streets, at night.

*Wednesday, Nov. 12th, Hotel d'or, Hyéres, France.*

We have at last arrived here where we may remain two or three weeks. We took a carriage at Toulon to see the arsenal and thence rode fourteen miles to this place. I will first describe what we saw there. What struck us first was the appearance of some of the men who were dressed in red and yellow. We found they were galley slaves, sentenced for some crime, to work for life or a certain number of years. It was a very sad sight. Some were chained two by two, others had separate chains, they all had to work for a certain part of the day, not at a trade, but in drudgery, and the dirtiest work possible. Upon their entrance here they lose their names and are known by a number, there are 4,200. The prisoners are allowed, in their leisure hours to make little articles for sale, and the profits, if not exceeding 10 francs per month they can use in buying extra food. For they have but a pound of black bread, and some little few vegetables, a day. We bought some of the carved cocoanut wood. They do it beautifully and also a kind of mosaic of straw which is very pretty indeed. Some look tolerably contented, but others hardened and wicked. I could not help shrinking a little, in passing through a crowd of them.

We saw the dry docks, and vessels, undergoing repairs in the lower parts others not yet ready for sea, on the stocks. The *Fontinois* was building, it was a large vessel, they are all war ships, some steam, others sail ships. We visited The different manufactories, from the forge, where the iron work is constructed, to the rope walk, where the cables are made. The Armoury was closed, but we saw many heaps of cannon balls, outside. There was a stack of Russian cannon taken at Sevastopol and four French ones, used in capturing them, formed posts, to enclose the others. We saw a peculiar kind of boat used in sieges, called a pontoon, covered with iron, so that no balls could penetrate it. The men who managed it were hidden inside, and could thus prove their fire in safety. One or two balls had struck it and left a dent. The roads were almost clear in the last war, so many ships went out. We all desired very much, too on board a man of war, and the *Bretagne* was lying in the harbour, so we obtained permission to visit it. We drove down to the wharf, where we took a little gaily painted boat, with a red sail, and were rowed out to her. It was quite a little sail, and we enjoyed it very much. The view of the town and hills beyond, was very fine, and the harbour was all alive with ships, large and small, and boats skimming over it. *La Bretagne* is a fine ship, it carries 130 guns in three rows. There are 1200 men belonging to it, sailors and marines. The latter were drilling on one of the decks. The sailors were all about, cooking, playing, shaving, etc. All had their land dress on, a tarpaulin hat, jacket, trousers, a broad blue collar turned over, and a blue and white shirt and seemed sober and well behaved. The little boy who showed us round, said he had been at the Crimea, and I suppose the others also. The cannon were all pointed outwards, and a lantern, and several swords and guns, hung by each. On the lower deck were the hooks for the hammocks and the beds were airing on the upper deck. This ship was all ready for sea. We were much interested, in all and embarked in our little skiff, feeling that we should understand a naval battle better than before. Across the harbour we saw the fortifications planned by Bonaparte, when the Republicans laid siege to Toulon. They command the city most fully. The French do not mean to lose it again I imagine.

We are very much pleased with the appearance of Hyéres. Our rooms are small but good. The view from the window is very lovely. We have not been out yet, but can see palm trees, aloes and cactuses growing in the open air, and in the distance the bay or sea. We have a chamberman instead of a woman. I have seen no modesty in France so far.

*Thursday, Nov. 13th, Hyéres.*

Spent the day in various occupations and made some changes in our rooms. The Hotel is very full. Many are English; one family has six servants, and a Lord occupies the room next to ours. We took a walk in the morning through the steep, crooked, narrow streets, and obtained from a terrace in the higher part of the town a very fine view of tower hills and sea. The castle looks down upon us from behind. We hope to ascend the steep crag some day. Letters from home; three all for me, it was quite a treat.

*Friday, Nov. 14th, Hyéres.*

We have regular occupations here. Uncle reads for perhaps two hours in Hallam's Middle Ages, while we sew. And then we have our private reading, writing, and exercising. We like the climate very much except the mistral, a cold wind which is blowing now and is not common we hear at this season of the year. We made, today, an excursion to the Hermitage of Notre Dame. We see it from our windows. We drove to near the top and then walked. I do not know who lived here, but processions are sometimes made to it, in honor of "our lady". The view is splendid from the top. We can see almost the whole circumference; the bay upon which I counted fifty sails, the blue sea beyond, the islands of Hyéres, and the mainland with a promontory jutting out, dotted with white cottages and covered with olive plantations. We found a number of new trees and flowers the cork tree was one, and a little pink daisy, or marguerite as the French call it, which was very pretty. We have the fruits of the country pomegranates, almonds, chestnuts and figs.

*Saturday, Nov. 15th, Hyéres.*

A pleasant day notwithstanding the mistral. We found a warm place in one of the gardens near, where we could sketch the castle. In some of the gardens the orange trees are laden with fruit and hedges of roses are in full bloom.

*Sunday, Nov. 16th, Hyéres.*

We went to the English Chapel which is very near. In the afternoon overtaken in returning, by a gentleman who introduced himself to Uncle, as an American. Mr. Bowdoin of Boston. He called in the evening. He is a connection of the Winthrops of Boston and knows my Aunt W. and Cousin E.W. he has been abroad five years with his mother, who is quite infirm.

*Monday, Nov. 17th, Hyéres.*

A bright, warm, sunny day. We took a drive to a chateau not many miles distant. It is quite a good specimen of a French chateau, four towers at the corners, long avenues of trees, hedges of laurel and many roses and other flowers. We continued through the valley of Sarebonne, making quite a circuit, and coming back, through the other end of town.

*Tuesday, Nov. 18th, Hyéres.*

   Contrary to our expectations when we came here, we are to leave on Thursday, having remained but a week. We made an excursion to the castle on the hill, today. We have found that it was built in the eighth cent. and considered so valuable, that, at a later period, Charles of Anjou gave 32 castles in exchange for this one. Auntie, M. and I rode on donkeys two of which had Spanish saddles, in which you sit, as on a chair. We wound round the hill, and dismounted, at the foot of a staircase, leading to the most precipitous part. It was exceedingly interesting to see how such a building was constructed. The walls stretch down the hills, enclosing the old town, and are in several lines inside of one another, making the approach very difficult. We peeped through a slit in a wall, where arrows were probably shot, and wandered up and down in various directions. One of my great wishes was accomplished in rambling among such ruins. The view of the sea and country was magnificent. We descended on a different side. Auntie fell off her donkey, but was not injured. We have some lovely roses on our mantel shelf, they grow in hedges and with great facility. The poor people here are suffering from disease in their olives, grapes, and oranges. If these should all fail I know not what they would do.

*Wednesday, Nov. 19th, Hyéres.*

   Took a walk in the paths, that lead about, among the fields. I here insert an account of the old castle, which Mr. Bowdoin gave Uncle, as I have not stated the facts correctly. "It is believed by antiquarians, that Hyéres is the site of the ancient Olbia. Excavations on the hill have from time to time, laid bare, old walls, whose cement proves a Roman origin, and mosaics, small bronze figures etc. have been found. The ruins as now seen judging from the form of the towers the thickness of the walls and arrangements of the stones bear the seal of the 5th cent., but the earliest written accounts of the town date only from the 10th. At that time it was considered a very strong place and bore the somewhat remarkable name of "Nobile Castrum Arocarum." Towards 970 Marseilles and the other towns along the coast, including Hyéres, were given in full sovereignty to Pons, by his brother, Bozon, 1st Count of Provence, and king of Arles. His family (De Fox.) held it till 1257 when it passed by treaty to Charles d'Anjou brother of Louis IX called St. Louis." Letters from home. Tomorrow we leave here.

_Thursday, Nov. 20th, Vidauban._

We are on our way to Nice. We stopped for lunch at Pignan, a miserable dirty little place, with narrow streets and brown houses. We managed to get a poor something and came on to this place which is quite comfortable. The mountains on our way looked finely in their light and shadow. Passed in Le Luc a tower or campanile, connected with a church, of the early Italian style, it was octagonal, and stood detached. It is Thanksgiving day at home, I wonder how they are spending it.

_Friday, Nov. 21st, Cannes._

Soon after we left Vidauban it began to be very damp and cold and rain fell, but ceased, by the time we reached Fregus, our stopping place, for noon. Here we took our dinner in the room which Napoleon occupied, when returning from his Egyptian expedition. There are considerable Roman remains in the place, but the rain prevented our examining them minutely. We saw from the carriage, what we supposed was the remains of the circus, and also the piles and arches of the aqueduct which has been traced for twenty four miles. They are very picturesque, some are covered with ivy. From Fregus the road was very fine indeed, it wound in and out among the mountains, looking down into a valley, and beyond at the hills, spreading out like a sea. There are mountains of Les Maures and the Pass of L'Estrelle formerly the haunt of Saracen brigands. The scenery was wild but the road was exceedingly well made. Along the roadside grew great quantities of the arbûtus tree from which the aquâ vitae if Italy is made. The berry is red and yellow and pleasant to the taste. In the mountains about here, porphyry is found; and the Roman quarry has been discovered.

_Saturday, Nov. 22nd, Nice, Italy._

In leaving Cannes we passed several pretty villas. We rode along the Mediterranean sea; it was very fascinating to see the waves, dashing upon the rocks. Opposite Cannes is one of the Lerin islands, upon which the "man with the iron mask" was long imprisoned, the only access to his cell, was through the Governor's room. Off, as it seemed at no great distance, we saw the Maritime Alps, with their peaks snow-covered; it was a beautiful sight, but a great contrast to the orange trees, roses, and soft air about us. We had quite a delay at the custom house, on the French side of the Var our passports were to be viséed; but the office did not open so early. The luggage was examined on the other side of the bridge, and then we were in Italy. While waiting here some of the family of the Dowager Queen of Russia passed us with outriders etc. The Victoria hotel was full so we took rooms at the Hotel de France. An English physician was summoned, for Mary who has been quite unwell.

*Sunday, Nov. 23rd, Nice.*

Went to the English church. It was very crowded as Nice is full of people. Heard Dr. Childers in the morning, and a fine sermon from his colleague Mr. Harris in the afternoon. On our return we had a call from my cousins Georgie, Eliza, and Mr. Howland. We were quite surprised to see them, as we thought they had gone on to Rome. They have been here a month. They are in this hotel in the story above us.

*Monday, Nov. 24th, Nice.*

Eliza came in to invite M. and I to a donkey ride; she could not go, but I went and enjoyed it very much. Georgie went with us and their courier, besides a boy and girl, to lead the donkeys. We went first to the Fountaine de Mousaille, it is a romantic little spot, like one of our little woody dells and the ride is pretty. Georgie's donkey began to roll, and broke the saddle girths, but she was quick enough in jumping off, and was not hurt. They are very ugly creatures sometimes. Afterwards we rode up to the old chateau. It is the castle, now formed into a promenade ground, whence there is a magnificent view of mountains and sea. We saw the Alps of the Colle de Tenda range. The highest in view was Monte Rosa. We went in the evening to the Howland's room and met there Mr. and Mrs. Pelat; he is the pastor of the Waldensian church here and she was a Miss Hitchcock of New Haven.

*Tuesday, Nov. 25th, Nice.*

Took a drive this morning to the Castle of St. Andre. Passed the site of the old town of Cimiers, and also of St. Pons perched on a steep crag. We walked over a foot bridge across a stream to the grotto of St. Andre. It is a very pretty spot, a cavern, hung with green fern leaves trembling at every breath of air, and water streaming down from the roof upon the pebbly floor. Hence we took a sweet path, through the cypresses, to the castle. It is the property of a Count St. Andre and has probably been long in the family. The salon with frescoes still on the roof, is now used as a place to store hay. A church and a school occupy part of the building. Returning to Nice we visited two stores for wood mosaics, and saw some very handsome things. Among others a table price 3,000 francs which took a prize, at the exhibition in London. The mosaic represents various battles, and English scenes. We saw again today the Russian Empress and had a good view of her face. She rides with a man in scarlet livery preceding her, and several carriages behind. She is here for her health.

*Wednesday, Nov. 26th, Nice.*
We drove out today to the Convent of Cimies the site of the old Roman town. Stopped at the ruins of the amphitheatre. The circle is still preserved though a road runs where a row of seats once was; several arches are quite perfect. The convent is inhabited by Franciscan monks, who wear a long brown dress tied by a rope round the waist and a cowl upon their heads. One of them showed the chapel to us. It is much ornamented with pictures, images, etc. He allowed us to look at the garden through the door, but it is forbidden ground to ladies, because surrounded by the monks' cloisters. Uncle only went in, and the monk brought us each, two roses to make up for the deprivation. Made a call on Mrs. Pelat. The Howlands spent the evening with us.

*Thursday, Nov. 27th, Nice.*
I went with Uncle to the dedication of the new Waldensian church here. It is a neat little building. The Sardinian flag hung near the door, showing that it is under protection of government. The services were exceedingly interesting. Mr. Pelat was assisted by four brother ministers, Mr. Ravel, M. Turin the Italian preacher of the church and two Italian Waldenses from the valley with jet black hair and moustaches and fine faces. Several prayers and the reading of the Scriptures were in Italian the rest in French. M. Ravel lead in a discourse expressing thanks first to the great Giver of all things and then to the human aid and countenance which they had had. He was followed by M. Pelat who gave a really eloquent sermon written we heard last night between twelve and three. The church owes 5000 dollars. We have had strawberries offered us in the street for sale. We leave tomorrow for Genoa.

*Friday, Nov. 28th, Mentone, Italy.*
We had a short day's journey, only five hours from Nice. We arrived between three and four and find a very nice hotel. We have enjoyed our

ride today exceedingly. It was the commencement of the celebrated Corniche road. We ascended first the heights above Nice, whence we had a fine view of the city, its bays, and convents, with the hills around. As we continued quite a range of the Col di Tenda came in sight, quite covered with snow in some parts. The road ascends for ten miles; but very gradually and is like a floor for smoothness. We looked down upon the sweet little town of Villefranche, and a promontory stretching out picturesquely into the sea. We passed Esa, perched up on the hill side and so like the rocks in color as hardly to be distinguished. There is an old Roman castle on a rocky hill near by; it was an ancient nest of the Saracens. Turbia is a town situated also on the hill side. Here we saw the Trophea Augusti, the lower part of which, was erected to commemorate the victories of Augustus over the Alpine tribes. It was in a circular form story above story and decreasing to a point. But now the foundation is surmounted by a ruined Gothic tower conspicuous for a long distance upon the winding road. Down on a promontory upon the shore is Monaco, the smallest kingdom in the world, as Mentone and Roccabruna which formerly belonged to it gave up its yoke in 1848, and became free towns. Florestan of the Matignon family, now reigns, the former kings were Grimaldi's. When more powerful, he was absurdly despotic. He took upon himself, to sell all the bread in his dominions, and workmen coming from without, were not allowed to bring their luncheon, but must buy of him. The town is very ancient supposed to have been founded by the Greeks, or as they say by Hercules. We passed Roccabruna where, I believe is a ruined castle. Soon after our arrival here, we took a walk about the town, and first entered the Church of San Michaele; here are some of the banners from Lepanto, for Prince Honorius Ist distinguished himself in the battle, at the head of his galleys. The church was first built, it is thought, in 1363. In one place we came upon a Piedmontere soldier sitting down, in the street, and reading a new testament. Auntie spoke to him, he looked up radiant with joy, and said "buono libro." It interested us very much.

*Saturday, Nov. 29th, Oneglia.*

Left Mentone at an early hour this morning, and had a splendid view of the sun rise from the sea. The sky was glorious, and sea and hills seemed bathed in its soft light. Our whole ride today has been delightful. We followed the bends of the shore, and could see the waves dash up upon the rocks and the white birds like sails in the horizon. It seems to me to be a peculiarly fascinating sea, the dark blue color in the distance and the emerald green on the nearer waves is so rich. We have been rather annoyed by the children who beg every-where. Some bring us flowers to sell. We had today a bunch of jasmines and yesterday roses and violets. We rode through many little towns. Ventimiglia was one of the larger size; it was once the capital of the Intermelians, a Ligurian tribe. We entered through a gateway and a drawbridge, and then had to get out and walk down a steep part of the city; for with our heavily laden vetturino riding was not quite safe. In crossing the river Nervia, we felt the cold wind, from the snow mountains coming down the valley. At Bordighera, we saw many palm trees bound up to prepare for Palm Sunday; for this town has the exclusive right to sell the palm leaves, for the following reason. In the time of Sextus Vth when the obelisk in the square of the Vatican, was being raised to its position, a point was reached, when they could move it no farther, a sailor from Bordighera called out to wet the ropes, and the experiment was successful. We stopped at St. Remo for dinner saw in the travelers book Mr. Silliman's and Cousin Edward's names. Passing various little places arrived here to spend Sunday. Andrea Doria was born here.

*Sunday, November 30th, Oneglia.*

The first rainy day for some time. There was no English or Protestant church so Uncle went for a little while to the Catholic. There was a subscription taken up for the tribute of the cities of Europe, to the Sultan for allowing Catholics in the Holy Land. Opposite our windows is a prison, and we see the men looking through the iron bars of their windows.

*Monday, December 1st, Savona.*

Left Oneglia before light and the sun did not appear for some time on account of a cloudy sky. All along the road we have seen at no great distance, mountains covered with snow; and a violent wind, blowing thence, made the air quite sharp. The scenery today has been very beautiful, more wild than before. In some places the road led us, at the foot of a high precipice, with another below, to the sea and round the projecting headlands, the wind blew violently. We rode through Albenga, which was Napoleon's headquarters in 1796. There are several old towers in the town; and indeed on almost every hill stood a tower, now falling to decay. At Finale we stopped two hours for our noon rest and lunch. In the middle of our table stood a vase of toothpicks. Before entering the town, we passed through a tunnel in the rocks. Noli we passed and reached here at a little past six. Have had a new fruit called Nespoli, it looks like a rotten apple but tastes pretty good. Savona is the birthplace of Chiabrera an Italian poet of the 17th cent. Near by, at Albisola, Pope Julian II was born. Tomorrow we shall reach Genoa. The boats are quite picturesque, many have slanting yard arms. The men wear Greek red caps and the women often a calico mantle. We have a very nice vetturino, it holds all our baggage, and is very roomy. The man who drives is followed by a dear little black dog who <u>will</u> <u>not</u> be left behind.

*Tuesday, Dec. 2nd, "la Superba," Genoa.*

Left Savona at eight, a fine, clear, cold, day; ice had formed on the rivers, and the snow on the mountains near us. Scenery as before, varied, and beautiful. The principal town of interest, was Cogoletto, where we stopped to see the house where, as tradition says, Christopher Columbus was born; Genoa too claims him. At Pegli we stopt two or three hours to visit the villa of the Marquis Pallavicini, for which we had obtained a permit. The house is nothing remarkable, but the grounds were in the true Italian style, much ornamented with architecture and a perfect labyrinth of paths. First following a path lined with Portuguese laurel, we came to a café, erected in honor of the visit, of some royal personage. It is exceedingly pretty. We ascended to the upper part where is a room, decorated in the Pompeian style, and a coffee service in imitation of the antique. Then passing a fountain we come to an arch of triumph of white marble decorated with goddesses. Upon it is an inscription in Latin to the effect that the owner here leaves behind his house, and all labor, and devotes himself to rustic pleasures, and the other side of the arch, is made rough and rustic; carrying out the sentiment of the inscription very prettily. We then came to a little Swiss chalet, with the walls frescoed, in imitation of the interior of such a dwelling. I can not attempt to describe everything, we were continually surprised by some new wonder. Little rustic summer houses, with seats and tables invited us to rest. Sometimes they were Swiss in form, sometimes Chinese, and there were often pretty views of the sea.

We wound round a hill to the summit, where was an imitation of an ancient castle. On the lower floor was a kitchen, a salle d'armes where hung old armor, upon the walls, a toilet room and two little dining rooms. Thence a winding staircase leads to the story above, where the windows are beautiful stained glass; and from the tower of the castle, is a splendid view of all the country round, and Genoa in the distance. Our guide, the gardener, who says his family have been there two hundred years, then led us to the grotto where he lighted a torch, and we wandered through. It is quite extensive, and formed of real stalactites, brought from various caverns, and so skillfully put together, that it can hardly be distinguished from Nature's works. After walking through we came to a lake, and here was a boatman ready to receive us in a little skiff. The marchioness' boat lay near, richly gilded. We rowed to a green island, where stood a Grecian temple of a graceful shape and made of white marble; in the centre was a statue of Diana. Upon one side of the lake, was a Chinese temple and on the other a Turkish one and on the hill above an ivy covered arbor. We walked through all these, after landing. The view of the city and the sea under one bridge, was exquisite; indeed it all was. In several of these little arbors, was a trick, to pour a little shower over one, and as you turn to escape, another follows, seemingly from invisible hands. It was not tried upon us but we saw how it worked. We saw a marble monument to Chiabrera and others to imaginary heroes. We went into a floral temple; which opened into a little garden and conservatory so arranged that you could see nothing until close upon it, and mostly with much taste. The principal part of these grounds was finished in eight years, employing 300 workmen. We went into the conservatories below the house and saw a number of rare and choice plants. The Norway pine with its graceful upturned branches. A thread and needle plant, a cinnamon, a camphor, a pepper and a coffee tree. A pinery with flourishing pineapples in it, banana trees and camellias growing in the open air seven or eight feet high, one was the camellia Andrea d'Oria. Orange trees, in abundance and a nespoli tree. Those in the other grounds were very beautiful the laurels, the hollys; a large paulonia with the fruit on, magnolias and rhododendrons with a cedar of Lebanon and a sort of tree heath. We came away well tired but every much delighted. There was a beautiful sunset just as we entered Genoa and the city looked finely. Commodore Breeze and his family are in this house. We have had a new fruit mandolines like a small orange, the flavor is pleasant.

*Wednesday, Dec. 3rd, Croix de Malte, Genoa.*

Our present hotel is built upon a Roman aqueduct, which forms an arcade along the street. It is a part of the old palace of the Knights of Malta, and the rooms being very lofty are difficult to warm. Beneath us is a store for gold and silver filigree work, which is very pretty. We took a carriage to see various objects of interest. This is indeed a city of palaces, almost everywhere, either is, or was, a palace. We visited first Andrea Doria's Palace. It was presented to him by the city, and in its day of glory, must have been a splendid place. It is upon the port, and the gardens extend to the water where are marble steps, and a balustrade, as if for a landing place, for the Admiral. The furniture was destroyed in the revolution, only two articles remain, a sort of throne given him by Charles Vth with whom he was allied, against the French and a gilt Prie Dieu. The ceilings are beautifully adorned, with frescoes, and stucco work. One entrance hall, has scenes, principally from the history of Rome, and classical or mythological; the work of Pierino del Vaga, a pupil of Raphael's. One hall had a painting of Andrea himself, in heroic costume, and around the sides, his ten sons in the same dress. One ceiling represented him as Camillus throwing his sword into the balances. Admiral Doria died in 1560. We saw in the city a monument, to Columbus, near the house in which he lived. It is a circular monument, not yet finished, with the beaks of ships, standing out from it, all around. Next we went to the Palazzo Balbi. The family still occupy a part of the house. The paintings were the chief interest. There was a portrait of a doge of the family. A bust, by Bartolini, of the present Marchioness who is a daughter of the Marquis Pallavicini. In a mosaic table of pearl and wood the arms of the two families are united, the three fishes of the Balbi with the three crosses and squares of Pallavicini. There was a Cleopatra and a Lucretia by Guido, several of Vandyke's portraits. The Saviour and John the Baptist as children by Rubens. Titian, Pierino del Vaga, Paul Veronese, were all represented, but we had little time, and shall study painting elsewhere. We saw the Church of the Annunziata, most gorgeously decorated, mostly gilt inside. St. Matteo is a very old church built in 1125 by one of the Doria's. It is constructed of the alternate black and white marble, which only the families of Doria, Grimaldi, Spinola and Tieschi were permitted to use. Andrea and other Doria's are buried here. His house is near by, with sculptured arabesques round the door. Finally we went to the Palazzo Ducale. The old tower, with its grated windows, is the only part that remains which belonged to the earliest doges. The council room is a splendid place, pillars of Ferrara and other choice marbles, surround it. Formerly statues of doges occupied the niches, but these were destroyed. The women here wear muslin scarves over their heads instead of bonnets.

*Thursday, Dec. 4th, Genoa.*

On first emerging from our dark rooms we saw the ground covered with snow, and it was very cold. Went to visit the Palazzo Durazzo. It is really magnificent. The entrance and stairway and halls are of white marble. The corridors and little gallery, overlooking the stairs are very beautiful. We saw some fine paintings, several of Guido's - viz. A fine Portia, the background and drapery black, and the white face in contrast, *Roman Charity*, a daughter nursing her father in prison. Vestal Virgin, and Cleopatra. A Magdalen, by Titian too wanton in expression. *The Tribute Money* by Guercino. The walls were frescoed to correspond to the paintings. Next we visited the Palazzo Bregnole. It was not by any means so magnificent as the former, but here too were fine pictures. A Madonna by Guido, blue drapery and soft fair countenance. Luca di Giordano, Olinda and Saphronia, with Clorinda on horseback. A Madonna said to be by Raphael and discovered a little while ago, covered by another painting. Titian's portrait of Philip II. The *Raising of Lazarus* by Annibal Caracci. At the Palazzo Serra which we saw next, we did not examine the paintings. There were several magnificently gilded rooms. One circular room was almost wholly gilt, pillars, mirrors, chandeliers and all. The gilding cost over a million francs. By the sides of the windows was a large piece of lapis lazuli, from Prussia, a blue stone, and quite precious. We saw the Old Bank of St. George. Before the door hung the Pisan chains. It was the earliest institution of the kind in Europe founded in 1346 and appears very ancient. The room we entered, was adorned with large statues placed in niches, of the great men of Genoa. The room was occupied by bankers. We wanted to have a view of Genoa from the top of Santa Maria di Carignano but the precipitous streets, were so slippery that it was thought dangerous for the horses to attempt it. Had a call in the evening from Com. Breeze, his wife and Capt. Sands his brother in law's brother.

*Friday, Dec. 5th, Genoa.*

Made a call at the Howlands' who came yesterday, they were not at home. Went to the Palazzo Beale or that of the king, when he comes here, which is quite seldom. He is coming on Monday to a fete, and has invited the ex-empress of Russia from Nice, whom he will accompany back. There are several very fine rooms. The Throne Room was hung with red Genoese velvet and furniture the same. A canopy overhung the richly gilded seat. The room prepared for the Russian empress, is very handsome.

The bed has white brocade curtains, the wardrobe was of gilded work, and the furniture covered with red and gold damask. Adjoining was a toilette chamber, hung and adorned with light blue, and gold. The contrast was very beautiful. The audience room was hung with tapestries. The room which the queen occupied when living was hung with red and white silk or satin. Saw two large paintings one of Medusa's head held out by Perseus, and another of Olinda and Sophronia tied to the stake, by Giordino. One hall is adorned with antique and modern statues. The ball room is very spacious, the floor is a mosaic of American woods.

We went again to St. Matteo's, as they were performing service before and we could not see much. We saw several inscriptions to Dorias, of the 15th cent. Over the high altar, and suspended over the baldakin is Andrea Doria's sword. In the cloister were fragments of colossal statues of Andrea Doria which once stood before his palace but were partly destroyed. We went to the Duomo or cathedral today. It is of striped black and white marble and of Italian Gothic style. One tower only has been built. Within in one of the chapels is, so they say, the charger upon which John the Baptist's head was brought to Herod. Females are not permitted to enter, on account of a decree to that effect, by Innocent III, in memory of Herodia's daughter. However Mary and I entered before we knew the interdict. Two of Canova's angels kneel in a little chapel behind the altar.

At the Palazzo Doria Tursi, now occupied by the municipality we saw some very interesting relics. The chief of these were the papers of Columbus. When we asked for them, the custodian inquired whether we were Americans, as they did not like to show them to any but such. They are kept in the pedestal of a bust of Columbus, and it requires three keys to unlock the little closet. We saw among the papers, the diplomas given by Ferdinand and Isabella to Columbus. It was a copy of the original, but very old. A letter to the Bank of St. George (1502) transmitting his will, which bequeathed to that institution, one tenth of his property, in order to lighten the city taxes. Some other letters of his, with his signature. We leave here tomorrow, for our journey to Pisa and Leghorn.

*Saturday, Dec. 6th, Sestri.*

We are here, on our journey, and shall spend Sunday in this place. We left Genoa at night, in the rain and this continued, so we lost all view of the towns through which we passed. We had a new vetturino and the spring was disordered, so we had to stop some time at a little place to have it mended. We arrived here after dark, and could only see that Sestri was on a promontory, which, the guide books says, was once an island.

*Sunday, Dec. 7th, Sestri.*

There was no church to attend; and a rainy day. However we read, and were comfortably situated and passed a pleasant day.

*Monday, Dec. 8th, Spezzia.*

Left Sestri at half-past seven and reached here at nearly half-past five. The sun has been again hidden, it is long since it has shone out brightly. The road has been wild and hilly, we were often turned at direct right, or rather acute angles, and have had six instead of our usual four horses. We took a lunch at Borghetti, and saw some women with the square cloths upon their heads, and their hair in a net. Spezzia is on a gulf of the same name. One of the U.S. ships anchors here, and the store house is here. In Spezzia the women wear little bits of straw hats, upon the crown of their heads, and much ornamented.

*Tuesday, Dec. 9th, Pietra-Santa.*

To our joy we have had the sun today, it rose beautifully, over the gulf of Spezzia, as we left. We rode about two hours and then came to the river Magra where we had to alight, and cross in a little boat. It was wet and dirty, so we had to stand up, the current is rapid, but we were safely landed on the opposite shore. The carriage and horses were carried over in a large flat boat, and then they dragged the carriage over a muddy part of the road where we walked on a little board path. One of the whiffletrees broke in the process and its place was supplied by a rope. A crowd of dirty men and beggars followed us the latter begging and the former were officious to assist us, in walking on the boards, and in the various leaps that it was necessary to make. It is said that they sometimes purposely break parts of carriages in order to detain travelers longer. We took a lunch at Sarzana. Soon after leaving Massa we crossed the boundaries of Sardinia and entered the Duchy of Modena. We were only detained a minute or two at the customs house, and soon after, entered Tuscany. Here, part of our baggage was examined and in about half an hour reached this place. We have seen more marble, about, showing the vicinity of Carrara, these quarries are the chief source of the revenue, of the Duke of Modena.

*Wednesday, Dec. 10th, Victoria House, Pisa.*

Leaving Pietra Santa at half-past eight we arrived in this famous and ancient city at about one. The ride was not very interesting, the road better than we have had lately but not equal to some. We crossed another river, the carriage and horses in one boat, and we in another, and waited some time on the other side, for the vetturino to be readjusted, while a crowd of children stood gazing at us. We have quite pleasant rooms here looking out upon the Arno, which, though muddy must be beautiful in a fine sunset, or by moonlight. I do not know whether we shall see either of these, for the weather has been cloudy, for several days. We saw the cathedral and its appendages, the baptistry, and Leaning Tower, as we drove into the city they appear familiar, from numerous representations made of them. From our windows this afternoon we saw a man with a black gown and mask, holding a little box up towards us. He looked frightfully and I believe belonged to an order, who go about to bury the dead, and was raising his box for money. Tomorrow we expect to go to Leghorn and return the same day, by railroad.

*Thursday, Dec. 11th, Pisa.*

A rainy day, but we started for Leghorn before it began. It is only half an hour in the cars which roll along with the greatest ease. We went to a few stores where marble and alabaster statues and vases are for sale. At one place we saw a beautiful copy of the dying gladiator in alabaster. At Micali's we saw a green vase upon swans and a Samuel, like those we have at home, and I believe they were bought here. We saw a large square, said to be the largest in Italy, at one end is the Duomo, the facade of which was designed by Inigo Jones. On the side of the Grand Dukes palace of yellow marbles, and others. The Reservoir of Leghorn is a very fine one, it is roofed, and has a promenade around it, under the arches. The water is carried from one compartment to another, to purify it, which is effected, by means of a porous stone, through which it passes. The water is so pure that an inscription on the bottom, can be read, through twenty feet of water. The Grand Duke gave a ball here, at the time of his second marriage, before the water was let in. Leghorn contains 80,000 people of whom 7,000 are Jews, many Greeks also. It is a busy place. We could not enjoy much of what we saw, because of the pouring rain, and came back at two o'clock.

*Friday, Dec. 12th, Pisa.*

The sun rose brightly, though it became cloudy afterwards. We visited the Duomo, baptistry, and campanile, and Campo Santo. The first, I will describe as we saw it. It is in the Latin cross, and the end towards the baptistry is covered with five rows of arches. It was erected in 1067 with spoils, which the Pisans gained from the Saracens of Sicily, in aiding the Normans against them. Over the high altar, in the vault of the apse, is a mosaic by Cimabue assisted by Gaddo Gaddi, of the Saviour with the Virgin and John one on each side; it is stiff and has some of the Byzantine style of the 13th cent. At each end of the transepts and on the facade were mosaics by Gaddo. The high altar was of valuable marbles, lapis lazuli, Spanish marble and a mosaic of agates. Over it hung a bronze crucifix by John of Bologna. He also made in 1602 the bronze doors of the Duomo which are very elaborate with scenes from the life of our Saviour and Mary surrounded by wreathes of fruit and flowers. In the choir, are bas reliefs of the history of Christ, by Giovanni Pisano (13th cent.). And four pictures St. Peter, St. John, St. Margaret and St. Catherine by Andrea del Sarto, who also painted, a beautiful St. Agnese, in the nave. The altars were said to have been designed by Michael Angelo; and a bronze chandelier in the centre, suggested to Galileo the idea of a pendulum, it has a little motion of that kind. At one end of a transept is the Chapel of St. Ranieri, the patron saint of Pisa; his bones are enclosed in a serpentine sarcophagus. The columns which form in the nave five, and the transepts three aisles, are mostly ancient Greek or Roman, and brought from different places. There is a triforium or woman's gallery running round the interior of the Duomo. The baptistry contains in the centre, a large font for adults and small ones for young persons, richly adorned with marbles and mosaics. The pulpit is of Parian marble, by Giovanni Pisano, and on five sides are bas reliefs of the Saviour's history. It rests upon columns of which the central one stands on griffins, and crouching figures. A gallery surrounds the building under the cupola. A very young infant was brought to be baptised, while we were there. We were beset by beggars on coming out of each building.

I turn next to the Campo Santo, the burial place, founded by Archbishop Ubaldo in 1188-1200. Driven from Jerusalem by Saladin, he brought fifty three ship-loads of earth, from the Holy Land, with which he covered, to the depth of ten feet, the area of the cemetery. The arcade, which surrounds this space, is decorated with frescoes, some of which are very ancient and interesting, as showing the progress of art. The South

*Plazza di Siena*

wall begins with those of Orcagna, the Triumph of Death, the Last Judgement, and Hell by his brother. The Hermits in the wilderness by Pietro Laurentii and others. The history of Job by Francesco da Voltura, is quite in Giotto's style. The west wall shows works of a later period, but not good. On the north are scenes from the Creation to the Deluge, begun by Pietro of Orvieto and completed by Benozzo Gozzoli. The east wall is much painted over and does not give much idea of the subject. Chapels are connected with the building, and on one side, hang some chains, taken from Pisa by Genoa, given by them to Florence and restored to Pisa, as a proof of concord, between these republics. There was a statue of Frederic Barbarossa, and a griffin of bronze, with an Arabic inscription, taken from the Balearic Isles; it stood formerly upon the top of the cathedral. The Tower we ascended as far as the bells; there was a perceptible leaning, but not so fearful as I thought. The largest bell is rung at executions. The view is very fine, Leghorn and the sea are visible. Here Galileo made experiments, as to falling bodies. We met the Howlands, half way up the tower. On returning we saw the palace of the Medici, the site of the tower where Count Ugolino was imprisoned. (See Dante.) Saw the old arsenal now the Duke's stables. I was excessively tired, with all I had seen.

*Saturday, Dec. 13th, Pisa.*

We had planned to go on today to Florence and take the Perugia route to Rome; but concluded to leave for Siena on Monday as there is no snow on the road as we feared. Took a little walk along the Arno.

*Sunday, Dec. 14th, Pisa.*

Did not feel well and only went to church in the afternoon.

*Monday, Dec. 15th, Siena.*

Having started early in the cars, two hours brought us to this place. Much disappointed to have to give up seeing the pictures and objects of interest in the city I felt very unwell and longed to get over the journey and reach Rome.

*Dec. 16th, La Scala.*

Passed Radicofani which is on a high hill.

*Dec. 17th, Bolsena.*

Near the lake of the same name, and here stood the Etruscan Volsinii. A miserable hotel.

*Dec. 18th, Viterbo.*

The journey nearly over. It was very painful.

*Friday, Dec. 19th 1856, Hotel de l'Europe, Rome.*

Entered this city by the Flaminian way, crossing the yellow Tiber on the Ponte Milve the site of the old Milvian bridge where the ambassadors of the Allobroges were arrested by Cicero's command. I could not feel much enthusiasm being so sick. I had the doctor immediately.

*Monday, Jan. 5th 1857, Rome.*

A long interval has elapsed since I wrote last but meanwhile I have been sick with the gastric fever. Doctor Gason thinks I had it a week before I arrived here and it runs three weeks. On Christmas Day I received from kind friends several bouquets of flowers, and New Year's Day we gave our presents and I could lie on the sofa. Letters from home were very delightful and also the children's daguerreotype. Today I rode out for the first time, in the old, or rather, the new part of Rome. Mary could not go for she has been quite unwell for a few days. We went through the Porta

*Temple of Vesta*

Pia, passing Torlonia's the Italian banker and as far as the Church of Sta. Agnese. Returning by the Coliseum and the Forum we saw Trajan's Pillar and the Fountain of Treve whose water we drink at the hotel. It represents Neptune drawn by sea horses the water is excellent. I am much better, indeed well, but still weak, and have to be very careful in diet.

*Tuesday, Jan. 6th, Rome.*

A rainy day so we staid at home. In the evening took an Italian lesson from Sig. Brocchi. We are to have them three times a week.

*Wednesday, Jan. 7th, Rome.*

All took a ride together. We saw St. Peter's; it is grand yet its true height does not appear. We took a pretty ride through Porta Angelica and had a fine view of the city.

*Thursday, Jan. 8th, Rome.*

Drove out to St. Paolo fuori le mure. It was burnt by fire some years ago and a little of the old part remains. Beyond according to tradition, Paul was put to death. We stopped at the Temple of Vesta, not the historical one, but a pretty round building with Corinthian pillars of Vespasian's time. We saw the tomb of Crius Cestus a tribune of the Augustan age, and the only pyramid in Rome. It is of Marble and adjoins the Protestant Burial Ground and was included in Aurelian's wall, which is seen, somewhat in ruins. The ruins of the Caesar's palace attracted us built on the site of Cicero's and Hortensius' houses. Saw the place where the Mamertine Prison is.

*Friday, Jan. 9th, Rome.*

Took a short walk for the first time on the Pincian hill. Drove upon Mt. Janiculum, through Porta Pangrazia had a fine view of the Sabine hills, and Mt. Albano, and the city spread out below us. Met Dr. Gason and his wife up there. It was cold and windy. The streets in Rome are very narrow, mostly without side-walks, and are not pleasant to walk in. Some of the peasants wear large blue cloaks and pointed hats and are quite picturesque. 5,000 French soldiers keep the people in check, and there are plenty more at command. I did not mention that we saw on our ride, the Fournarina's house, Raphael's lady love, a barber's daughter. Raphael's house is near St. Peter's.

*Saturday, Jan. 10th, Rome.*

Went this morning for the first time to St. Peter's. In the vestibule of this magnificent building is the Navicella a mosaic of Giotto's designing, but much altered since. It is the Saviour, walking on the water, to his disciples. The size of the church did not at all impress me, one can only appreciate it by comparison. On the mosaic floor is marked the comparative length of the largest churches in the world. St. Paul's London comes next to this in size. To describe St. Peter's is beyond my powers if indeed it is possible for any one to do it, satisfactorily. I shall speak only of the different objects we saw. We were interested in the Pieta of Michael Angelo, a sculpture of the Virgin holding in her lap the dead body of our Saviour. The utter lifelessness of his form with the arm hanging down is very striking. We saw the monument to Clemt XIII by Canova at the front of which crouch his celebrated lions. They are perfect, so true to nature, the sleeping one especially has so much strength in his face. An angel with a sad countenance leans upon the monument with his torch reversed, Religion stand opposite and above is the kneeling figure of the pope. The walls are adorned with beautiful mosaics, copies of paintings. We looked at the Communion of St. Jerome, Peter healing the lame, and Guido's Michael and the Dragon. I have not seen the originals but these I admired very much. The marbles of the church are very rich and costly. The monument of the late Pope Gregory XVI has slabs of Oriental alabaster upon it. The grand altar is supported by bronze pillars, of which the bronze, was taken from the Pantheon. Behind, at the end of the tribune, is a chair, enclosing as they say Peter's chair upon which the pope, who reigns twenty five years, is to have his body embalmed, and placed, for a certain period of time. The bronze statue of St. Peter in the nave is a very ugly one. Antonio told us it was a proconsul of which the head and hand were altered. The toe is kissed by the people, on enter-ing, and looks quite worn, the pope per-forms the same cere-mony, when he pays his devotions here. The colors of the dome are beautifully soft, it is covered with mosaics. Below in the four spandrels of the arches are the four evangelists. The pen which Mark holds is six feet long, but from its great height appears no more than one. We visited only the right aisle, and shall see it again sometime, as well as the other parts. Took

*Foro Trojano*

a drive after lunch in the grounds of the Villa Borghese and upon the Pincian where a band played very good music.

*Sunday, Jan. 11th 1857, Rome.*
    Went in the morning to the chapel in Mr. Cass' house and heard Mr. Hall the American clergyman who married Dr. Malan's daughter.

*Monday, Jan. 12th, Rome.*
    Just finished writing home to Grandmama and to Laura. Went this morning to see the obelisk in the Piazza del Popolo. It was brought from

the Temple of the Sun at Heliopolis, in Egypt by Augustus and placed in its present position by Sixtus Vth. It is covered with hieroglyphics. Just outside of this gate is the English Chapel. Then we went to see the Pillar of Trajan which stands in the forum of the same name. This is sunk, much below the level of the street and has broken pillars and bases scattered over it. We made a few calls but everybody is out in Rome when it is at all fit to go out. We then looked at the column of Marcus Aurelius Antoninus, erected by the senate and Roman people. It stands in the Piazza Colonna, and celebrates victories over the Armenians Parthians and other nations. Not far from this is the temple, which formerly stood on the same forum with the column. It is called the temple of Neptune and has several Corinthian pillars and a rich freeze and cornice, it has been filled up, and is used as a custom house. We saw besides, on the Campus Martius, an Egyptian obelisk, with only a few hieroglyphics, but these very distinct, and probably of the age of Psammeticus. After lunch we went to the Vatican and as it closes at three had but little time. It was a public day, and we had to take a long walk through various halls, and corridors, to reach the picture gallery.

We spent all our time before the Transfiguration, of Raphael, and it was little indeed for such a picture which needs the study of hours. What beauty is in the Saviour's countenance! and the figure is so slight, and spiritual, it seems as if all, earthly, had been left below. The apostles seem awestruck. The scene at the foot of the mount too. The Father looks at the disciples, with such entreating looks, that they would heal his son, while they point upward to the one alone able, to effect this. It was Raphael's last work and perhaps greatest. We were driven out by a company of Swiss guards most unceremoniously. The Whitneys were there and we brought Mrs. W. home. She has met with a sad loss, in the death of her brother.

_Tuesday, Jan. 13th, Rome._

A rainy day, but notwithstanding we went to the Doria Pamfili Palace to see the gallery. It is a gallery of 15 rooms and a very fine collection. Several paintings interested us much. One was a landscape of Nicholas Poussin's, a large picture, and representing a pretty country scene, a brook, river, cattle figures, old bridge etc. We saw a number of Bassano's works, they consist chiefly of animals. One, _The Supper at Emmaus_, had a kitchen in the fore-front and the chief scene way in the background. A portrait of Holbein by himself. A picture said to be by Giotto of a cruci-

*Castle S. Angelo*

fixion on a gold ground. A Madonna and child, with two saints on each side and players on instruments, quite in the old style; the painter was Taddeo di Bartolo of the Sienese school, 15th cent. Below this is an Annunciation by Fra Filippo Lippi, the countenances are soft and pleasing but the drapery and wings of the angels gaudy. St. John drinking water in the wilderness, by Guercino, and by the same St. Agnese just about to be burnt. She was very young and beautiful, looking up to heaven with an angelic expression, her little lamb stood sorrowfully by, and a rough man was lighting the pile of wood. We saw the espousal of the infant Saviour, with St. Catherine by Beccafumi. I hope to visit this place again for I was very weary before half through.

We afterwards visited the site of the Mausoleum of Augustus, where he and many of his family lie entombed. Some of the old reticulated wall remains, and a few of the sepulchral chambers. The present building is in imitation of the old. We ascended a flight of stairs and came out upon an open circular place. It is very large and was supposed to have a cone of earth on the top where trees were planted. It resembles Hadrian's Tomb or the Castle of St. Angelo as it is now called, which we pass, on our way to the Vatican, or St. Peter's, situated at one end of the Bridge of St. Angelo. After lunch we rode and walked on the Pincian and took an Italian lesson in the evening.

*Wednesday, Jan. 14th, Rome.*

Took a walk while M. was at the riding school. We went to Sig.
Benzoni's studio, at Eliza's request, to see Mr. Howland's bust. It was
only the brown clay model, but we liked it very much. It is a present to
their mother. The studio is quite extensive; we saw some beautiful works.
The four seasons; busts, were exceedingly beautiful. One was Spring, a
young girl with a sweet face, and primroses and other early flowers in her
hair. Summer, more mature, with grain upon her head. Autumn, a full
rich head, with a bunch of grapes, and leaves,
on each side. Winter, a stern old man, his long
bear blown by the wind. A statue of Eve looking at the apple; and the serpent wound about
the tree. Gratitude, a young girl, taking a thorn
from her dog's foot, while he licks her hand. A
mate to this, was the girl fallen asleep over a
half-finished wreath, and the dog with his foot
upon a viper endeavoring to wake his mistress.
Cupid in disguise, covered with a sheep skin, A
monument to Cardinal Mai, and many more,
worth seeing, in various stages of completion.
At two o'clock we made some calls, on Mrs.
Hooker, wife of the banker. She was a Miss
Winthrop and very lively and chatty. Then on
the Le Roys who were out. Mrs. Singer and
Mrs. Sargent were at home. Auntie met them in
Europe, before. We then drove to St. Peter's
and visited that part which we had before omit-
ted. We were interested in Canova's monument to the Pretenders James
III, Charles Edward, and Henry IX of Eng. There is a monument also to
the wife of James. George IV paid part of the expenses. Two angels, with
torches reversed, stand at the base. We saw the monument to the
Countess Matilda, who in the 12th or 13th cents., gave lands to the pope
There is almost no end to the monuments to the popes, some of them
are quite fine. Sunday is a fête day, so the pope will officiate, and rich
hangings are being put up for the occasion. There is a rumor of the death
of the King of Naples, probably untrue [Editor's note: Ferdinand II of
Naples was called "King Bomba" after bombing his own people to quell
an insurrection. In December 1656, a soldier tried to kill him, but was
arrested and executed.]. There are few strangers there now, many fear to

*Campidoglio*

go. Mr. Treat Sect. of the A.B.C.F.M. called in the evening. He is going to Constantinople. He says there are several thousand priests here. The people hate them, especially the men, who for the most part despise the Roman Catholic religion.

*Thursday, Jan. 15th, Rome.*

We are still in the Hotel d' Europe. We find it impossible to get sunny rooms out of a hotel. The troubles in Naples keep many here. We went notwithstanding the rain to the Campidoglio or Museum of the Capitol. It contains mostly Greek and Roman statues busts and relics of various sorts. We dwelt long on the *Dying Gladiator*. It is a splendid thing. The last life blood is gushing from his wound, and he sinks, lower, and lower, to the ground. He has a cord about his neck, and thence, is supposed to be a Gaul. We saw a fine Amazon, with delicate drapery, just stringing her bow. A pretty Flora holding tulips, and other flowers, in her hands. In the next room was a bronze tablet, containing the Lex Regia, by which the senate conferred imperial power, upon Vespasian; which Rienzi who was killed at the foot of the Capitol stairs, expounded to the people. A fine sarcophagus with an alto relievo of Theseus at war with the Amazons. Another, Diana alighting from her car to look at the sleeping Endymion. A little boy with a comic mask, very natural. We saw a gilt, bronze statue of Hercules, and one in basalt, of him, when an infant. Hippocrates the god of medicine with a snake. There were busts of celebrated men, all the Roman Emperors, Socrates, Blind Homer and many other Greeks and Romans. In another room was the Iliac Table, with very small delicate bas reliefs, of the Fall of Troy and history of AEneas, of the time of Nero. Pliny's *Doves* a mosaic with a border very beautifully done for so ancient a work. It is supposed to be one, mentioned by Pliny and the work of Socus. A mosaic of two masks, found on the Aventine. Several stiles for writing on wax. A large ornamented vase of white marble found near Caecilia Metella's tomb. A colossal bust of Juno. On each side of the staircase are plans of Rome that have been found, and inscriptions. We saw below, a sarcophagus with bas reliefs from Achilles history, within this, was found the Portland Vase.

Afterwards we ascended a flight of steps that led to the Church of Aracoeli a building of the 6th cent. and on the site of the Temple of Jupiter Capitolinus. The pillars along the aisles are brought from different places, one, from the Palace of the Caesar's has inscribed upon it "A cubiculo Augustorum." It was here, that Gibbon, resolved to write his history of Rome. We saw here kept under lock and key the "sanctissimo bambino" a wooden doll representing the infant Jesus, said to have been made centuries ago by a monk, and painted by St. Luke. It is kept in a box richly adorned, and is covered with diamonds and other precious stones, presented by sick persons whom it had cured, for it is said to possess this wonderful power. In one chapel were some frescoes by Pinturiccio, the life of St. Bernard. In another was the tomb of Cardinal Matteo, mentioned by Dante in *Paradiso* canto 12. In another still, the tomb of Cardinal Sigismondo Conte, for whom Raphael painted his *Madonna di Figlino.* Under the high altar is an altar said to have been erected by Augustus, to celebrate, the prophecy of the Delphic oracle, of Christ's coming.

*Friday, Jan. 16th, Rome.*

A clear cold day, I took a walk with Uncle on Monte Pincio while Mary was at her riding lesson. At half-past twelve we went to the Vatican, and this being a private day were admitted to the picture gallery, without making the circuit of the statuary. We saw again the Transfiguration, and were able to compare it with some of Raphael's earlier works. Near by is the *Madonna di Figlino.* She is seated in the clouds, and has a half-sad look. Below are Cardinal Sigismondo Conte, St. Francis, and several other figures. A cherub in the foreground, with a lovely face holds up a tablet. One of Raphael's earliest pictures is the *Coronation of the Virgin.*

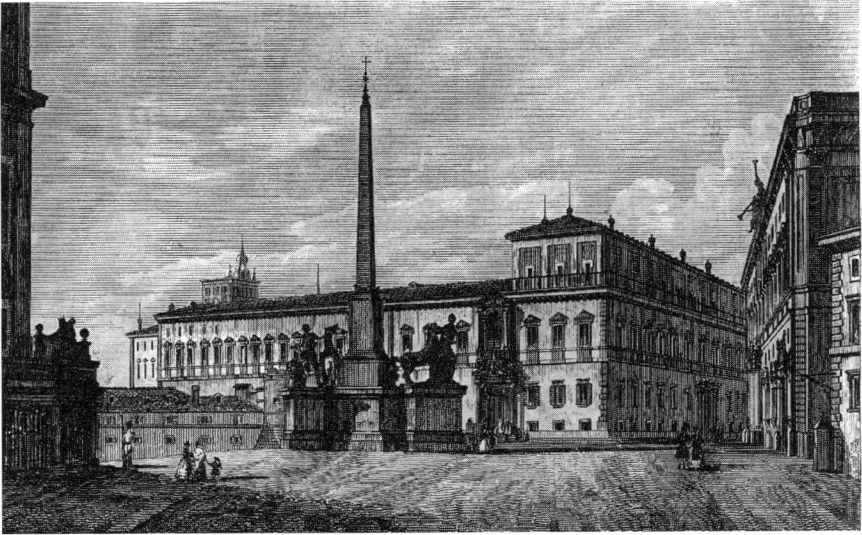

*Plazza Di Monte Cavallo*

She is raised in the clouds and below is an empty tomb surrounded by apostles. Domenicino's *Communion of St. Jerome* in this room is considered by far his finest work. In the next room we particularly admired a Madonna by Guido, with Sts. Jerome and Thomas below. Another by the same is the *Crucifixion of Peter*, with his head downwards. The *Entombment* by Caraveggio was quite fine. We saw in another room a picture by Fra Angelico da Fiesole, of the Sienese school, *The Miracles of St. Nicholas of Baei. The incredulity of Thomas*, by Guercino, was very beautiful. There was a Coronation of the Virgin with saints and bishops in adoration by Pinturicchio. Pietro Perugino painted a Resurrection; The Virgin is seated on a throne with two saints on each side, around the tomb below, are soldiers in various attitudes, one flying in fear, has the face of Raphael's master, and one who sleeps still, the lovely countenance of Raphael himself. There were Medallions of Faith, Hope and Charity by Perugino. After leaving the Vatican, we went to the base of the Capitol to look at the Tarpeian rock. It has been much filled in with earth, but we could see what the original height must have been, and called to mind the dreadful scenes which had been enacted here. We then went upon Monte Cavallo, where the Quirinal Palace stands in a fine situation. The popes are chosen here. In the piazza are the horses of Phidias or Praxiteles as they are called though upon slight grounds. At all events he must have been a skillful artist who modelled these finely rearing animals. By the side of each, stands a man, with hand raised, is if to reign in the horses. They are black with age. We have at last a prospect of sunny rooms in the Hotel de Russie and we shall leave here tomorrow.

*Saturday, Jan. 17th, Hotel de Russie, Rome.*

We are here in very comfortable apartments, where we shall have the sun, and, when settled, I think we shall enjoy the change. We have today visited the Schiarra Palace which is only open on Saturdays. The picture gallery is small but choice. We saw two of Claude Lorraine's early landscapes and two later ones. They pleased us much, for who can help admiring that soft warm glow, which he throws over his pictures. There were several landscapes by Brill and peasant scenes. *The Magdalen of the Roots* by Guido, represents her as a recluse, kneeling in penitence before heaven. A Moses by Guido is an early work and has more strength of expression, than of beauty. A pretty Madonna by Titian and his *Bella Donna*. A Madonna by Perugino, the infant holds a bird in his hand. We saw there also Leonardo da Vinci's *Vanity and Modesty*. The latter with a grave face, and covered with a veil, beckons to her sister, who richly decked seems by her affected smile to court admiration. The three Gamesters by Caraveggio was in his peculiar style. After this having still time we visited the forum and explored on foot some of its ruins. We read the inscription on the arch of Septimius Severus, and saw where

*Saturn Vespasian Tempio della Concordia e de Giove Tonante*

Caracalla had erased his murdered brother Gaeta's name and replaced it with other words. The old forum is much below the present level. We went down, and walked on the ancient pavement through the arch and up the steps of the temple of Vespasian and into the temple of Saturn of which a row of five pillars remains. There is some dispute about these names, but I believe those I have given are the correct ones. We saw the ruins of the tabularia, where the records were kept. On our return we passed the remains of Nerva's forum and the temple of Nerva a line of three or four columns connecting with the wall of the forum.

*Sunday, Jan. 18th, Rome.*
Went to church all day. Heard Mr. Hall in the morning, and an excellent Episcopal clergyman in the afternoon. After the service we stopt for a few moments at St. Peter's to hear the vespers, which were to be very fine. But a crowd was there, and we did not think it right to spend much of the holy day there.

*Monday, Jan. 19th, Rome.*
We planned to go today to the Capitol Tower to see the view from there. We ascended the marble steps, that lead to the top of the Capitol hill, in face of Castor and Pollux with their horses, and after a wearisome ascent reached the summit of the tower and began to study out the localities, especially in the forum below us. We saw the temples of Saturn and Vespasian; of the temple of Concord, where Cicero made his orations, nothing now remains, it stood opposite the Arch of Sept. Severus. Between the Arch, and the temple of Saturn, was the milliarum aureum, whence distances within the city were calculated. Near the Arch stood the Column of Duilius; and between the two temples, passed the clivus capitolinus. This part of the forum must have been quite crowded. We saw the direction of the via sacra; it passed through the arch of Titus at the further end of the forum, and joined the clivus capitolinus, near the column of Phocas. The Basilica Julia, which lay on its side has been partly uncovered, under Canina's direction, and exposes a white marble pavement, with low steps leading to it, from the via sacra. It was terminated by the temple of Minerva Chalcidica, of which, three Corinthian columns in a line, remain. We saw, from our high position, various buildings and ruins in the city; the tower where Nero played the fiddle, while Rome was burning, the Pantheon, the desolate campagna, and the snowy mountains beyond. We saw winding up the road to the Capitol, three

senator's carriages. They were red and gilt and looked very gay. In the afternoon we again visited the forum and walked about, examining more particularly, the various buildings. The Scuola Xanthica or notary's room, was near the tabularia, which joined the Capitol. We looked at the Basilica of Constantine, of which little more than three apses remain. The columns of Antonius and Faustina are fine, they are of Egyptian character, with griffins etc. on the frieze. We continued on, passing numberless French soldiers drilling until we came to the Coliseum. We did not stay long there as we are to go again to examine it thoroughly.

Then, returning through the Forum, we went into the Church of Saints Cosmo and Damiano, to look at a mosaic of the 6th cent. It represents the Saviour, with a scroll in his uplifted hand, and St. Peter and St. Paul leading the saints to him; with Pope Felix and St. Theodore behind. Below is a symbolic procession of sheep. See Kugler Vol. I. The church faces the Forum, and stands on the site of that of Romulus and Remus. Then we went to the Church of Sta. Maria Maggiore to see a mosaic of the 12th cent. the coronation of the Virgin by our Saviour. Along the centre aisle and arch were small mosaics of an earlier date but the light was so bad we could see little. The Borghese Chapel is very rich; a gilt picture represents a pope, shoveling snow, by a miracle, in August. The gilt roof is of the gold, first brought from America and given by Ferdinand and Isabella of Spain.

*Tuesday, Jan. 20th, Rome.*

No letters yet, I fear we shall have none this week. We went out quite early this morning, and visited first the Janus Quadrifrons, a sort of portico where the merchants used to assemble. It is in the forum boarium, and was built I believe by Sept. Severus. Near by is an arch, erected to him by the goldsmiths, and covered with bas reliefs. Farther on we stopt to examine the Cloaca Maxima, of which, only the ruined arches remain. It was the work of Tarquin the elder, and is one of the few kingly relics. Then we rode on, to the Church of the Knights of St. John and walking through their garden (they used the whole Aventine hill) which overlooked the Tiber, at quite an elevation, had a very fine view of the city. We saw the probable position of the Pons Publicius, memorable for the exploits of Horatius Cocles.

We had intended to visit the Baths of Caracalla, but finding the door locked, went instead to the Palace of the Caesars. We ascended several flights of steps and reached a high point, probably the second story,

*Pantheon*

where we looked off over the country. The Coliseum looked grandly; we saw at some distance the circular building where the wild beasts were kept for the shows and let in, by an underground passage, to the Coliseum. We enjoyed very much wandering about here; there is not much shape to these ruins, weeds and rubbish cover them, but they are very interesting. We picked up bits of mosaic, and ivy leaves, as mementoes. This is on the Palatine hill. Cicero's house stood near. Once probably it was a magnificent pile of buildings, now what a wreck! In the afternoon Mary and I went to the Pantheon. The portico is very fine. The top is open to the air. The roof has been despoiled of the bronze with which it was once covered. Raphael is buried here and near by Hannibal Caracci, Pierino del Vaga and Taddeo Zucchero. The marbles in the church are very rich; there are columns of gialo antico and a mosaic pavement. After this we went to the Church of the Capuchins to see Guido's Michael and the dragon. It was very beautiful, we dwelt long and earnestly upon it, and could hardly leave it. Opposite is a picture by Pietro di Cortona, of the conversation of Paul, and Annanias touching his eyes. In the basement of the convent is the cemetery; it is a horrible place. Skeletons stood round the sides, and bones were used, like mosaics, to make figures of. We took a speedy departure.

*Wednesday, Jan. 21st, Rome.*

We have had little sun today and some rain, but we went to the Palazzo Borghese. The gallery is one of the richest and most extensive in Rome; there are over eight-hundred pictures and some are very fine. We saw a Madonna by Sandro Botticelli 15th cent. Vases of flowers stood behind her head and several female figures surrounded her. We saw some Madonnas by Perugino and Francia his contemporary. One, by Imola a close imitation of Raphael; his faces glow, with richness of color. The history of Joseph in many parts, by Pinturiccio. There were two apostles, said to be by Michael Angelo, in his early style. An entombment of our Saviour, by Garafolo. But Raphael's *Entombment* surpassed this, in most respects. Two men carry the body of our Saviour, and the virgin has fainted in the arms of some women, while the Magdalen and the apostles lean over their Lord's lifeless body. Raphael also painted the portraits of Caesar Borgia and a cardinal. A holy family by Andrea del Sarto has smiles on all the faces, and they are very soft and pleasing. A Madonna by Carlo Dolce, in the style of his, Mary with the alabaster box. I saw here one thing that reminded me of home; it was Domenicino's Sibyl. Our copy is very like the original though the expression differs somewhat. Another of his is Diana in the chase. The goddess is giving a prize of a bow, to one of her nymphs, who has hit a bird fastened to a pole. Others are grouped about in various attitudes, two are in the water bathing. It is a graceful pretty thing. A head of St. Joseph by Guido, is very fine indeed with white hair, and beard, and very life like. By Caravaggio was St. Anna and the Virgin and child, the two latter placing their feet upon a serpent. This picture shows the strong contrasts, of dark and light, of which this artist was so fond. In one room was a very large and handsome mosaic table, formed of lapis lazuli, malachite, verd antique, gialo antico, Oriental alabaster and every variety of marble.

In the afternoon we stopt at the Church of St. Augustine. A sculptured Madonna and child adorned with jewels and a man who once tried to steal them, broke his leg, so that now none dare touch them. Silver hearts presented as offerings are fastened all over the walls. In this church is a prophet Isaiah, by Raphael, in imitation of Michael Angelo, but not equal to him. We then went to the Church of St. Agnese within the walls, where she was beheaded. It is her fete day, and the church was so crowded with poor miserable men and women, that it made us nervous to go among them. Beneath the church was a bas relief of the saint, representing he, when, as Antonio said, she was placed naked in prison, and hair was made to grow out miraculously to cover her. We entered the prison also, where she was kept. Then we went to the Church of St. Mark, to see a mosaic in its tribune, of the 9th cent., when early Christian art, had begun to decline. The figures are of Byzantine stiffness each on a

*Basilica di S. Giovanni in Laterano*

pedestal, as if the feet alone, were insufficient to support it. The Saviour is in the centre and on each side saints and apostles; on the arch of triumph, are symbols of the evangelists. This is a very old church first erected in the 3rd cent. and rebuilt in the 14th cent. There are three aisles and three apses, the pillars are covered with red and white jasper.

### Thursday, Jan. 22nd, Rome.

Took a walk before lunch, after that we set off for our day's sights. We went first to see the Church of St. Clemente one of the oldest in Rome. It is especially interesting from its form, which is exactly the old basilica, converted to a church. In the tribune is a mosaic of the Romanesque school 12th cent. More attention is paid to decoration that before. Vines issue from the foot of the cross, and birds and figures are interspersed. Above on the arch, were the symbols of the evangelists, and Peter, Paul Isaiah and Jeremiah, two on each side, and lambs beneath. Behind the altar was the bishop's seat, and circular benches of marble, on each side, for the elders. In the nave is a richly decorated choir, covered with fishes, and other early Christian symbols; the two pulpits one for the reading of the evangelists, and the other for the gospels. The floor was mosaic in a neat pattern of green, red, and white marbles. In the chapel of St. Catherine were some frescoes of Masaccio 15th cent. showing scenes from the life of St. Catherine, one, was the saint disputing with the doctors. Also a Madonna by Sassoferato, praying with folded hands.

From the church, we went into the old atrium, an open space, surrounded by pillars; it was altogether very interesting. We then went out to the Church of St. John Lateran. The palace was occupied by the popes until they went to Avignon, and the church ranks next to St. Peter's. It is much ornamented; along the nave are statues of the apostles by different artists. The Corsini chapel is very rich; its walls are adorned with elegant marbles, one kind that I have not seen before is called peach blossom. It comes from Africa and is of a purplish color, and the contrast with the verd antique is very pretty. There is a bronze monument here to a pope of the family, and another is enclosed in a porphyry sarcophagus, which came from the Pantheon. Torlonia's chapel too was very rich with malachite, lapis lazuli, etc. There were monuments to Torlonia's father and mother and a Pieta by Tenerani the first Italian artist in Rome. In the crypt of the church we saw a Pieta said to be by Bernini but the guide book gives a different name. It was the most perfect thing of the kind that I have ever seen. The lifeless expression of our Saviour's face, and its death like paleness were very vivid, and the veins of the hands and feet and the print of the nails were perfect. The virgin's face was very lovely.

We went out into the cloisters, which had been attached to the old church, and saw many remains of mosaic pavement, altars, etc. We were shown an altar where, they say, a monk, who did not believe in the bread being the true body of Christ, was convinced by seeing blood issuing thence, and percolating through the marble. The well where Jesus talked with the Samaritan woman. Part of the wood of the altar where Paul performed mass and part of the table where the last supper was eaten. The "heads of Peter and Paul" are kept above the high altar. We listened in silence to these absurd stories, thinking it useless to contradict them, we hear them everywhere in Rome. In the baptistry we saw several mosaics. In the vestibule was one with green gold tendrils upon a blue ground of the 5th cent. another of the 7th quite stiff and Byzantine like. This baptistry was built by Constantine, and the marble basin is still there, in which he is said to have been baptised. The interior part of the building has been restored, and is quite handsome, with porphyry columns. Near by is the Santa Scala up which so many poor deluded mortals climb on their knees. It is under a portico and is said to be Pilate's staircase. We saw several ascending it; it gives them indulgence for nine years. Here it was that Luther toiled up, 9 times and made his knees bleed. The popes are crowned at St. John Lateran's and take formal possession of it. Near by are many ruins of aqueducts and we stopt on our return to see the monument of the baker, discovered within twenty years, close by the Porta Maggiore the largest gate in Rome.

*Friday, Jan. 23rd 1857, Rome.*

We went to the Vatican today, and spent more than two hours in the stanze of Raphael, consisting of three rooms, and a saloon or larger one. We began with the one first executed by him. Jurisprudence, Theology, Philosophy, and Poetry, were symbolized by female figures in four parts of the ceiling, under them, on the four sides of the room were representations of the same, in a large form. Theology is in two parts; above, the Saviour enthroned in heaven, and surrounded by apostles, patriarchs, and saints. Below, are seated the four fathers of the Latin church discussing and behind them, learned theologians, spectators, and listeners in various attitudes, among these Dante, Perugino, and Raphael himself. Jurisprudence showed on one side the explanation of ecclesiastical law, and on the other of civil law; Justinian giving his pandects to Trebonius. Poetry represented Apollo and the muses under a tree, others grouped about in various ways, among them blind Homer pouring forth his inspired words behind Virgil, and Dante, while below Petrarch, Sappho and Corinna converse together. It forms a beautiful picture. Philosophy was the school of Athens a most interesting group of distinguished personages. In the next room was the plunder of the temple, by Heliodorus and the angels driving him out, it is a most spirited piece with the exception of a group, of the pope and his followers, put in as a compliment to Julius II, which is rather tame, for spectators of such a scene. Over the window is the Mass of Bolsena the finest of all, for coloring. On another wall is the scene, of Attila driven from the papal seat, by Peter and Paul, coming down from heaven. Attila himself looks up terrified, and of his army, some retreat, some look on in wonder. Over the other window is the deliverance from prison of Peter. The light is very beautiful, in the prison it seems to emanate from the angel above, and in another part from the moon and the torches of the sleeping guards. The Sala di Constantine shows first the Apparition of the cross; then in an immense, and a most animated picture the battle near the Milvian bridge, between Constantine and Maxentius; the figures are admirable, but it would take long, to study each one thoroughly. The baptism of Constantine, and the presentation of Rome to the bishop occupying three large walls, and a space between two windows are designed by Raphael but painted by Giulio Romano. The last stanza contained the burning of Rome, and shows the pope in the act of staying the fire, as it approached the Vatican, by making the sign of a cross. Several persons bear water, to extinguish the flames one naked figure is letting himself down from a wall another carries his aged father, upon his back. The other pictures in the room are Leo III crowning Charlemagne; Leo III justifying himself, before the emperor, and the battle of Ostia, over the Saracens. The ceilings are by Perugino and were left at the request of Raphael.

This afternoon we went to Tenerani's studio and saw him modeling a colossal Christ, full of dignity. An angel waiting to sound the last trumpet was fine, his wings were beautifully made, they looked like real feathers. After this we went to the Church of S. Pietro in Vincolo where is a splendid statue of Moses, by Michael Angelo. He is seated, leaning on the stone tablets and holding his long beard in one hand. The muscles are extraordinary for power and development. Two female figures of Religion and Virtue on each side are not particularly pleasing. These were all intended for a monument to Julius II but have never fulfilled their original intention. In the sacristy was Guido's *Hope*, a sweet face with clasped hands and Domenichino's deliverance of Peter from prison a fine picture. Over the altar was St. Margaret by Guercino, by holding up her cross, she subdues a fierce dragon, who was opening his mouth to devour her. We came home in a violent thunder-storm, hail and rain in torrents, which lasted about two hours.

*Saturday, Jan. 24th, Rome.*

Took a little rest this morning from sight seeing, but had a nice walk on the Pincian and Corso, though the ground has been wet today, after the rain. We found violets and periwinkles in blossom in the flower beds. This afternoon we went to the Rispigliosi Palace to see Guido's *Aurora*. It is in a Pavilion, which we reached, by passing through a garden, in the Italian style. The *Aurora* is on the ceiling and we found it difficult to look up so high, but there is a mirror arranged so as to bring down the reflection. Many artists were engaged in copying it. It is indeed a most beautiful thing, I believe I like it better than any-thing else, I have seen. The colors are most brilliant and the figures are gracefully dancing through the air. Phoebus is surrounded by the golden light of day, and Aurora scatters flowers before his chariot. In an adjoining room was a picture by Domenichino of David with the head of Goliath and a company of women singing "Saul hath slain his thousands, but David his ten-thousands." In another room Adam and Eve picking fig-leaves to cover themselves with. We afterwards visited the Barberini Palace, there are but three rooms of pictures. Guido's *Beatrice Cenci* is there, a lovely interesting face, though sad. One story is, that it was taken the night before her execution; another that it was done from memory. Next is Raphael's *Fornarina* the face is a little coarse, but not bad, the figure almost naked. There were four pretty Claudes, and a bella Donna of Titian called *l' esclave*. Behind the palace is an inscription to commemorate a victory of the emperor Claudius, the latter part is, Quod reges Brittaniae absque ulla jactura d omuerit, gentesque Barbaras primas indicio subigint. We made a few calls on Mrs. Hall, the Whitneys, and the Wheelers, and then returned to the hotel.

*Sunday, Jan. 25th, Rome.*

Went to church all day as usual. Mrs. Hall lent us some every good French tracts.

*Monday,* Jan. 26th, Rome.

Received four delightful letters from home, from Father, Mother, Laura and Lillie W. all New Year letters. We went again to the Borghese Gallery, to see the remaining rooms. We saw a landscape of Salvator Rosa's; he was once a bandit and generally paints wild scenes. In one room were some frescoes by Raphael recently detached from the walls of the Villa Olgiati. One represents boys shooting at a mark with Cupid's arrows, stolen while he sleeps. Titian's three graces which I did not admire. By Paul Veronese, was St. John preaching in the wilderness with three Arabs about him another by the same was St. Antonio preaching to the fishes, who put their heads out of the water, to listen. Several by Geraldo della notte, who is said to have always painted by night and the light in his pictures is always that of a lamp. This afternoon notwithstanding a pouring rain we went to the Colonna Palace. In one room were gobelin and arras tapestry. There were several good pictures. One, was by the father of Raphael, Giovanni Sanzio, a portrait of a boy. There were two landscapes by Albani, whose pictures are particularly characterized by elegance. A sweet Madonna by Giulio Romano. The *Guardian Angel* by Guercino; an angel leading a little boy, and pointing him to heaven. A fine large sea-view by Salvator Rosa and a pretty little Claude. A battle by Wouvermans etc. There were two beautiful cabinets in this room, one, made of Florentine marbles, and the other with 27 bas reliefs in ivory, of the *Last Judgement* of Michael Angelo, and scenes from the

Loggie. There is here a large hall, called the largest in the world, or rather, one of the finest. It is ornamented with Venetian mirrors, frescoed with beautiful flowers and cupids, and scenes from the family history of the Colonnas, and portraits of their distinguished men. One of the marble steps leading to this hall was broken out by a cannon ball from the French in 1848.

*Tuesday, Jan. 27th, Rome.*

We went again to Belzoni's studio, to meet Eliza Howland, and see her bust, which has been modeled in clay. I think it very good. After this we went to Tadolini's studio, but were not particularly struck with anythin. There was however, a large figure of David, with his harp, to be placed at one corner of the new column to the Virgin. We made a call in the afternoon at Dr. Gason's and then went to Filippi's in the via Condotti, a store full of pretty bronzes, mosaics and cameos. After this we visited the Baths of Diocletian. All that remains of these, that we could see, is the calidarium; which was turned by Michael Angelo, into the Church of Sta. Maria degli Angeli. It makes a splendid church. The roof was groined, and we saw the brass rings, where the lamps hung formerly. We entered by the vestibule, supposed to have been used for the cold baths. Here is the tomb of Salvator Rosa. The tribune facing the vestibule was the place for the swimming baths, and at the end of each transept, was a small circular room. Eight old granite columns remain in the transept. The floor was raised several feet, being below the level of the ground. We obtained from this, some little idea of the magnificence of these Roman baths. And when we consider that those of Diocletian, covered a mile in extent, our wonder is increased. We stopt at St. Bernardo a moment which was probably the circular room adjoining the theatre it is much like the pantheon in form, with the same opening in the round dome. Attached to the Church of the Angeli, is a convent, and in its garden are some cypresses planted by Michael Angelo; the monks are Carthusians and robed in white. We afterwards visited the "Pretorian Camp"; it is little more than an open field.

*Wednesday, Jan. 28th, Rome.*

Made another excursion to the "Palace of the Caesars"; entering from the forum. We saw first the supposed ruins, of the house of Agrippina, the mother of Nero. They have been formed into a low tower by Prince Farnese in whose grounds these ruins are included. Near these was situated the palace of Caligula, and on a corner overlooking the city Cicero's house, and that of Tiberius. This is the site of the Rome of Romulus built on the Palatine hill. At one side, was the garden of the Knights of Malta, where we went the other day. Crossing then the grounds to the other side, we came to the remains of the temple of Apollo, erected to commemorate the victory at Actium. Near by, is what the guide called the "Baths of Livia." It is underground, and we explored it, by means of a lighted torch, as far as it has been opened. It was evidently a bathing place, a tub was found in it, and statues in their niches, but these are all removed. The gilding of the ceiling remains in some places, and also little frescoes, in arabesque forms, quite pretty, as far as we could see. It was an interesting little spot, all the more, as we had no idea, from the outside, of its existence. The library was a circular room, in fact there were two, one Greek and the other Latin. We could trace the shape of one and, as it were, little places for alcoves. In the Convent of St. Bonaventura, which we could not enter, are some remains of Nero's "golden house," which formerly extended over this hill, and the space where the Coliseum now stands, to the Esquiline. Returning down the via St. Bonaventura, we passed on our right the temple of Adonis and came out at the arch of Titus, which is supposed to have been, the grand entrance to the old palaces. It requires much imagination to get an idea of the different buildings that stood on this hill, and their relation to one another, but we enjoyed the excursion very much. Mr. Lansing called in the evening, and Mr. Howland came to tell us, that they were going to Egypt and to start for Naples on Tuesday. We went to dine with the Howlands and saw all their pretty purchases and presents. Mr. Bartholemew and Mr. Wright came in while we were there.

*Thursday, Jan. 29th, Rome.*

    Went to Fioppi's, to have a paper weight made, from the marbles we had collected. Thence to Rosetti's studio and saw a very beautiful statue. It was the crazy Ophelia carrying flowers to her father's grave. She has flowers upon her head, and in her dress, which she holds up with one hand, and which has the appearance of satin, while in the other, she holds a single daisy. Her face has a crazy look, but it perfectly beautiful. The drapery is modest, and the whole figure has such a delicacy and life-like expression, that we could hardly leave it, but have carried it away, in our memories. Another thing is the Greek Slave bowing her head in sorrow at her captivity. The delicacy of this too is exquisite, she sits upon a mat, but has little drapery. Esmiralda and her goat, from a story of Victor Hugo was another. We then went to the Corsini gallery. A miniature painter was taking most exquisite little copies of the pictures. We saw here a sweet Madonna, leaning over her sleeping child, by Carlo Dolci. Three "ecce homo's" one by Guido, one Guercino and one by Carlo Dolce, the last I rather preferred. A portrait of Philip II of Spain by Titian. St. Apollonia by Carlo Dolce holding in her hand a tooth and pincers, the method of her persecution. In the afternoon we drove out to the Church of St. Agnese "fuori le mure." The church is below the level of the ground and we descended by a long flight of steps, on each side of which, were inscriptions from the catacombs beneath. It is a pretty church and is remarkable for having an upper gallery which is not common here. In the tribune is a mosaic of Byzantine rigidity; Sta. Agnese between two popes. Above the pillars of the nave, are portraits of some of the later popes in mosaic. They were repairing part of the church, where at some fête, the floor had given way, and let down the pope, cardinals, and all; but none were killed. Very near this church is Sta. Costanza, now used as its baptistry. Originally built by Constantine as the tomb of his daughter Costanza, it is an example of a circular Roman tomb, quite plain externally. Within, the centre was enclosed by a double row of columns, and the ambulatory outside of these was decorated with mosaics of the 4th cent., arabesques, with genii, birds, etc., among vine branches. On each side of the entrance, are remains of the circular ends of the Forum, which was usually added to such tombs. In returning we walked home as far as the Ports Pia and met the daughter of the Queen of Spain; and two cardinals, with their attendant priests, all taking the air.

*Friday, Jan. 30th, Rome.*

A bright pleasant day. We went to the Coliseum and wandered in its ruins, among the rows of seats. We ascended the steps, as far as we could, and had a fine view of the building and the country around. There were five rows of seats; first the Emperor's, and nobles', next the citizen's and common people's and lastly the women's. We stopt in the Forum and picked up some marbles, on the site of the Temple of Concord. Then we spent an hour at the Doria Palace, which is so extensive, we have not yet seen it all. We saw a portrait of Joanna of Arragon, by Leonardo da Vinci, rich, glowing, and beautiful. A holy family, by Giovanni Bellini, of which the child is very expressive; he seems to be speaking. A rustic peasant scene by Teniers, and a curious picture, on Oriental alabaster of the destruction of Pharaoh's host. Other pictures of less interest.

In the afternoon we went to the Baths of Caracalla, but it was damp and looked like rain, and we had not time to examine them as we wished. The ruins are very splendid, and the halls immense; we saw the cella caladaria and the vapour bath and the pinacotheca. The surface of some of the rooms has been removed, and shows a pretty mosaic floor, in one red porphyry, and a green stone, in the "fish scale" pattern; and in another black and white marbles. In one room were discovered, the Toro Farnese, the Torso and the Flora. We saw a mosaic of a griffin, which had fallen, I believe, from the roof. These are the finest ruins in Rome next to the Coliseum. There are plenty of pretty bits of marbles lying about, and we improved our opportunity to get some. The rain began, so we hurried away. In riding home we stopt to see Rienzi's house; the frieze is very rich. Near by, is the temple of Fortuna Virilis, with its Ionic columns and in sight of the temple of Vesta. We rode through the Ghetto or Jew's quarter, the gates of which are now allowed to be open by Pius IX. Near this is situated the Cenci Palace, where the unhappy Beatrice lived. The exterior is very plain, and we saw nothing more. We passed the theatre of Marcellus, of which, only remains, two rows of columns, one above the another, and built in with masonry. On returning we saw a funeral; priests chanting, and bearing a bier, covered with velvet, and silver ornaments, and preceded by priests and monks carrying torches.

*Saturday, Jan. 31st, Rome.*

Finished the sight seeing of the week by going to the Museum of St. John Lateran. It contains what the Vatican could not hold. Upon the ground floor, in a number of rooms, were the old Roman remains. We saw a mosaic of two gladiators which had formed a pavement in the Baths of Caracalla. Also a bas relief of senators and lictors found in the form of Trajan, another two boxers with their boxing gloves on. We saw some very beautiful capitals, Corinthian and Ionic, little altars, and funeral urns with inscriptions, friezes, and pillars, all collected from various parts. We admired exceedingly a statue, eleven feet high, of Antinous found in Hadrian's Villa; it is still very white and of Carrara marble. The head is crowned with a wreath of ivy leaves and berries; the drapery hangs gracefully over one shoulder, and in his hand he holds a sort of thyrsus. We saw a fine statue of Sophocles, he has one hand in his toga, and one behind him. A statue of Drusus, and one of Germanicus, in armor both with fine faces. A colossal head of Jupiter. A repetition of Praxiteles faun. A large stag in grey marble, and a cow in white. A bas relief showing a crane for lifting stones. Another with the arch of Titus carved upon it. We saw an unfinished statue called a captive barbarian; it had the sculptor's marks for his workmen still remaining. There is none to tell, who was the sculptor, why it is unfinished, or when it was begun.

We left the heathen monuments, and turned to the Christian. They began on each side of a staircase, leading to the second story. There were many sarcophagi, and inscriptions found in the Catacombs. They portrayed scenes from the Old and New Testament, one as typical as the other. Such as Jonah thrown into the sea and again upon the land. Abraham about to slay his son. Moses striking the rock. Elijah ascending to heaven Elisha receiving his mantle, and the sons of the prophets looking on. The miracle of the loaves. The entry into Jerusalem. There was generally a medallion separating two of these views on each sarcophagus, with a portrait of the deceased. Those of later date, were separated by pillars only. Some had only Christ and his disciples, each one, divided off, by a pillar. There were many inscriptions of an early period, mostly marked in red, sometimes in bad Latin and having the cup, olive branch, or monogram, as symbols. One had, as it seemed, the instrument of the martyr's death and almost all ended with "in pace," or "requescat in pace." There was a sitting figure, of Bishop Hippolytus, of Porto of the 3rd cent. In another room were copies of frescoes found in the catacombs. They were very interesting as showing the infancy of Christian art. We saw Christ as a youthful shepherd bearing a lamb on his shoulders and followed by others. Some frescoes were in their original state, but so much injured, that we could see little. There were mosaics, found in excavating near one of the gates of Rome. Upon a white ground were bones, of fishes, nuts, fruit etc. all in mosaic, with their shadows faithfully delineated. They represent the art in its first stages. There were several cartoons of large paintings; one, *The Incredulity of Thomas*, by Guercino. There were other paintings, but it was very cold on the stone floors, and raining hard, so we came away.

*Sunday, Feb. 1st, Rome.*

February opened with a fair sky, tried walking to church in the afternoon but found it very disagreeable on account of the wet, crowded, and dirty streets, and scant pavements.

*Monday, Feb. 2nd, "Candlemas Day," Rome.*

We rose early to prepare for our excursion to St. Peter's for it is the day on which the pope blesses the candles. The ceremonies began at ten, but we started at nine in order to be there in season. We were obliged to wear black or dark dresses, and only black lace veils, upon our heads. We sat upon a staging, in the right transept, of the church. There was plenty of time to look about us and we improved it very agreeably. Soldiers abounded: Swiss guards in their variegated red and yellow uniform, others with dark coats, white trousers, and white plumes, some in crimson, and the common French in their blue jackets and dull red trousers. The chamberlain, who showed the ladies to their seats, and kept us in order, was a man with a Spanish cast of face and reminded me of pictures of old times, of Elizabeth's or Henry's reign. He had on a black coat, trimmed at the wrists, with lace, a large, double white ruff, around his neck, a sword at his waist and black stockings with buckled shoes, and a short velvet cloak hanging behind him, a chain and several ornaments suspended about his neck. Chanting was heard and the long procession came in. First came the different orders of ecclesiastics in red, purple black and white, I could not distinguish them by name. Then the cardinals, in white silk, with gold and purple capes, and white mitres. Among these were the Greek and Armenian Bishops with rich tiaras, and I thought I saw the hated Antonelli, in a richer dress than the others and wearing spectacles. Then came poor Pio Nono borne aloft in a chair, dressed in red and gold, and a white silver mitre. He waved his hand gently about, blessing his flock and most of the people knelt as he passed. He had a very benevolent countenance. He was placed in his throne, at the end of the church, which was white, and he had the singular appearance, of being in a glass case, so entirely was he inclosed by the chair. The cardinals had their candles blessed first. Each in turn, knelt before his

*PIO IX. P.O.M.*

Holiness, and kissed his hand, while the pope raised a candle from his lap, over the head of the cardinal. Then the inferior ecclesiastics received one, only kissing the toe, instead of the hand. Lastly private gentlemen, soldiers, and even some British Officers. This took a long time, then the procession formed again, all with lighted candles and then they returned to their places. Mass was performed by a cardinal, the choir sang, and the pope did something, (I could not tell what) standing up, sitting down, and having his mitre taken off, and put on again. His dress was changed to white with a gilt mitre. The officiating cardinal three times emptied the glass of wine, wiped his fingers on a little napkin which was then used to wipe out the cup. He raised the wafers, or as it is called, "elevated the host," read and sang, etc. We came away after this, to avoid the crowd, as we had no gentleman with us. Auntie, M. and I, had to go down the whole length of the broad aisle, between two files of soldiers, which was far from agreeable. We heard that afterwards the pope came to the altar, and took some snuff. And that at the mass, the cardinal, or priest always drinks the wine himself, and distributes the bread alone among the people. So much for the Catholic ceremonies, once is enough for me. Received letters from home. Made some calls, but found everyone out. The Howlands came to bid us goodbye, they leave tomorrow for Egypt. The Wheelers also have been here.

*Tuesday, Feb. 3rd, Rome.*

Went to the Vatican today, and spent as much time as we could, before one. We entered through the Hall of the inscriptions, covered on each side for a long space with both heathen and Christian remains. Then passed into the next hall or gallery filled with antiques, statues, sarcophagi, and busts. We saw Autumn reclining, her head adorned with grapes, and genii in various attitudes around her. The muse Clio was a female seated, and holding in one hand a trumpet, and in the other a scroll. There were two large seated statues of Tiberius, both fine, one was crowned with an oak wreath. We saw the celebrated head of the young Augustus taken at 14. It is exquisite, very white for so ancient a thing, there is much thought in the brow, and the nose and mouth are beautiful. Many busts of celebrated men Cato, Cicero etc. A colossal Hercules lying upon his lion's skin. Hygea's feeding serpents from their cups. A fisher boy asleep with his basket of fishes by his side. A swan. A phoenix on a burning pile. A wild boar in nero antico. A bas relief, with the shield of Medusa and scenes representing a hunt for wild animals. I have mentioned a few of the principal objects in this room, but they are innumerable.

Then we entered the little circular room where the Torso is to be seen. There is no head, no arms, no legs below the knees, and part of the back is sliced off, but it is much admired for the knowledge of anatomy it shows, and was a favorite study of Michael Angelo. The artist was Apolonius of Athens as found from an inscription. The tomb of Scipio is in the same room. It is of Doric style, and made of grey tufa, and it is a well known relic of republican Rome. It stood upon the Via Appia. It is to Lucius C. Scipio Barbatus, conqueror of the Samnites, and great-grandfather of Scipio Africanus. There are many other records of the Scipio family. In the circular room adjoining was a very large marble vase or more resembling a basin or fountain, but I do not know what it was. A little balcony opens out from here, whence there is a splendid view of the city and hills around which gives this part of the Vatican, the name of Belvedere. In this balcony was an ancient sun dial, with the cardinal points, and the winds, marked upon it. In an adjoining room is the Meleager, a beautiful statue. His dog looks up wistfully in his face and a boar's head lies beside him. The story is, that he led in the Caledonian boar hunt but died afterwards, in consequence of a decree of the fates, that he should live, till a piece of wood on the hearth was consumed. Another room was occupied by three of Canova's works. Perseus, holding the Gorgon's head in one hand, and his sword in the other. Also the two boxers Creugas and Demoxenus, on opposite sides of the room, as if fiercely running to meet one another. The one has his boxing gloves on, the other has thrown them on the floor. There is much muscular power in both, Canova himself, thought they compared well with the antique Apollo. Finally we went into another little room where is the Antinous. He was a youth of remarkable beauty, and a great favorite of the Emperor Hadrian, who deified him, after death. It is partly mutilated; but Domenichino is said to have declared, that all his knowledge of the beautiful, was derived from that. We were then obliged to leave; it hailed, and rained hard, as we rode home.

In the afternoon we went upon the Coelian Hill to the Church of St. Gregorio, built on the site of the family mansion of Gregory the Great. We saw the chair of the saint. It was of white marble and looked very old and worn. We each took a seat in it and found it easy. In the chapel of St. Silvia, in the apse, was a fresco by Guido, representing a choir of angels. The Father is seen above, and all the angels around a sort of balcony. Three little boy angels stand in the centre, singing, the middle one, having his arms about the necks of the other two. The rest had various instruments, and some were very beautiful, and graceful, in their movements. The chapel of St. Andrew contains two works, rival productions one by Guido and one by Domenichino. The first represents St. Andrew led to crucifixion, and adoring the cross in the distance while brutal soldiers try to force him on. Domenichino's is the scourging of the saint, who lies stretched upon a bench. I liked both very well, but the first, I think, the best. They were very large frescoes. Another door was opened, and we saw the table, where the saint fed, every day, twelve poor pilgrims; it is a large one of marble, and is kept with scared care.

*Wednesday, Feb. 4th, Rome.*

Went again to the Vatican and passing through the halls we visited yesterday, commenced anew at the Apollo Belvedere. It is a most exquisite, fascinating thing, such beauty mingled with slight disdain, as he waits the result of his unerring shaft. It was found at Antium, and supposed to have stood in the imperial baths. I can not describe it more. The Laocoon is an image of horror. The father and two sons, enveloped in the awful folds of two serpents, whose fangs buried in their hearts, cause them to heave in agony. Oh! it is horrible to think of. It was found on the Esquiline Hill.

We went next, into the Hall of Animals. These are sculptured horses, lions, tigers, dogs, asses, and every imaginable animal. We saw a fine lion of black marble, holding an ox's head in his paws and crouching upon his front feet. It is quite fine. A greyhound running at full speed. A stag with a hound upon its back, gripping it, with a death grasp. Another of the same, breathing its last. Two mosaic pavements, with fishes, fruit etc., upon them. The next room we entered was the Hall of Muses. Some were very beautiful. They were Euterpe, (Lyric Poetry), Urania (Astronomy), Clio (History), Thalia (Comedy), Polymnia (Sublime Hymn), Calliope (Epic Poetry), Erato (Erotic Poetry), Melpomene (Tragic Poetry). In a little passage way was a statue of Lycurgus, and a fine bust of Pericles helmeted, one of Aspasia also, not so pleasing.

The next is the Rotunda, a small but beautiful hall, circular in form. The centre is occupied by a large round mosaic pavement found in the baths of Titus and quite celebrated. It represents the battle of the Centaurs and Lapithae; with sea gods, and a beautiful wreath of fruit and flowers about it. In the middle stands a large porphyry basin, also found in these baths. Around the room are statues and busts of divinities and celebrities. A bust of Faustina. One, of the beautiful Antinous. Juno Sospiter, with a bronze shield and spear. On the left, is the Hall of the Greek Cross. The principal objects here are two immense sarcophagi of Helena the mother, and Constantia the daughter of Constantine. The former was found, near the Porta Maggiore and the latter in the Church of Sta. Costanza near Sta. Agnese. They were quite injured but have been restored. The porphyry one, occupied 20 years in making. There is a cippus or funeral monument in this room to Syphax, its authenticity has been doubted; but if genuine is very interesting. The inscription is, "Syphax Numidiae rex. - A Scipione. Afrc . Jur . Bel . Causa . Rom . in . triumph . sum . ornu . capitus . preductus . In . triburtino . terri . religatu . suamque servit v . in ani . revol . - supremam . d. clausit - etalis . ann.XLVII.M.V.D.XI . captitio V . obrut . -P.C. Scipio condito sepul." It was found at Tivoli. There were two sphinxes of Egyptian granite, found near the Vatican. A mosaic pavement, found in Cicero's Villa at Tusculum with Minerva's and Medusa's heads in the centre and arabesques and ornaments surrounding them. Another, a basket of flowers was very pretty and the flowers quite natural.

We walked through the Braccio Nuovo, but left it, for another time. It opens out from the long hall of statues through which we always pass called, Chiarmonti. We took some rolls in our pockets, and instead of returning for lunch, went out to the Church of St. Paolo fuori le mure. It was burnt down about 25 years ago and is now nearly rebuilt in a very beautiful style. In the tribune, are the mosaics of the old church, Christ and the apostles, dating from the 13th cent. Upon the "Arch of Galla Placidia" beyond the transept are mosaics of the fifth century. A head of our Saviour and angels lowering their wands before him, almost the first known representations, of these beings; on each side a crowd of saints bow before their Lord. The grand altar is very splendid. A gilded canopy overarches it, supported by four beautiful columns of Oriental alabaster, presented to Pius IX by Mahomet Ali Vizir of Egypt. The altar is a pleasing combination of gold and white, with rich marbles. Heads of the popes will adorn the whole length of the church, above the pillars of which there are 80, of rose granite, from near Lago Maggiore. These heads are of mosaic, and not all finished yet. They are being made in the Vatican Manufactory. The altars at the ends of the transept are most magnificently adorned with slabs of the splendid malachite with lapis lazuli. Under the arch of triumph, are two very fine granite columns of the

Ionic order, which had belonged to the old building. The whole effect of the church is splendid. We saw the cloisters through a window, they show every possible variety of columns, twisted, spiral, fluted, etc. In one of the small chapels we saw the half-burnt, wooden statue of St. Paul. Workmen are still employed in the building. We came home well tired, with our interesting day. Weather rainy still. O for sunny skies, and good sidewalks. Mt. Pincian is the only place here, fit for ladies to walk in.

*Thursday, Feb. 5th, Rome.*

Started today to visit the Sistine Chapel, but not being able to get in; visited the lower church, or cloisters of St. Peters as we had obtained a permit. We saw a statue of St. Peter seated in a chair and holding his keys. It was formerly a proconsul but was altered by Constantine who built a St. Peter's in 306. In a little locked chapel is Peter's tomb, and Paul's too, they say, whose body was brought from the Catacombs of St. Calixtus? There were a number of bas reliefs of scriptural subjects - frescoes, statues, and mosaics also the heart of Christina in a semi-circular tomb, a statue of Benedict IX, and remains of many other popes. The only English one was Henry. The tombs of the Pretender, and his two sons, with their usurped titles. The light of our guide's torch, did not admit of very close inspection of these objects and we passed rapidly through the crypt or Grotto Vaticano as it is called. It is all, under the dome alone, of the church above, which occupied 350 years in building. We then went into the sacristy of the basilica from which opened on each side, vestries for the cannons and rooms where the robes of the cardinals, and priest, are kept and put on. In a little chapel adjoining one vestry is a picture of the Madonna and Child, with John, the faces are very sweet. It is by Giulio Romano, and is one of his most careful early works. Another angel raising Peter in the prison, is by Giambattista Caracciolo, and very highly colored. In the council room of the ecclesiastics were frescoes which had been removed here from some church and divided up, and framed. They are angels singing, and playing on instruments, by Melozzo da Forli a scholar of Squarcione of the 15th cent. The faces of some are very beautiful, three cherubs, singing with folded hands, or crossed upon the breast, were lovely. They may have been the model to Guido, of his choir of Angels. There is a good deal of foreshortening in the figures, and the attitudes are not common.

Then, we visited the mosaic manufactory of the Vatican. The workmen were principally employed on the heads of the popes, for the

Church of St. Paul. They have a copy painted upon a gilt ground, and marked in squares. Each one has a circular frame filled with plaster upon the surface of which they draw the head. They then fill up the ground, with the bits of composition covered with gilt, and cut out the plaster, piece by piece, as they proceed in the face. Into the spaces, thus cut out, they put a sort of clay or putty and the mosaics are set into this, after the workman has selected from 20,000, one, of the right form and color. When viewed near at hand these pictures are quite coarse, but at a little distance they have the effect of a well finished painting. The process seems quite mechanical, but the selection of colors requires much skill and practice. We saw some other mosaics, which were so fine that it required a pincers, to take up, and set in their places the minute bits. The colors are obtained by a chemical process. In the afternoon we went again to the Baths of Caracalla, not feeling satisfied, with our former hurried visit. We followed out the plan, and obtained quite a good idea of it. The entrance leads into the gladiatorial room. Next is the swimming room and the pinacotheca. There were many smaller chambers, a vapour bath, dressing rooms, etc. We went up by a staircase to the top of the ruins and obtained a fine view. The mountains are beautiful, but still snow clad.

*Friday, Feb. 6th, Rome.*

A most beautiful day. The finest throughout that we have had since we have been here I think. We improved it, by walking for an hour, on the Pincian, and then we went to the Vatican for the sixth time, to visit the Sistine Chapel. I was quite familiar with some of the frescoes here and was very desirous of seeing the originals. At the end by which we entered is Michael Angelo's *Last Judgment*. It is 60 feet high and occupied seven years. It is blackened by smoke, and not a pleasing picture at all, but it shows the power of the master, and accorded with the religious feelings of his day, more than it does with ours. It is the *dies irae*. The Saviour is a Judge alone, and no lovely forms, appear among the angels, or the saints, who surround the throne. The Virgin only has a countenance of pity and tenderness. The ceiling adorned by the same artist, shows the history of the human race since the deluge. Naked human figures, hold up frescoed architecture, and the Prophets and Sibyls are in the curve of the roof, and more easily examined then the ceiling though at so great a height. They are most of them very grand. In the corners are, the brazen serpent, Judith with the head of Holofernes, the death of Haman, and

David slaying Goliath. In the triangles between the prophets, are scenes from the life of the Virgin and in the arches underneath kings of Israel and Judah. Beneath the windows are earlier works, those on the one side the history of Moses, typifying those on the other the life of Christ. First, on the right, Moses and his wife on their way into Egypt, Luca Signorelli. On the left the baptism of Christ. Perugino. Moses helping Jethro's daughters at the well, Sandro Botticelli. The temptation of Christ, the same artist. Crossing the Red Sea, Cosimo Rosselli. Calling of the Apostles, Ghirlandajo. Moses giving the commandments from Mt. Sinai, Christ's sermon on the mount, both by Rosselli. The punishment of Korah etc., Sandro Botticelli Christ giving the keys to Peter. Moses giving the last commands to Joshua. The Last Supper. Michael bearing away Moses's body. The Resurrection Michael Angelo's pictures are intended to carry out the typical meaning of these.

In the afternoon we went to the Baths of Titus. These were built over the remains of Nero's Golden House. We had a guide who led us first into a long corridor, which as well as most of the other rooms, probably belonged to Nero's house; of the baths, there are few remains, as they were hastily built. We saw some remains of frescoes in the form of arabesques, birds, and small figures. In one room were frescoed two figures and a tripod basin. In another, were some basins for bathing purposes; and in another still, several feet below the surface, a pavement which is supposed to have belonged to Maecena's house, which was anterior to Nero's. Some parts are not yet explored. The floors are swept clean and fragments locked up. In one room, the great porphyry Vase in the Rotunda of the Vatican was found. And upon this hill the Laocoon was discovered and also the Meleager and Antinous of the Vatican. On our return we stopt at St. Stephano Rotundo where was nothing very interesting. Some horrible martyr pictures surround the walls. It has the appearance of having been a baptistry. In the evening as there was a splendid moon, we went to see the Coliseum by moonlight. It looked very finely. Others were there as well as we. We walked about for a while, and then went upon the Capitol hill, and then to St. Peter's, which looked very splendid, and its fountains too, were very pretty in the moonlight.

_Saturday, Feb. 6th, Rome._

Took a walk in the morning, and went in the afternoon to the Museum of the Borghese Villa. In the lower story the rooms are frescoed; and filled with antique statuary and the floor covered with mosaics, representing hunts of various kinds. One room was called the Hercules room; having busts and statues of this hero. The Apollo Saloon, has a figure of the God in the centre. In this room are also the muses Polymnia, Erato, Clio and Melpomene, Anacreon seated, with his lyre and a figure of Daphne, just turning into laurel as Apollo overtakes her; the only known ancient representation of this subject. There were some splendid vases two square ones of nero antico, one of oophite, a precious stone of a greenish color, upon a green and porphyry base, and one of rouge antique. A graceful nude Venus, a gypsy of the 16th cent. in black and white marble, and several nymphs and other figures among which was a boy plucking a thorn from his foot. On the upper floor were paintings and modern sculpture. David throwing his sling at Goliath. Daphne and Apollo again with beautiful faces, and bark growing over her limbs. Finally AEneas carrying his father Anchises, who holds the Penates in his hands, and little Ascanius runs by the side. These are all by Bernini and are very fine. We saw the celebrated Venus Victrix, by Canova. It is a figure reclining on a couch, and is the likeness of the Princess Pauline Borghese, sister of Napoleon I. There are several very beautiful marble vases. We have had a call from Dr. and Mrs. Fisk of Northampton.

*Sunday, Feb. 8th, Rome.*
Went to church as usual. There were many persons present. Rome begins to be still more full, in expectation of Carnival.

*Monday, Feb. 9th, Rome.*
Went to the Quirinal or Pope's Palace, and garden. The garden is quite stiff, but the mode of arrangement was curious. The walks are mostly through hedges of green box, which had grown to the great height of 18 or even 20 feet, and was trimmed so as to present a surface like a wall. It must make very cool and delightful walks for summer. That is the season when the popes occupy this palace. The present one has not been here, for some time, for his last troubles had their commencement here; but in the coming summer, he intends to honor it with his presence. We went into a little Casina, where distinguished visitors are sometimes received. All around are fountains, and beds of flowers, arranged in regular forms. We descended to the lower garden, by a flight of steps, or inclined walk. We saw there, a grotto, covered with a sort of stucco mosaic; at one side was a vulcan's forge with statues and fountains on each

side, and in the centre an organ. A screw was turned, and it played several tunes, on either side was an angel, in marble, or plaster, with at trumpet, and they blew long blasts upon them. All this was done by water works. Everywhere were statues fountains and gardens. In one of these, the beds were laid out, so as to form the coat of arms, of the present pope, we could distinguish the lion in it.

Then we went into the palace, and entered first a long hall, lined with benches and having on each side the inscription of Pius IX Pont. Max. In the hall of the consistory was a mosaic picture of the Madonna and Child by Carlo Moratta, which has been copied in mosaic, and placed under the clock of the palace tower. In one room were interior views of the four basilicas in their former state. We saw some Gobelin tapestry presented by Napoleon I to Pius VII. Some was old, but one piece new, a representation of Caravaggio's entombment in the Vatican. There was a throne room, and an antechamber and another throne room and the antechamber of the noble-guards, who are sons of the nobles. In the pope's private chapel was an Annunciation by Guido. The virgin's countenance is very expressive, of meek submission, the angel points upwards, and offers her a lily-branch and a band of lovely cherubs appear in the sky. It is a very beautiful picture. There were some vases of Sevres porcelain given by Nap. III to Pio. Nono. the figures were genii, gathering grapes. There were also two full length figures, of Peter and Paul, by Fra Bartolommeo, which we saw copied in a tapestry at Genoa. The rooms were tasteful and the walls of some were hung with crimson velvet and silk. The pope's bedroom had a brass bedstead, (here Pius VII died) and such furniture as the successor of St. Peter needs, as much as common mortals. In this room was a picture, having a very pretty frame of velvet, and Genoese, silver, filigree work. The dining room and writing room were nothing remarkable, the pope's chair was always stuffed comfortably and had a canopy more or less gilded over the top. We saw some ecclesiastical vestments of Clement XVIII a gold ground splendidly embroidered, with fruit, flowers, and figures. We were not able to see the room, where the pope is elected, only to look through the key-hole. The balcony upon which he appears to the people, is in front.

After seeing the palace we crossed the square to the stables or harness rooms, where we saw a very elegant horse-cloth presented by the Sultan of Turkey. It had been very richly adorned with diamonds, but they were given away as presents by the pope and their place supplied by imitations. This afternoon we went to the Villa Albani. The day has been exquisite, and the air in the sun, balmy and spring-like, so that we enjoyed walking about the grounds. The Villa and Coffee house are separated by a garden, in the Italian style. The latter is a semi-circular building, statues and herms adorn the vestibule, within is a large basin of Egyptian breccia, and in an inner room are mosaics, one found in Cicero's Villa called The School of Medicine.

We came, in our walk about the grounds, to another building, where were lounges and seats, tables, statues, etc. and a fine view. I should like to take a book and read there, in full view of the splendid mountains, which never looked finer, to me, than today. The villa is in parts, rather neglected, it belongs to a Milanese nobleman, who never occupies it. There are a number of antiques to be seen here. Two Etruscan Priests and Priestesses. A bas relief of Antinous, holding flowers, considered to rank in value, next to the Apollo and Laocoon. A bas relief of Diogenes in his tub and Alexander standing before him. Another in rouge antique of Dedalus making his wings and Icarus standing by. Poor deformed AEsop, the only known representation of him, the face was very good. An Apollo Sauroctonos, supposed to be the original bronze statue, by Praxiteles, described by Pliny, and found on the Aventine. A painting by Carlo Dolce, of the Saviour blessing the bread, which Sig. Petragnani has copied, in miniature. One room was fitted up, in the Chinese style, tables and tea sets etc. We saw two figures of Diana of Ephesus, very ugly indeed. In a glass case, we saw some beautiful flowers, varieties of camellias red, pink, and white. Some of the walks here, were very beautiful, through dark alleys, of trees. In one, the sun shone across the mossy path, and it seemed a poet's walk.

*Tuesday, Feb. 10th.*

Started at half-past twelve for the Via Appia and its accessories. It commences at the Porta Capena. We stopt first at the Scipios' tomb, which is on the left side of the present road and formerly had an entrance from a vicola connecting the Via Appia and Via Latina. We each took a candle and followed a guide to examine it. The sarcophagus of L. Scipio Barbatus is in the Vatican and here remain only some copied inscriptions of several members of the family a son of Sc. Africanus and others. We saw where the eternally burning lamp was hung. Statues of L. Scipio and Ennius are said to have adorned the front of the sepulchre. It was an interesting place. After this we came to the columbaria of the freedmen of Caesar's household. We went down a long flight of steps, to a deep chamber, lined on each side with niches, like dove cotes, for sepulchral urns. Many of these remains, of various shapes and sizes. There were also little lamps of terra cotta, figures, bits of statues, bas reliefs of two figures joining hands and other little objects. It gave us a complete idea of the columbaria, or common burial places for the burnt ashes. Near by was another called Pompey's but similar in form. A little museum contained seals, bronzes, vases, and coins, found, round about here. Beyond, we passed under the Arch of Drusus, over which an aqueduct, was, in later times, carried. We passed the Church of "Domine quo vadis" where, the Catholics say, Peter met the Lord, and asked him this question and he replied "to Rome, to be again crucified." A little beyond is the Church of St. Sebastian, where they keep the arrow with which the Saint was pierced, and a stone, with the foot prints of our Lord, when he met Peter, as they say.

The catacombs are entered beneath the church. A monk gave us each a taper, and we followed him first, into a little chapel, where the saint was buried and then into the narrow dark passage of tombs. Each side is lined with excavations, and the niches are broad at the head, for the shoulders, and narrowed down for the feet. They are very rude and some are closed up with slabs; most of the inscriptions are removed. In some places the passage is enlarged to a chapel, where were altars, and we saw the hinges of a door, in one. Passages branched off from the one we were upon, but we could not explore them, and indeed the thought of the accidents that had happened in these places, from losing the way, or the lamp going out, was very fearful. Some paths were stopped up, to avoid accidents. We saw where the body of St. Cecilia was found, and also the place of sepulchre, of two or three popes or bishops of Rome, for, even they, fled here for refuge, in times of persecution. I thought of the holy men and women who chose rather to endure persecution and suffering, than to deny their Saviour. The air was close, and though of most deeply absorbing interest, there was something fearful, about the place. We were there about twenty minutes, and came up the ancient stairway, to the other side of the church.

We walked on from here, to the Circus of Maxentius or Romulus. It is an oblong space, with the ruins of walls surrounding it, and has in the centre the remains of the spina, around which the chariots passed in the race, and which was once ornamented with statues and columns. The Emperor's seat was on one side. Not far distant, is the well known, and yet really unknown tomb, of Cecilia Matella, the most perfect one on the

Via Appia. It is like a fortress. On entering you look down into the deep hollow, where the single sarcophagus was found, now in the Farnese Palace. The inscription throws no light upon her history; except that she was the daughter of the wealthiest Roman. The road from this point has been opened lately, under Canina's superintendence; the former one ran to the left. The sides of the road are perfectly lined, with funeral altars, statues, pieces of cornices, and huge masses of brick work, and it presents a singular sight; a ruined cemetery. We saw the supposed tomb of Seneca. There is no inscription, but a bas-relief, symbolical of the instability of human life, represents the death of Atys by Adrastus, who kneels before Croesus the father of Atys. As Seneca was murdered at this precise distance from Rome, and they probably did not dare to write an inscription during Nero's lifetime, it is quite possible that this may be the true sepulchre. We drove on as far as the tombs of Horatii. These are conical mounds, so called, though without, probably, any foundation. We know that they fought there, and perhaps the victor brother honored his brother's memory, by some such monument. They stand side by side, partly surrounded by funeral altars of peperino. This was the extent of our excursion and we turned back. The Via Appia continues in a perfectly straight line to Albano, we could see it crossing the hills in the distance. This has been I think our warmest day, the sun was almost oppressive. The Italians avoid the sun at this season, they say only Englishmen and dogs walk in it.

*Wednesday, Feb. 11th, Rome.*

Mary and I went again today to the Corsini Palace to see the rest of the pictures we had left on Jan. 29th. We saw a vestal Virgin by Carlo Moratta and beneath it a Magdalen by Carlo Dolce, and a St. Agnes as a child with her lamb. A Madonna by Murillo. There was a picture with two wings, by Angelico da Fiesole, of the Last Judgement, the Ascension and the descent of the Holy Ghost, the blessed in the first picture are embracing one another and looking to heaven, the condemned, who are all monks, are driven by demons. We saw several of Salvator Rosa's landscapes, some were battle scenes but one a quiet little nook in the woods near a lake. There were portraits of Luther and his wife by Holbein. An early landscape by Claude and many more by other artists. In one room was an ancient Etruscan chair, of marble and somewhat carved. This afternoon we have been to the Church of St. Onofrio on Janiculum, in the Lungano. It is approached by a very steep street. In this church

Torquato Tasso is buried. He died in the convent adjoining, having come to Rome, to receive a crown in the Capitol. We saw the tablet above his grave, on which is an inscription to him memory. To our great disappointment ladies are not allowed to enter the room where he died, we could only see the windows from below, for it is in the convent.

We went also to the Palazzo Spada to see Pompey's statue of parian marble 11 feet high. It stood formerly in the curia of Pompey and was removed thence by Augustus. It was found broken in two under a house. It is supposed with some probability, to be the statue at whose base "great Caesar fell." The figure is quite imposing, nearly naked, holding one arm extended, and in the other a globe. The face is stern, and severe in expression. Near the left knee, is a red stain, which some call Caesar's blood. We stopt on our way out, to look at a portico, from which the one leading to the Sistine Chapel was copied. There was a curious optical illusion here, a person passing through the arch, looks at the farther end immensely large, and a small statue there, looks large also. It is probably owing to the sudden decrease in size of the arch, making the distance appear greater than it really is, and the eye making its usual allowance for that, causes the illusion. Carnival begins on Saturday. Mrs. Hooker has been telling us about it today. We hear of a great snow storm, between N.H. and Boston, by which the cars were delayed two or three days, and our letters from home also.

*Thursday, Feb. 12th, Rome.*

Went this morning at rather a later hour than usual to the Church of Sta. Maria della Pace, to see Raphael's Sibyls which I should regret very much to have missed seeing. They are in fresco, over the arch of a side chapel to the right, on entering. The Sibyls are all different and receiving their oracles in various attitudes, the two cherubs are lovely, one on the left leaning on a tablet, has a most heavenly countenance. It is well to compare the sibyls of Raphael with those of Michael Angelo; there is such a difference, the mind of each, developing itself, in its peculiar manner. Then we went into the Trastevere to the Church of St. Cecilia.

Under the altar was a marble figure of the saint, of great beauty. It represents her in the attitude in which she was found on this spot many years after she was killed? The work is of the 17th cent. by Stephano Maderno. She lies upon her face which is hidden, with her arms extended. There is a wonderful appearance of death about the figure even without the face. The drapery is excellent and the arms and hands exquisitely delicate, the gash in her neck is also represented. The church stands upon the site of her house. She was put to death by her father's order and buried in the catacombs. At one side of the church is the ancient bath room, which was in her house, and where, they say, she was placed in boiling water before her execution. There are marks of a bath and copper plates on the wall, where the vapour came up. The floor is of rather rude mosaic, and lower than the church. In a little chapel are frescoes by Pinturiccio in another part of the martyrdom of the saint, by Guido, and mosaics on the apse of Byzantine stiffness.

We have been this afternoon to the Mamartine Prison. It is at the base of the Capitol beneath the Church of St. Joseph. In the floor of the church, which is called the site of the old tribunal, is a hole through which the prisoners were drawn up. The first cell was of the age of Ancus Martius, it is of Etruscan architecture, massive blocks of stone meeting in an arched ceiling. In the centre of this, is also a hole, which leads into a lower cell, built by Servius Tullius. We descended by a modern staircase. The floor is damp and the ceiling low, the walls much the same as the one above, only, in part excavated of solid rock. This is rendered memorable by more than one noted prisoner. Peter was said to have been confined here, and there is a well in the floor which sprung up (the legend says ) that he might baptize his fellow prisoners, who were converted. Here Jugurtha was starved to death, and the accomplices of Catiline strangled by Cicero's order. And here also Sijanus, minister of Tiberius was executed. It is a horrible dungeon, no light can penetrate its massive walls and hence by some sort of staircase, the dead bodies were removed when the work was accomplished. In the upper cell is a rude impression in the wall of a face and we were gravely informed, that it was made by Peter, when, refusing to descend to the dungeon below, he was pushed against the wall, by the jailer. It was a most interesting spot though so dreadful in association.

*Friday, Feb. 13th, Rome.*
Went this morning at twelve to the Museum of the Palazzo Campana

across the street. Met the Wheelers in the little garden in the court. We saw there a number of large Angora cats running about. They were mostly pure white, with long fur. The museum which is open once a week and then only to friends or by special permission consists principally of Etruscan remains. We did not see the jewelry, at which we were disappointed, but saw a very large number of Etruscan terra cotta vases, some of quite pretty workmanship, red, with black figures, or vice versâ. There was a sort of iron brazier or fire place, and a curious contrivance for heating water, consisting of a pedestal with a fire below and a huge kettle on the top. There were several cinerary monuments, one to a father and his children made of earthen ware, the heads taken off and the ashes are deposited within. We saw spears, swords or daggers, shields with a face in the centre, helmets and greaves. There were mummied skeletons, and an iron bed much like the modern ones, with a low pillow of iron, scales like those we have except the weights were heads or animals, kettles and pateras and a gridiron. Two helmets of fine work, one having a wreath of gold filigree leaves, said to have belonged to Ulysses? or Achilles?!! There were many antique lamps, statues of Antinous Seneca and Socrates. Many of these things were dug up on the estates of the owner.

After this we made our seventh visit, to the Vatican, and went into the Braccio Nuovo. This is a very fine hall indeed. Two of its columns are of gialo antico, and one is from the tomb of Cecilia Metella. We admired particularly a statue of Livia crowned with a diadem and holding one hand to her face in a very easy attitude. Minerva Medica was a fine thing; she has the aegis on her breast a helmet upon her head and her serpent at her feet. A pretty Diana in an attitude as if watching the upward flight of her arrow. A colossal figure of Nile personified, with sixteen pretty little beings, crawling over him, or playing around him. An athlete scraping himself with a strigil after his exercise. A fine figure of Demosthenes, about to make a speech, as it seems, one shoulder bare and the drapery fine. From this room we went into the hall of the Biga, to which we ascended by a staircase from the Greek Cross. This is so named from a Roman chariot and horses in marble, mostly restored. A quoit player is here also throwing his quoit. Passing then through the hall of animals we came to a long gallery of statues. At one end is the sleeping Ariadne. One hand is over her head, and the drapery is excellent. The look of sleep about the figure is really wonderful. The Cupid of Praxiteles, called the *Genius of the Vatican* has a very sweet face, only the upper half of the statue remains. The celebrated Apollo Sauroctonos of Praxiteles with arms extended. An Amazon much like the one in the Capitol, one of the finest draped statues in the Vatican. Jupiter with the thunderbolt, a savage face. The hall of masks is so named from some scenic masks, in mosaic on the floor.

*Saturday, Feb. 14th, Rome.*

Started at a quarter before eight for an excursion to Tivoli, a ride of eighteen miles. Uncle did not go. We found it quite cool so early in the morning. We rode over the broad campagna, quite flat, with the exception of only an undulating spot here and there. We passed a lake whose incrustations form the travertine and another a solfatera lake, of which the sulphur smell was anything but agreeable. In two hours and a half we came to a road that turned off to Hadrian's villa, about a mile distant. We went there, and spent some time in examining the ruins, which are in quite a perfect state. There was a "vale of Tempe" in imitation of the Thessalian vale of that name, and I believe it was the fashion to have one, in all such country seats, in old times. There was once a splendid villa, covering eight or ten miles. The paecile which seemed to have been a long portico, had its wall remaining, some of the columns were in the Sta. M. Maggiore. We saw what were called the philosophers' and mariners' theatres, remains also of baths and of the library. The Thermae of the Emperor, had some pretty stucco work still remaining and in these ruins were found Pliny's doves. We went into a sort of crypt or secret chamber of the palace where were visible some remains of painting. The part where the Emperor resided was over a long line of corridors, for the servants. At a little distance, we saw the Serapeon of Canopus, a temple built in imitation of one at Alexandria, and where were found many of the Egyptian curiosities of the Vatican. Then crossing a raised walk we came to the cente camere or barracks for the praetorian guard, upon which we looked down. Then we entered the Naumachia, a place 600 ft. long, and used for a circus. Fine large stone pines were growing in this field.

We came out by the paecile and returning to our carriage reached the main road again. Here we found the donkeys awaiting us, for we were to visit the falls before we went into the town of Tivoli, by taking a circuitous route. We made quite a cavalcade each seated on our own ass and having a man or boy to lead them. We crossed the ancient road, which led from Rome to Tivoli, and a bridge which brought us into the Sabine territory. Then skirting a hill we came in sight of the first fall. It seemed to flow out of some ruins which were called the villa of Maecenas, then dividing, poured over the rocks beneath into the Anio forming a broad surface of little tumbling rills. It was very beautiful indeed and so also was the next one, which was larger. The valley between us, and the town, was so deep that we could hardly see the bottom of it. We were shown upon the hill-side, the remains of Horace's villa or as is more probable Salust's and that of L. Quinctilius Varus; the ruins were quite insignificant. The next waterfall was an artificial one, which was turned from its channel, by Gregory XVI, and made to pass through two long galleries, cut in the rock, into which we could look, from a platform, built out at one side. Behind this, is another fall. Leaving our donkeys, we went down, to see the Grotto of Neptune. It is a channel in the rock, through which the stream rushes, with a tremendous roar. Then remounting our lazy beasts we climbed to the top of the rugged path where sits, perched upon a rock, the pretty little round Temple of the Tiburtine Sibyl. On our way up we saw a pretty rainbow, made by spray from the falls. Next to this temple is another called Vesta by some, or Drusilla by others. It is oblong in shape, with Ionic columns and is now used as a church. We went into the Sibyl's temple. The back part has fallen, but the rest is quite perfect. Then passing through the town, we spent a few minutes in visiting the Villa dÉste, a forsaken abode. The doors and windows stood open, and the rooms were deserted, and bare. Trees grew wild upon the terraces, and in one court was a fountain, and a statue of a woman lying alone, the water guardian of the place. It was a melancholy spot; but from a portico in the house, there was a very fine view of the campagna and hills. St. Peter's dome was to be seen in the far distance and that was all of Rome that was visible. We went to the inn afterwards for a lunch and stared on our return. We saw the sun go down with a beautiful sky, faint tints of green lilac and pink. Then a brilliant star appeared and at seven we reached home finding Uncle quite anxious at our long stay. It was a fatiguing, but very delightful, day.

*Sunday, Feb. 15, Rome.*

Went to church as usual. The chapel was more full than ever before.

*Monday, Feb. 16th, Rome.*

We went this morning at ten to ascend the dome of St. Peter's and finding the Wheelers on the same expedition we joined them and found it very pleasant. First you ascend by an easy slope to the roof. On reaching the first gallery we looked down upon the interior of the church. People looked like pigmies, and the mosaics about us, which from below were barely distinguishable, were very coarse and ugly. At the next gallery just below the dome itself we looked down again. The mosaic floor looked well, we could see the pattern of it. From this point the ascent became more difficult, and narrower and narrower, so that we had hardly room to wind up the stairs. We stopt at an outer gallery before going to the very summit and looked at the view. It was very fine. The piazza looked beautifully with its colonnade, and the minute soldiers moving over it. The campagna beyond the city, looked like a sea, being very flat, and a little misty. From this point we went up a narrow staircase and a narrower ladder into the very ball on the top where we sat five of us together. It is said to be able to hold eighteen but I should think not very comfortably. It was very close; four little cracks let in all the air there was. Upon the dome we saw the places for the lights in the Illumination of Holy Week. Several hundred men are employed in the dangerous duty of lighting the lamps at a given moment. The effect must be splendid. We descended without accident to the roof where we made a short stay. This is quite a village in itself, there is even a fountain there. The statues on the front look quite rude, when closely examined. We found it very warm in the sun, and were well tired when we reached the ground.

Carnival began on Saturday, and we went to our balcony on the Corso to see the fun, but were above the reach of much, being in the second story. The dresses were as amusing as anything, there were men dressed in woman's clothes, and walking about the streets, and some acting the fool, in many colored garments. The ladies in carriages were dressed, some as peasants, others with white cloaks and hoods trimmed with bright colors. Almost all wore wire visors to protect their eyes, while they dealt out flowers, confetti or flour by the handful. We became rather weary waiting to see the horse race that closes each day's sports. It took some time to clear the street and it was over in a few seconds, the five or six horses flying, with the speed of the wind up the Corso. We returned home and found letters. They have had dreadful storms and cold at home, while we have lately been suffering from the sun's hot rays.

*Tuesday, Feb. 17th, Rome.*

Went to the Vatican for the eighth time and took a review of the picture gallery. We saw again Correggio's *Saviour in the Clouds* done in very light colors. A marriage of the Virgin by Murillo, the Virgin and child and the saint have all dark hair and eyes and very sweet expressions. We looked afterwards at the tapestries. Ten are from Raphael's designs the remaining thirteen from those of his scholars. The first represent scenes from the life of Paul, and the murder of the innocents the rest are from the life of our Saviour. We passed through the stanze of Raphael and then went into the Loggie. This is a hall with one side covered in with glass and open to the light. The ceiling is divided into thirteen arcades, and has in each, four scenes from the Bible beginning with the Creation, and ending with Solomon, and the four last are New Testament scenes. They were mostly executed by Raphael's scholars, from his designs. The arabesques which adorn the walls in every possible place are very pretty. They are vines, with birds and animals among them, fruit in festoons and every possible variety of subjects, but unfortunately they are much injured. Whilst here, we saw in the court below, the minister of the King of Bavaria come, to pay a visit to the pope. He and his suite were richly dressed in blue, and Swiss guards, chamberlains, and priests, came out to receive them.

We went in the afternoon out upon the Via Appia and turned off to visit Egeria's fountain. After walking some distance in a field, we came to a fountain, arched over with brick. There were niches in the walls, and a reclining figure, called the nymph herself. Tradition says this is the fountain where king Numa resorted, but modern antiquaries place it elsewhere. It looks pretty at a little distance, being overhung with green vines. We drank of the water of the fountain, and then went into a cork grove, on a hill near by. On our way home we stopped at the Villa Negrone where Crawford used to reside, to see the remains of the wall of Servius Tullius called his agger. It is a mere mound with trees growing upon it. We have taken this morning our last Italian lesson from Sig. Brocchi. We are to leave here on Wednesday next. Poor Frances went to ride in the Corso today and had some lime thrown into her eyes. It pains her very much, it ought to be prohibited at Carnival.

*Wednesday, Feb. 18th, Rome.*

Started off early, for a long excursion, to Frascati Tusculum and Albano. We went out of the Porta Giovanni near St. John Lateran's and soon passed the spot, where the Claudian and Maecian aqueducts cross; from the former of which the Aqua Felice has been constructed, which supplies twenty six fountains in the city. Beyond we passed the ruins called Casale de Roma Vecchia, probably the site of the temple of Fortuna Muliebris, erected in honor of the wife and mother of Coriolanus, who here dissuaded him from his intended attack on Rome.

As soon as we reached Frascati which is about twelve miles from Rome we ordered donkeys to be prepared. This town has risen up since the old town of Tusculum was destroyed in the twelfth century and is now, as it was then, the favorite resort of the Roman nobles. I had no sooner mounted my donkey than he fell down and I jumped off and took another which trotted along very briskly. We ascended at first and had fine views of the country. The mountains were covered with snow; and sent us chilly winds. We rode for quite a distance through an avenue of box and evergreens with views on either side. Once or twice we came to a piece of the old pavement, the "Via Tusculana," and passed the amphitheatre one of the later ruins. We turned off on to the old Prenestina and saw part of the ancient wall of Tusculum, and a reservoir for water, of the age of the Mamertine prisons, and constructed before the principle of the key stone was known. They laid the stones horizontally, and then cut them off to form the vault. near by are the bases of the pillars of the gate of Tusculum.

Returning then to our former road, we came to the theatre, the best preserved of all the ruins. The stage for the actors, the seats for the spectators and the passages between; all remain in a perfect semi-circle. It began to rain a little, but we kept on, and scrambled to the top of the arx or citadel, from whose summit a grand view is obtained, and where are some of the ancient fortifications. Looking towards Rome which was plainly seen in the distance, we could discern beyond the Mediterranean Sea, and the position of Civitavecchia the old Ostia. To the right were the Sabine hills near which lie Tivoli, and Labicum, which was a Volscian town, and taken by Coriolanus. Beyond the hill where this was situated Lake Regillus was pointed out to us or rather its position for it has been lately almost drained. There is some doubt whether this was the place where the famous battle was fought. On the lower part of the mount where we were, we saw the Camaldolese Convent and Villa Dragona, now, I believe deserted. Turning then to the left we saw stretching out behind us the Volscian Mts. and Monte Cavo. On a flat plain half way down this latter peak is the Camp of Hannibal so called, where the 47 Confederate Latin Cities held their assemblies. On a lower peak is perched Rocca di Papa which can only be reached by donkeys or on foot. Beyond lie Grotta Ferrata, Marino, Castel Grandolfo, and the long ridge where Alba Long was once, stretching from the farther side of the Alban mount. The view was splendid, and our imagination peopled the country with its ancient inhabitants and seemed to carry us back, centuries, to days long past.

*Rocca di Papa*

On our return we passed some ruins called Cicero's Villa but probably only the site of that, and really the Villa of Tiberius. Upon the Arx, Cicero composed his tusculan disputations, and in Tusculum Cato was born. We stopt at the Villa Allobrandini, instead of returning to Frascati, and met our carriage at the gate. It is owned by Prince Borghese as well as 22 towns around. The situation is beautiful, commanding the Compagna and quite a circuit around, and it has been called Villa Belvedere. There is a pretty contrivance of water, upon the steep hill side. It is made to flow over steps, forming waterfalls, on different levels, and then at the bottom, throws up three beautiful jets of water. The dining room looks out upon it and the sound of the water must be very refreshing, on a hot day. The family spend six months here. We walked through the lower floor, it seems comfortable, with no great pretensions. The chapel, which is a building by itself, contains some modern paintings.

Proceeding on our way, we arrived at Grotta Ferrata, and went to the monastery of Basilian monks; the only one of this order in the States of the Pope. We looked at some of Domenichino's finest frescoes the history of St. Nilus which are here. The meeting of the Saint and the Emp.

Otho III is quite fine. In it the artist has introduced portraits of himself, Guido, Guercino, and some others. In other pictures miracles performed by the saint are represented. We passed through the town of Marina and stopt after descending a very steep hill to look for the source of the Aqua Farentina; a pool of water where Tarquinius drowned his former ally Turnus, king of Aricia, in revenge for an insult received. We walked through an avenue of trees in the Parco di Colonna, where the Latin assemblies were held, and looked in vain for the pool. Finally Uncle left us, and found it, after quite a scramble; we saw the little stream that flowed from it, but did not go further. Then riding on we came to Castel Grandolfo and Lake Albano. This was once the crater of a volcano and is surrounded by hills. It is a pretty place. We looked down at the emmissarium and walking through the town rejoined the carriage in another part. This emmissarium is a subterranean canal and was built in 394 B.C. in obedience to a Delphic oracle which commanded them to draw off the waters of the Lake. By this work the Romans learnt how to sink a mine and thus took Veii which had before resisted them. The short ride hence to Albano is very pretty under the shade of some trees. Just before entering the town we saw the tomb of Pompey, the ruins show that it must have been four stories high. His body was brought here from Egypt. After some refreshment at Albano we started for Rome. It was eighteen miles, and on the Via Latina; we arrived at about eight o'clock after a day of great enjoyment.

*Thursday, Feb. 19, Rome.*

Went in the morning to the Vatican to the Library which is only part open, on account of Carnival. It consists of two magnificent halls. The one crossing the first hall, at the end, is 2,000 feet long. The books are invisible being locked up in ornamental bookcases. There were some magnificent vases here, one of Sevres porcelain given by Napoleon I another of malachite, from the Emp. of Russia. We saw some antique cameos, and bronzes, and some relics, from the Catacombs of St. Sebastian. We were also permitted to see some very interesting, and valuable manuscripts which are kept locked in a cabinet. The first was an illuminated Virgil of the 5th cent., then a Palimpsest, a treatise of Cicero de Republica, and over it the Commentary of the Psalms by Augustine; it was discovered by Cardinal Mai. A Terence on parchment of the 9th cent. A copy of Dante by Boccaccio and sent by him to Petrarch. Some love letters of Henry VIII to Anne Boleyn in his own handwriting. There is the copy of Henry's book against Luther, presented by him to Leo X and having his handwriting on the fly leaf. We saw a few old painting on wood by Cimabue, Giotto and Massacio. Also pictures cut in black rock crystal, from the life of our Saviour done most exquisitely. The Library is certainly worthy of its place in the Vatican.

After lunch we went with Mrs. and Miss Whitney to the Ludovici Villa, for which we had received permit, for this day. It was rainy, and we had little time, so we did not see much, of the grounds, but they seemed pleasant. We went first into the Casino of sculpture where are several fine things mostly antiques. One was a barbarian who has just killed his wife, whom he holds up by one arm, while he thrusts the dagger into himself. Then there was the colossal Ludovisi Juno, the only goddess, as Hillard says, that we saw. I should think the head alone was three feet high; it is certainly very fine. Another, Pluto, carrying off Proserpine, is by Bernini. The other casina which is at quite a distance, contains Guercino's frescoes of Aurora, Night, and Day. The Aurora is on the arched ceiling; it does not equal Guido's but is quite fine, and some of the faces are very sweet. One figures drops dew from the vase which she holds and another chases the stars into the dwelling of night. This latter is represented on the end wall, by a cave, and two sleeping children, with a woman who has dropt asleep over her book, and an owl and a bat. We have at home an engraving of this. Opposite to this is Day, a youth holding in his hand a lighted torch.

We have been again to the Corso and had a shower of confetti poured upon our heads in walking to the balcony. It was much gayer than before. We saw the procession of Senators and Conservatives in their gorgeous dresses and carriages. The horses in the race, make the sparks fly from striking the pavement with their hoofs. Mrs. Stowe and Mrs. Perkins were with us, today. They arrived at twelve the night before and have had perils by land and sea. [Editor's note: As their steamer had entered Naples Harbor, it was rammed by another boat. The paddle-wheel went to the bottom. The land accident was the breakdown of their carriage as they entered Rome.] In the evening we went by invitation, with the Whitneys to a box they had engaged at the Argentine Theatre to witness the masquerade ball which is the great entertainment of the Carnival. There are two others but they, thought finer, were not to commence till after midnight. We were quite amused with the costumes, though there were too many, black coats unmasked, to make it very brilliant. Some wore black, white or pink dominos, others had costumes and masks and some lace, feathers, and diamonds. The fun is in speaking to any and every one, and being so disguised that no one shall recognize you. M. and I did not go down, but some of the ladies of our party put on black masks, and made the circuit of the brilliantly lighted rooms, to see and hear what was going on. A niece and nephew of Lord Raglan were there. He was dressed as a harlequin in red and white stripes. We became rather tired of it, after a while, and came away at eleven.

*Friday, Feb. 20th, Rome.*

In the morning we went to the Vatican, to the Etruscan room. There were many terra cotta vases some showing an Egyptian influence, and one or two of a Grecian cast. Some pateras also, and urns in the shape of huts in which still remain the ashes of the dead. There were iron pots and tripods, and bronzes, several sarcophagi with rude bas-reliefs upon the lids. There were frescoes found in an Etruscan tomb, which had quite an Oriental character; hunt, games and races are represented. The gold ornaments were quite rich. Two gold-embossed breast plates for the high priests, bracelets, necklaces, rings, chains, and wreathes of gold for helmets. We saw an ink horn or vase with Pelasgic characters upon it, considered the earliest form of the Greek Alphabet. The Egyptian Hall contains no very remarkable objects, the usual mummies etc. One room has figures of Roman work, an imitation of Egyptian found in Hadrian's Villa, Tivoli. In the Hall of Candelabra were some handsome vases of marble. After leaving the Vatican, we drove over to the Island of the Tiber. But could not see what we wished, for the water was so high, that it covered the stones of the foundation, which were in the shape of a boat, and sculptured with a serpent, and besides it was in a convent's grounds and ladies were not allowed. Afterwards we drove to a bridge, where we could see down the stream, the position of the old Pons Sublicius, defended by Horatius, against Lars Porsenna.

We then visited the studio of Gibson an English sculptor. He has practiced coloring his statues. We saw his Venus, it has a slight flesh tint, the eyes are blue, and she has flaxen hair. The effect of this is quite pleasing, but I do not prefer it, to snowy purity. A colored cupid is not very good. He had several statues or busts of Victoria. One is for the new houses of parliament. A Pandora of his is quite pretty. She holds a small casket in her hand. Miss Hosmer a young American sculptress has a studio near, but she was ill and we could not see it. However we saw her finest work, Beatrice Cenci lying in prison asleep, on the night before her execution. She holds her rosary in her hand. The position and subject are difficult, but it is a very fine thing. We saw a bust of Daphne and a model of Puck, a funny little thing. This lady is very independent; she lives alone, and rides on the Campagna with pistols and unaccompanied. She has a high name as an artist.

*Saturday, Feb. 21st, Rome.*

Went to the Capitol today, through the rooms where we had been before and into a small Cabinet where *the Venus of the Capitol* is kept. It is a perfectly beautiful thing. There is much modesty in the position, though she is wholly naked. It is very lifelike and exquisite in form and proportions. It was found in a walled up room in the Suburra of Rome, and was quite perfect, all but the tip of the nose and one finger. We saw the Marforio or river god, on which the replies to the pasquinades were pasted, in the 18th cent. Then we went over to the Palace of the Conservatori where were some interesting objects. In one hall is all that remains of the Duilian columns, which stood formerly on the forum, near the temple of Concord, and celebrated the first Roman naval victory. The inscription alone remains the rest is restored by Michael Angelo, with the six beaks of ships, and anchors, in marble. Another interesting relic was the bronze wolf with Romulus and Remus a very ancient work and with marks of lightening on two of the legs of the animal said to have happened when great Caesar fell. The halls were decorated with frescoes, from the early history of Rome; the battles of the Horatii the defense of the Sublician bridge etc. We saw a bust of Michael Angelo in bronze by himself; a frightful head of Medusa with snaky hair, almost enough to turn one to stone, by Bernini. A bronze statue of a boy taking a thorn from his foot, a very pretty thing and quite ancient. A fine bust of L. Junius Brutus, and one of Appius Claudius in rosso antico. The fasti consulares covered the walls of one room, they tell the years of the consuls and are an instructive and interesting memorial. In the gallery of paintings was a large picture of St. Petronilla by Guercino. It represents her burial, and above, her reception into heaven. Among others a young Roman Senator to whom she was betrothed is seated by the grave. It is considered the chef d'oeuvre of the Capitol. A Persian Sibyl is also by Guercino, and Augustus, with Cleopatra kneeling before him.

Afterwards we went again to the Sistine Chapel. They are preparing for Ash Wednesday which terminates Carnival laying down carpets arranging seats etc. In the afternoon M. and I rode up the Pincian to the

Trinita del Monte to see the *Descent from the Cross* a large fresco by Daniele da Volterra. The door was opened to us by a smiling Jesuit nun, for a convent is connected with the church where vespers are sung, every Sunday evening. We admired the picture very much, though it is much defaced. We went then to Crawford's studio to see the works of this fine sculptor, who is himself in Paris, suffering and in a critical condition. We saw the model for his Richmond monument. Also that of the pediment of the Capitol at Washington and some of the figures that compose it. One was a western emigrant, hewing a tree, another a woman with her babe sitting by a grave. An Indian in a melancholy attitude, and a fine colossal figure of America with her shield and spear in one hand. Among other things were the *babes in the wood* an exquisite thing, a little bird has just scattered a few leaves over the sleeping children and repose is in every part. Also a little boy with his books strapped on his back and a bird nest in his hands into which his little sister is peeping. A splendid statue of Beethoven the model of one in Boston, and many other beautiful things.

We went then to the Farnese Palace to see some frescoes on the ceiling by the Caracci. They represent mythological subjects. Mercury giving the apple to Paris. Hercules and Iole. Bacchus and Ariadne in triumphal chariots, with fauns nymphs and satyrs etc. They are bright and pleasing, the colors are rich, and the countenances, for the most part beautiful. The palace was begun by Pope Paul III and built principally from blocks, and columns, taken from the Coliseum, and the entrance is in imitation of those of that building.

*Sunday, Feb. 22nd, Rome.*

Went to church but half the day. It is our last service in Rome. We have been much favored in having such good preaching here.

*Monday, Feb. 23rd, Rome.*

Took our last walk on Mt. Pincian. The sun was very hot and there were two cherry trees in full blossom. Made some parting calls but no sight seeing as we are preparing to depart.

*Tuesday, Feb. 24th, Rome.*

Took our last ride, over the Ponte Molle by which we first entered Rome; then upon the Monte Mario to the grounds of Villa Mellini where we had a splendid view of the city and hills, lying about it in a semi-cir-

*Sora di Compagna*

cle. The villa is neglected but has some pretty shady avenues so very acceptable, in the hot Italian sun. About five, we went to the Corso. The confetti were still flying and we watched them for some time. Saw some very picturesque costumes; one was dressed like a bandit with his gun. After the horse race as it began to grow dark the moquelette began; the final sport of carnival. We each had a lighted candle and Mr. and Mrs. and Miss Whitney, Mrs. Stowe, Mrs. Perkins, and Mr. Hall were all with us on the balcony. The fun is to blow out one another's candles and we enjoyed the sport quite well. But the best part was the beautiful effect of the thousands of tapers up and down the street. There was one mass of lights, all up the sides of the houses and in the streets. People in carriages carried them. Some had long sticks with a row of candles, others little chandeliers of four. Thus ended Carnival and Lent comes in.

*Wednesday, Feb. 25th, Cistina.*

Thus far have we reached on our first day's journey. This is the site of the Tres Tabernae where Paul's friends came from Rome, to meet him. We left Rome at seven so as to be on the road in good season, as many leave, after Carnival. We went out by the Porta San Giovanni and took the road to Albano. Here in order to save time we took another carriage while the vetture rested, and went on to Genzano where we were to meet it again. We stopt to look at the tomb of Arun son of Lars Porsenna just outside of the gate of Albano. It is a massive work and remains in very good preservation. It had a square base and a large cone in the centre, and one on each end. Further on we crossed one of the finest viaducts, in Europe. The center is three or four arches high and it joins Albano and Laricchia. To the right of our road, rose a conical hill surmounted by a tower. It is Monte Giove, the site of Corioli from whence, after conquering it, Coriolanus took his name. We could see the Sea, from our high position and, what seems an island, but is the Circeian promontory, where the witch Circe lived, in fabulous times.

At Genzano we went into the Villa Cesarini situated on the very edge of the Lago di Nemi. This is enclosed by hills and is even smaller than the Alban lake, but is very lovely. The walks in the grounds of the Villa, wind about in a pretty manner giving glimpses of the water. We found crocuses in profusion, growing wild, some deep yellow flowers and one violet. The lake is three miles in circumference. After joining our vetturino we passed through the Volscian Velitri, whence came, as a conquered people the Trasteverini of Rome. We arrived here at, between three and four. Since our arrival eleven carriages have driven up. We have done well to engage beforehand our accommodations.

### Thursday, Feb. 26th, Mola di Gaeta.

We left Cistina very early this morning before it was light, as we had a long day before us. Almost immediately we came upon the Pontine Marshes, which we traversed for about 32 miles as far as Terracina. It was a perfectly flat marshy ground uncultivated except where the land had been redeemed by drainage. Few people live here, those we saw were a wild-looking set living for the most part in straw huts. Herds of cows, horses and buffaloes were grazing and we saw a myriad of black and white crows. It is a very pestilential region in summer. A post house that we passed is said to be the position of the Appii Forum of Paul. Here begins a canal upon which Horace sailed on his journey to Brundisium.

Several miles from Terracina, we met a man who told us of a new regulation, that a vetturino must be a certain time on the road, or pay a fine of 50 dollars. We slackened our speed, and found on arriving at Terracina, that the required time, was two nights between there, and Rome. It is an abominably tyrannical law. In order to compel post traveling by which they are enriched, the government make the poor stranger spend a much longer time, than he needs upon the road, or force the unfortunate driver who commit the sin, of driving too fast, to pay a fine which would almost use up his earnings, on the road. The worst thing is, that no notice is given of it beforehand, so that no one knows of it until too late to conform to it. We were much vexed. But the difficulty was overcome. Our passport did not mention our time of starting, from Rome so that, though Antonio told the officer the truth; by means of the all powerful money, he permitted us to go on; seeing there would be no proof of his failure in duty. Beyond Terracina is the narrow pass of Lautulae where a battle was fought between the Sammites and

Romans. In the second Punic war it was the stronghold of Fabius Maximus who held it against Hannibal. It is a narrow pass between steep rocks and the Mediterranean Sea. Beyond, near Itri perched on a crag, is a long hill, bordered by rugged rocks and formerly the haunt of Robbers, whose chief Marco Sciarra once offered to Tasso a safe conduct, from his admiration for the poet. Before reaching this place we passed a fertile valley called the Campania Felix where the Neapolitan territory begins. As we advanced we perceived a change in the vegetation. There were peas four or five feet high and in blossom; violets, crocus's daisies etc. on the roadside, and the fruit trees were in blossom. Near this place we passed a tower with a square base and conical top like many on the Via Appia. It is probably the tomb of Cicero, who was killed in escaping from Rome. Mola di Gaeta is on a long peninsular, which forms a bay, and the hotel is situated upon that, as the town is quite out of the road. Our view of it is very pretty, we also see Ischia, and Procida. From our windows we look out upon the Sea, separated only by a beautiful orange grove. We have abundance of these, sweeter than in Rome, and very fresh.

*Friday, Feb. 27th, Naples.*

We left Mola di Gaeta at seven this morning. Crossed a level plain; on one side near the road was a ruined amphitheatre and theatre, the site of Minturnae. We crossed the Garigliano over a pretty suspension bridge. It is the ancient Liris and still a "silent river." On its bank was fought a battle between the French, and Spanish under Gonsalvo di Cordova, in which the latter were victorious. Campagna is a very fertile country, men and women were busy in the fields. At noon we stopt at St. Agata, an unattractive place. On leaving three or four little boys followed us tumbling head over heels and singing "Signora, Signorine date qualche cosa." They seemed as happy as could be. We entered Capua by a very wide straight road meeting carts and curious vehicles of every description. It is a dirty place on the Volturno, we walked through it, to take the cars and let the vetturino come on, tomorrow morning. We found Italian cars comfortable though not luxurious, and very slow. We were two hours in going about 22 miles. We stopt often, once was at Caserta where the king now resides. The smoking Vesuvius was to be seen in the distance. It is not just as I expected, rather higher and perhaps less smoke. It has snow on its sides even now. We have not seen much here as yet. The people have a gay lively air, we have seen the lemonade sellers, with their painted booths, and Byzantine Madonna on the top. A kind of high gig is common here, upon two bright colored wheels. We do not face the bay here, in the Vittoria Hotel, but tomorrow we hope to go to pleasanter rooms, in another hotel.

*Saturday, Feb. 28, Hotel des Iles Britannique, Naples.*

We have a charming view of the bay here and can watch the ever changing lights and shades. We took a very pleasant walk on the Chiaja, a public promenade directly on the lovely bay and adorned with trees, shrubs, flowers, and statues and fountains with shady walks. It is called the Villa Reale and is part of what is called the Riviera di Chiaja. After lunch we took a drive along the bay to the Grotto of Posilippo where we walked up a steep hill to visit the tomb of Virgil. It is a single room with windows, and niches in the wall. The monument with his epitaph is modern "Mantua me genuit, Calabri rapuere tenet nunc Parthenope, cecini pas cu, rura, duces." It is built just over the Grotto of Posilippo. Petrarch is said to have once planted a laurel here, and it has been a venerated place.

Thence continuing on, we had a fine view of the Islands Ischia Procida and Nisita and on a peninsula of the mainland saw Baiae and Pozzuoli. On the left was Naples stretching along the bay for some distance and at the foot of Vesuvius, Portici, Risina or Herculaneum, Castellamare and Sorrento, Caprae an island visible from all points, was also a picturesque object. We went through the Grotto of Sejanus, which is a very long and dark tunnel lighted only by our torches. We came out upon a ground covered with ruins, and were led about everywhere by a very disagreeable guide. Bec the engineer of Pompeii had a house near by and has made some excavations. They are supposed to belong to a villa of Pollio, of the time of Augustus. We saw the fish pools, arched chambers, where, the story is, he kept his eels and fed them with human flesh, thrown in at a hole in the ceiling. Among the other ruins were, some stucco figures that were quite perfect, but it is mostly a shapeless mass. We saw a large and small theatre, both quite well preserved, and Sejanus' house was pointed out to us. The sea view was very fine. We returned by a different route, and rejoined our carriage.

*Sunday, March 1st, Naples.*

Went all day to the English Church. It is in a palace and is a regular church with pews. We heard two rather indifferent sermons. The streets are gay with people. We have had musicians of different kinds, before our windows, most of the morning. One was playing the bag-pipe, another dancing.

*Monday, March 2nd, Naples.*

We have today made an excursion to Baiae. We rode first through the Grotto of Posilippo. It is dusty, and so poorly lighted, that the drivers keep calling out, for fear of running against some-one. It is an ancient excavation in the tufa rock, enlarged and improved in modern times. We passed Bagnoli which in summer is a resort for bathing, and arrived at Pozzuoli, or Puteoli, as it was formerly called. This was a colony from Cumae many centuries B.C. and a station of the Tyrians. Here Paul spent a week having come in a ship of Alexandria, with which place, there was trade. We visited the ruins of the temple of Serapis. But few columns remain standing, but, sufficient to show the shape. The sea was once much higher than now, and its effect is seen on the columns which have also been bored by lithodomi. The ground too has sunk, and water now covers two mosaic pavements, which were successively laid, as the change took place. Two or three mineral springs are also connected with this, useful, for external and internal affections.

We saw also in Puteoli the amphitheatre and Solfatara Mountain after our return from Baiae, however I will describe them here. The first is a most interesting object. It has been excavated only twenty years from the clay thrown upon it from the neighboring volcano. The shape is oval and the seats are ranged round in tiers, steps lead from the corridor beneath to each row of seats, and in the central area are air holes for the beasts kept beneath. We went below; the arches and corridors are very perfect still. We could see, there, the effect of the earthquake which had broken the columns, and then of the volcano, which had thrown in, its deposits. Huns and Goths had also pillaged it of marbles. We rode part way up the Solfatara Mountain, on donkeys, which were particularly disagreeable, and we descended on foot. The mountain is not high. We walked about in the old crater which has now trees and flowering heath growing within it. The soil is white and Alum and sulphur are found here. At the farther end we saw hot steam issuing from a rock. It had done so for twenty days, and people think there may be an eruption. It has long been silent. A heavy stone was thrown on the ground and caused a hollow resounding noise, and a foot or so down, the earth was warm. Puteoli itself, is a disagreeable, unflourishing Italian town. Along the hillside, were ruins called Cicero's villa.

Continuing on, we turned off at a branch road, to visit Lake Avernus. We passed the Lucrine Lake, once so famous for its oysters. It is separated from the sea only by a narrow piece of land, the mole of Hercules, and was once connected by a canal, and used as a port for the Roman fleet. There was a connection of the same kind with Avernus, but, the raising up of Monte Nuova, in three days, by an earthquake, filled the canal, and cut off communication by water. Lake Avernus was in fabulous times, a spot of great veneration, and horror. Dark woods surrounded the lake, and the volcanic agencies around, were invested with mystery and awe. The hills are full of caverns and one very long one was thought to be the descent into Hell. Near by dwelt the Cumaean Sibyl and delivered her oracles. The trees are now cut down, and the ground cultivated, and it is a lovely piece of water. We explored the cave for some distance, which is a tunnel, connecting Avernus, and Cumae I believe. The mouth of Hell opens off one side, and the room of the Sibyl is reached by crossing some water, on men's backs; but we were content to forgo this novel mode of locomotion.

Continuing, on our way we stopt at grotto containing at its farther end a hot spring, whence the steam came issuing forth. A man half naked ran in, and returned panting and covered with perspiration, with a bucket of hot water, in which an egg was boiled. Many have endeavored to follow this man, but have not been able. It is called "Stufe di Nerone" as there are ruins of Nero's villa on the ground above. Riding through modern Baiae which consists of mere hovels, and a fort built by the Viceroy Toledo we came to the temple of Venus, octagonal in shape, situated on the seashore. It was probably once a bath house. The baths of Venus were two darkened chambers, black with smoke, but having some stucco ornaments, an eruption of Lava from Monte Nuova, had coated the walls. The temple of Mercury was a circular building with an opening in the roof. The echo there, was very fine. Some peasant children followed us in and danced the tarentella to the music of a tambourine. We were quite troubled by their importunity in offering us stones, and flowers. Baiae is so called from Baius, AEneas' pilot, who died here.

We went upon the promontory of Misenum where we saw the Piscina Mirabilis, the ancient reservoir, to supply the fleet in the harbour. The reservoir at Leghorn is in part an imitation of this. It is in very good preservation, the arches remain entire, and in the roof are holes, through which the water was drawn up. The Cento Camerelle is not far off, it is supposed to have been a prison for seamen. We began to explore it, but a cold wind drove us back. On our way the Mare Morto was pointed out to us, where, they say, the souls embarked in Charon's boat and were ferried into Avernus. We were in the Elysian Fields, and we saw a skull, found there, with a piece of money in its mouth, as toll for the grim ferryman. We took donkeys for these last sights, but found it difficult to keep on them, they were so ugly. From the promontory, we had a fine view of Ischia and Procida, as indeed all through our ride, more or less but there was some mist over the sea. We were tormented with beggars at one place and the usual cry was "una piccola moneta per maccaroni."

*Tuesday, March 3rd, Naples.*
The weather not very clear today. Did not go out.

*Wednesday, March 4th, Naples.*
At home all the morning. In the afternoon we took a drive along the bay. Vesuvius looked finely with much smoke, issuing from it. The sea looked rough and very blue. We passed through some of the dirty market streets, and saw all kinds of operations from the cleaning and arranging of hair, to selling eels and macaroni, indeed every-thing seems to be done out doors. The fisherman's wives and daughters were making nets at their doors. We passed the theatre of St. Carlo, one of the finest in Europe, and the palace is near by. We afterwards went into a lava and coral store, and saw branches of the latter, in its natural state; the pink is the most prized.

*Thursday, March 5th, Naples.*
Took a drive over Capo di Monte, and by the Ponte Rosso an old aqueduct. The Toledo is one of the principal streets here. We see many musicians in the streets also tumblers, bag-pipers, Punch and Judy etc.

*Friday, March 6th, Naples.*
Went again over Capo di Monte and into the grounds. It is one of the king's palaces. The grounds are beautiful, having pretty views, winding shady walks, avenues, and woods, more English in parts, than Italian. The Casino was pretty, with white velvet, and painted furniture.

*Saturday, March 7th, Naples.*
We drove up to the Castle of St. Elmo a fort which crowns the city, in its highest parts. We were not allowed to enter, but saw a lovely view

of the city bay and Vesuvius from a villa near by. Then Uncle and Mary went on, to see a fine view, from the Camaldoli Convent, an excursion which took them two hours, or more while Auntie and I waited below.

*Sunday, March 8th, Naples.*
Went as usual to church.

*Monday, March 9th, Salerno.*
A cloudy morning, but, hoping for a better day, and fearing to defer it longer, we started on our excursion to Pompeii and Poestum. We drove through Portici, Resina, Torre del Greco, and Torre del Annunziata for fourteen miles to the ruins of Pompeii. We made two visits, one going and the other returning, from Poestum; but to avoid confusion I shall describe it all, now. We entered at the Herculanean gate, by the street of tombs. We saw a roadside seat with an arched roof, in which skeletons were found. There were several tombs still remaining, one had a curule chair sculptured upon it, another had a marble door of which part of the iron latch remains. The places where the bodies were burned and where the funeral feast was eaten, were shown to us. Diomedes' Villa is without the walls. It is quite extensive; having a garden below, and a very large cellar the only one we saw, in which several amphorae or jars were found, imbedded in lava, and also seventeen skeletons. The impression of one of these is on the wall. At the street entrance there was a sort of portico. Of the Villa called Cicero's there is nothing but an open court and staircase to be seen; some pretty dancing figures found here, are in the Museum. Some arches make what is called, the suburban country inn. Near the gate in his sentry box was found the faithful sentinel in armour. The streets have the ancient Roman pavements, very narrow and in some parts deeply rutted. Large stepping stones are to be seen, for foot passengers, and there are a few sidewalks paved with smaller stones. One street has a large stone put up to prevent passage, as it was not finished or undergoing repairs. We saw a marble cornice, that a sculptor had been at work upon; and his model.

We entered many houses, to which various names have been given. Pansa's house is large and regular, even to the kitchen with a marble sink, or table, to wash upon. In front of Sallust's house was an oil shop; the counters of oil or wine still remaining. There were two or three bake houses. The mills for grinding corn, were of singular construction, made of lava, in shape: like an hour glass set into a hollowed-out stone, and turned, by men or asses. The ovens also were there. The house of Apollo had a pretty contrivance for a fountain. The stone was cut into many rows of steps, over which water was to flow and at the back was a fresco of water with fishes. The houses were all much on the same plan, an atrium, cavedium, triclinium, and cubiculae and often a garden beyond, either a large square one, or a mere trough of stone, to set a few plants in, as in Sallust's house. The house of the Sonatrice has been left as found, it is a large double house. Around the fountain are many little marble figures of fishes, etc., and also frescoes. We saw some extremely pretty frescoes, arabesques and figures, of which, some, were in perfect preservation. The house of the Tragic Poet had some little masks in one room, in another frescoes. The house of the labyrinth had a rusty iron chest which contained coins, and also, upon the floor, a mosaic of Theseus killing the Minataur, around which had been made in mosaic, a labyrinth, whence the house was named. Meleager's house has a fresco of him, with his boar by his side. The house of Adonis is so named from a fresco of Adonis dying, with Venus by his side, and cupid holding up his arm; it is perfect, and very well done. One is called the house of the Vestals from an altar, where the sacred fire is supposed to have been kept. Then there are the houses of the great and little fountains. These are quite fanciful being made of colored mosaics and shells. We explored many more houses, the same, in the general plan, the walls painted with figures, fruit, birds and flowers and sometimes imitating marble. The mosaic pavements were often very beautiful. The forum is quite long; with the pedestals of statues, ranged on each side; into it, opened the basilica, containing also pedestals, and at one end the tribune, under which was a little prison. In the Pantheon, or temple of all the gods, are still frescoes of Ulysses recognized by Penelope, and of Theseus and Acthea his mother, both, well executed. The washing place for the women contained a large pool in the centre, and one or two scrubbing stones rough and worn by constant use. The temple of Iris was in the same quarter, with altars, a secret passage for the priestess etc.

There were many other temples and two theatres; under the corridor of one we sheltered ourselves for a while, from the rain then pouring down. Across one street is a triumphal arch. The public bath house contains a room, with a large basin in the floor, for washing, and little dressing rooms; also a room with niches, to hold the clothes, oil, and ointments of the bathers, with a long bronze brazier and a bench. The next room was the caladarium or vapour bath, the walls were double and at one end was a deep marble basin, ascended by steps. On some of the buildings were notices or advertisements in red paint. Only about a third of the city is yet uncovered. We walked upon a part of the mound, and also went by steps to the city wall from which there was a fine view of the country and the desolate city. Our excursion had been deeply interesting and filled our minds with strange and wondering thoughts. We took lunch at a little inn, in a pouring rain and then continued on our way to Salerno. The road is very picturesque and we enjoyed it in spite of the rain. Mediaeval castles were perched on the neighboring peaks and the road wound about until it came out upon the lovely bay of Salerno.

*Tuesday, March 10th, Salerno.*

It was still cloudy when we woke in the morning, but did not rain much the first part of our way. We crossed the Silanus or Sile in a ferry-boat. After heavy storms the river is often impassable. The road is over a plain, lonely and not very interesting. The temples of Poestum stand in solitary grandeur, on the shore of the sea, in the midst of a flat plain. There are only a few houses to be seen at a distance. The first one is the temple of Ceres or Vesta, and the smallest in size. The other two stand near together and of these the Temple of Neptune is the finest. There are six columns on each end, and twelve on the sides, of perfect Doric with a slight swell in them. The pediments are entire, made of travertine, and very fine. The Basilica is not so well preserved; in both there is a centre part, also surrounded by pillars, perhaps for an altar. We saw remains of the town walls and of one gate. The masonry is very solid and fitting closely. We found the violets that are so celebrated, but it is too early for roses. In one of the houses nearby, we saw copies of some of the paintings found in the tombs. One represented a warrior received in triumph, and crowned with flowers. Others were of the same style. We returned to Salerno at night. In the evening it thundered, and lightened, and the waves dashed furiously upon the shore.

*Wednesday, March 11th, Naples.*

Still raining as we left Salerno. We stopt on our return at Pompeii, to see the amphitheatre, which is outside of the town. It is elliptical in form and quite perfect except a few seats that are wanting. We visited the ruins again, as I have before mentioned, and spent two hours very pleasantly, there. At Resina which is built over Herculaneum, we descended to view by means of torches, the ancient theatre. There was an accumulation of

80 feet of volcanic mud, so that it has been difficult to excavate this city. The theatre has had to be supported by piers, to prevent the ground above from falling in. The stage for the orchestra, is longer than that at St. Carlo's and in the room behind is the impression made in the mud of a bronze mask. Then emerging, we followed one of the streets of Resina, to a part of the ruins, much like those of Pompeii. There were some frescoes, porticos in front of the houses, and some street benches. We saw a prison where two skeletons were found in chains. Also a chapel, beneath a house, with an altar, and niche for a statue. The town extended to the water's edge. We had a splendid view of Vesuvius, on our way home, in the peculiar sunset color lilac or pink.

*Thursday, March 12th, Naples.*

Visited today the Museo Borbonico and entered first the Pompeian fresco room. They were of all kinds, and some, very perfect. There was a grasshopper in a chariot driving a parrot, a caricature of Seneca and Nero, because the latter preferred driving in the circus, to ruling the state. The dancing figures were graceful, but much injured. Venus fishing and Cupid looking on, Ulysses taking the cup from Circe, the death of Adonis. The sacrifice of Iphigenia, besides birds, fishes fruit flowers and arabesques and a myriad of others, also mosaics, one of a cat killing a bird, excellently well done. The next room contained a queer combination of valuables and charred eatables. There were bracelets for the arms and legs. One was found on Julia Diomedes, rings with immense stones, and two, with the bones of the fingers that they encircled. There was a rich collection of gems, cameos, amethysts, and sardonyx as large as a plate and carved on both sides. A piece of asbestos, in which bodies to be burned, were wrapt and which does not itself burn. We saw charred figs, prunes, seeds, English walnuts, two loaves of bread like loaf cake, a skillet containing the meat ready to be cooked, now cooked to a cinder. A wine jar, olives in a bottle, sponges, soap, a straw covering for bottles, ropes, linen, thread and many paints, one a very beautiful pink used for rouge and, one green from an unknown mineral, and a purple the royal color, netting needles, a little press for ricotta, a cake and a piece of pie, oil, raisons, some still unbroken eggs, dates, almonds, shells for ornaments, and a purse containing money. To think of all these things being 1800 years old make it seem perfectly wonderful, that they can still be recognized.

In the bronze room was an oven or portable kitchen shaped like a castle, the central court was to contain the fire. There were all sorts of kitchen articles, some very pretty lamps, a marble table and a bronze chandelier, found in Diomedes' house. Urns for water, vases, a curule chair and two others like sedan chairs, the skull and helmet of the sentinel, found at his post, and several suits of Roman armour. There was also armour found in the tombs at Poestum; very ancient looking, and much lighter than the Roman. A lady's toilet utensils consisting of a comb, rouge in a little box, ivory hair pins and a brass looking glass. Some quite valuable surgical instruments. Spoons, and a bronze contrivance with hollows in it for cooking eggs, delicate scales, a lantern, tickets for the theater, dice to play with. A thimble and some pills! It seems from all these things, as if they lived, much as we now do, with many of the conveniences of life.

### Friday, March 13th, Naples.

Again to the museum, and into the torso and Hercules room. The first is the celebrated group of Dirce, just released from the bull, to which she had been bound by the sons of Antiope, who stands behind commanding them to desist. It was the work of the Greeks Apollonius, and Tauriscus and was restored. There is a good deal of spirit in the movements of the young men, one holds the mouth of the furious animal and a cord is bound to the hair of Dirce. The Hercules however, interested me more; he is such a ponderous creature, resting on his club, which bends under the weight of his enormous arm. In one hand he holds three apples. All the muscles are much developed and the feet are huge. It has the name of the Greek sculptor Glycon, and was much admired by the ancients. These two works were found in the baths of Caracalla at Rome, and belonged to the Farnese family.

We then went into the room of bronzes. Here we saw a fine meditative head of Plato. Also a fine bust of Scipio Africanus in his old age. Mercury reposing after great fatigue, considered the most perfect bronze statue in the world, he is bending over, and there is a slight distension of the nostril, as if breathing hard. A water cock for an aqueduct hermetically sealed, and still containing water, as, if shaken, is manifest. There were also more statues and busts, a mounted Amazon raising her lance, a huge horse's head, the body was an object of superstition, to the common people, so it was destroyed in 1322. A large horse belonging to a chariot of Nero. In several other halls are also fine statues; one of Aristides much celebrated, found at Herculaneum. There is much dignity in the form and face, the drapery is simple, one hand in his toga, and one behind him. An Antinous much like the one in the Capitol at Rome. A wounded Amazon on horseback, and falling backwards. A hunter in a coarse coat of sheepskin, birds hang from his belt, and a hare over his shoulders. A colossal Flora a very beautiful thing, holding up her robe lightly with one hand, and treading with airy step. In front of this, on the floor, is the mosaic of the battle of Issus or Granicus, found at Pompeii in the house of the Faun. The scene is animated, Alexander and Darius are in active fight as well as their respective armies. There was a statue of Atlas, bending under the weight of the terrestrial globe. Several of the Muses were fine, especially Polymnia, crowned with flowers. There were several of the Balbi family, the Father, Mother, and daughters, the hair had once been gilded. There were many others, but too numerous to mention. We then went into the glass, and terra cotta room. One of the vessels was of cameo glass, white figures, on a blue ground. We saw also children's playthings, horses, birds etc.

*Saturday, March 14th, Naples.*

We visited today the vase rooms of the Museum. Some of these are very beautiful. Those with black or dark ground, and red figures, are Greek, and on these the figures are the natural color of the clay, and the ground painted. The light grounds and variegated figures are Egyptian; and the red grounds and black figures painted on them are Etruscan. Some of the shapes are very elegant, and the execution delicate. One, cost eight-thousand dollars. They were found in the kingdom of Naples and mostly in tombs. The subjects are generally mythological. In the gallery, we saw some fine paintings. A cartoon of Raphael's Madonna col divin' amore. Also Moses on the mount, holding his hands before his eyes. A cartoon of Michael Angelo's, three soldiers, as a study, they were in the bold muscular style of the artist. The Madonna della Gatta was being restored, so we could not see it; but there was a drawing in imitation of it by Giulio Romano. The descent from the cross by Andrea da Salerno a pupil of Raphael. St. Jerome taking a thorn from a lion's foot by Van Eyck. St. Francis, St. Jerome and the Madonna, by Leo Zingaro, or the Gypsy. Jesus among the Doctors by Salvator Rosa, and another the mote and beam very literally represented by a beam protruding from a Pharisee's eye, and a straw from that of a poor man. Several of Salvator Rosa's landscapes were also to be seen, in his usual bandit style. One of Claude Lorraine's landscapes and several domestic scenes by Teniers. Raphael's Madonna col divin' amore pleased me much, it is beautifully soft and delicate. We saw a copy seven and a half feet high of *the last judgement* by Marcello Venustri, executed under the eye of the Master and more satisfactory to examine than the large one. A fine full length portrait of Philip II by Titian, with a very disagreeable expression, but I presume natural. Correggio's marriage of St. Catherine to the infant Saviour is very lovely. Also by the same artist the *Egyptian Madonna* with turbaned head, on her way into Egypt. In the afternoon we took a walk in the Villa Reale. We were preparing for a journey to Rome on Monday. Vesuvius is now quite active, red flames issue from the highest peak. We have not been able to ascend it for two or three reasons. I did not mention in my account of Friday a ride to the cemetery. There are here, numberless little chapels where the members of the different fraternities are buried, and in some spots, the nameless poor are heaped, one upon another. We heard a monk preaching, he gave a short sermon at each station, where was a picture to represent some event, in Christ's progress to Calvary. He was earnest and had quite a crowd of listeners.

*Sunday, March 15th, Naples.*
    Went for the last time here, to church, and heard a good sermon.

*Monday, March 16th, Terracina.*
    We left Naples at half-past six, in a snug little hired diligence. We have tried posting for the first time; it is a much quicker and more lively mode of traveling. The posts are eight miles apart and we generally took one in an hour. We had a small accident, in the falling down, of our two back horses, with the post boy, and the carriage nearly rolled upon him. The vegetation had made great progress since we passed before. The almond trees are in blossom, and other trees leafing out.

*Tuesday, March 17th, Rome.*
    Again in Rome! I little expected to be here again so soon. It seems quite like home to me. We reached here at 4 o'clock, and find there is no post horses for us on the Perugia route, so we shall probably go by Siena.

*Wednesday, March 18th, Rome.*
    We have concluded to stay till tomorrow. We went to a cameo store, up stairs in a side street, and saw some very exquisite things. Visited also Mr. Brown's studio. He is an American artist of great merit, and has sent home a number of his landscapes. One of his pictures was the aqueduct

of Claudius and the hills around Rome, and one of a rugged promontory at Sorrento. There was a view of Florence looking down the river from
some high point and some fine stone pines in the foreground. There
were several others and they all had a peculiar softness and hazy light,
which was very beautiful. His pictures show a study of nature, in her varied forms. He means to settle down at home in five or six years, when he
shall have gained more, from the advantages which Rome affords. It is a
true artist atmosphere, here, he says.

We then visited Mr. Terry's studio, he is a Hartford man. One of his
works was Tobit with the angel, bidding adieu to his parents. The most
pleasing was the *Artist's Dream* A painter with a brown velvet coat and
cap, very naturally represented, with brush in hand, had fallen asleep and
sees in a dream, three graces, each one, of great beauty. One, lifting aside
a green curtain, was a brunette with purple drapery, the middle one was
in white, very fair and wearing pearls in her hair, while the third, leaning
upon her, had auburn hair, black eyes, and a blue drapery with buff lin-
ing. They were all exceedingly graceful and lively. The other picture was
a peasant girl, in the Roman costume. Her eyes were lustrous and her jet
black hair braided around her ears. Mr. Terry took care of Mr. Crawford
at one time, he has heard lately from Mrs. C. who thinks he is no worse.
We were disappointed to find Mr. Ives' studio closed, as were desirous of
seeing it.

*Thursday, March 19th, Viterbo.*

We left Rome in a light carriage so as to stop at Veii on our way, and
meet the diligence there. It is a distant twelve miles; we turned from the
main road near La Sorta, the carriage was left at Isola Farnese, a miserable little place, which some think the citadel of Veii and we took donkeys for our excursion among the ruins. There were no ladies' saddles, so
we rode sideways upon others, but managed to keep on very well. Along
the roadside, were some pretty flowers a pink cyclamen, and some purple aster-like flowers. We crossed a stream the "Fosso di due Fossi,"
where was a lovely little waterfall, and then entered a triangular space,
formed by this stream and the Cremera, which was probably the position
of Etruscan Veii. Saw remains of a pavement, and columbarium of
Roman times, then, close to the brook, a piece of massive Etruscan wall.

Continuing on over the fields, we came to the "painted tomb" a very
curious and interesting relic, of this most ancient people. It belongs to
the Marquis Campana. It is approached by a passage cut through the

rock and guarded by lions, these are placed also at the entrance of the tomb, in a crouching position, of rough execution and now mutilated. When opened, the tomb had two skeletons laid on benches of stone, but these have now crumbled away. The helmet of one remains with a piece of a spear sticking through it, by which probably the unknown warrior received his death wound. The other skeleton was probably a woman. There were, in the tomb, several terra cotta urns, a bronze lamp, and upon the wall frescoes, showing the rude state of the arts, at this period. They represent men, horses, a leopard, cats, and dogs, mostly red or yellow, of long thin figures, and rather eastern in character. Another chamber beyond, and opening into this, had upon the wall round discs of red and yellow, for what purpose is unknown. There were urns, and little terra-cotta chests for funeral ashes, and a bronze brazier here, and golden crowns had been found, but removed to a safer place. The door ways were formed of rough polygonal stones, with, not a key stone, but a top stone resting on two horizontal ones, notched out to hold it.

From hence we went to the Ponte Sodo, a tunnel through which a stream passes; it is 240 feel long and for what purpose is unknown. Uncle suggested that it might be part of the tunnel of Camillus, which was the means of taking Veii. Near by is a part of the wall, showing that was close to the city. We afterwards crossed the Ponte di Fornello made of Roman brick work upon Etruscan piers, and rejoined our carriage and then met our posting diligence and began the journey to Siena, so trying a one to me before. The scenery was pleasing. One of our horses fell down dead and we had to leave him on the road. The hills were quite steep, and we had for a while nine horses, and afterwards six horses and two oxen. We have found Viterbo a comfortable lodging place. M. and I had the room which the Emperor Nicholas of Russia occupied once, and over the bed was a crown.

*Friday, March 20th, Radicofani.*
Passed today the Lake of Bolsenna, it is very unhealthy in summer. We saw many basaltic columns cropping from the hill-side. One road for most of the way has been dreary and desolate, beyond description, especially in ascending the mountain where we now are; it was a hard pull, for even our seven horses. There was no verdure, nothing but a succession of barren hills and the wind blowing cold and strong. The hotel is a queer old place. It was formerly a hunting lodge for the dukes of Tuscany, and is ornamented with frescoes of castles, terraces, and birds.

The halls and rooms are large, and the wind howls through the key holes. Tomorrow we reach Florence, by a hard day's journey.

*Saturday, March 21st, Hotel d'Italie, Florence.*
Left Radicofani at six, with a cold wind, and flurry of snow. It was dreary enough, descending the mountain the sky seemed to match the barren earth. A little after noon we reached Siena, and waited there nearly two hours for the cars. We changed cars at Empali and reached Florence at eight. The hotel is comfortable and looks directly upon the Arno. A packet of letters greeted us on our arrival.

*Sunday, March 22nd, Florence.*
Attended in the morning the French service in a church on the other side of the Arno. The sermon was by M. Colomb. In the afternoon in the same church we heard Mr. Hanna a Scotch Presbyterian whom Uncle met in London at Mr. Hamilton's.

*Monday, March 23rd, Florence.*
We began today to have some idea of La bella Firenze and like it very much. We first visited the Uffizi Gallery. One of the rooms was almost entirely filled by portraits of artists by themselves, indeed there were two such rooms. There was Leonardo da Vinci, a beautiful portrait, with a long soft beard. Salvator Rosa, C. Allori wearing a light blue cap on his head. The Caracci, Guido, Rubens, Raphael in his cap and long hair, Pietro Perugino, Michael Angelo, Sir Joshua Reynolds, etc. We then went into the tribune as it is called, a small room which contains the gems of the collection. There was the Madonna with the Goldfinch, one of Raphael's earlier pictures. And his Madonna with the infant St. John, presenting a little scroll to the Saviour. Also the Fornarina as it is called, the portrait of a beautiful lady holding with one finely formed hand her fur trimming. The portrait of Julius II by Raphael. An altar piece by Andrea del Sarto, one of his best works. The Madonna stands over an altar, supported by two cherubs, on one side is St. Francis and on the other St. John. Herodias' daughter, with the head of John the Baptist, by Luini a scholar of L. da Vinci and much resembling him. A Holy Family one of Michael Angelo's few easel pictures and very ugly. The attitudes are unnatural and difficult. Mary is taking the child from Joseph who stands behind. Job and the prophet Isaiah by Bartolommeo. St. John in the desert by Raphael. A Madonna adoring the Saviour by

Correggio; a very sweet thing but without much depth of expression. Endymion asleep, with the moon shining overhead, by Guercino. Also a pretty Sibyl by the same. An altar Madonna with saints on each side by Perugino. The statues here are first and chief the Venus di Medici it is smaller than the Venus of the Capitol at Rome and I am so bold as to say I do not like it as well. There was another Venus, also naked. Two wrestlers. Apollo and a Faun.

After this we took a pleasant drive and walk in the Cascina, a public promenade, a little out of the city, on the bank of the Arno. There were plenty of trees and walks through the woods, the birds sing in delightful freedom and wild flowers grew abundantly. Here is the royal dairy; the family of the Grand Duke are supplied and what remains is sold. This afternoon we have been to the Duomo. On one side it is richly covered with marbles, but the facade is unfinished, or was taken down and has never been renewed. The dome is a little larger than St. Peter's, it was planned by Bruneleschi and was the first undertaking of the kind. The building is in the form of a Latin cross, and was built, partly by Anolfo, partly by Giotto. Within, it seems plain and dark. The walls are brown stone or stucco, or white, with few ornaments besides cornices. Behind the high altar, which stands beneath the dome, is a Pieta, Michael Angelo's last work and intended for his own monument, it was left unfinished, on account of a defect in the marble. Nicodemus and two Marys are bearing the body to the tomb. There are in the church, monuments to Anolfo and Giotto, and in the square surrounding the Duomo, are statues of these two, leaning against a building, and gazing, as it were, at their work. The Cupola is painted by Vasari and Zucchero. I do not like it. Michael Angelo admired the shape of the dome very much, and when setting off to build St. Peters, he said, to it "Come ad te non voglio, meglio di te non posso."

The baptistry was the old cathedral; it is built of black and white marble, laid alternately. The interior has a gallery, with windows, running round it, all the children of Florence are baptised here. Some think, this was an ancient temple, as the columns are very old. On the outside are two porphyry columns, which fell to the shares of the Florentines from the spoil of Majorca, when they helped defend Pisa. The three bronze doors, by A. Pisano and Ghiberti are quite celebrated, the two latter Michael Angelo considered worthy to be the gates of Paradise. The one on the north, represents scenes from the life of Christ, one of the others, scenes from the life of John Baptist and the third we could not see very well. The ornaments of birds and flowers about the doors are very rich and beautiful. Dante calls this baptistry "mio bel' San Giovanni." The campanile was built by Giotto it is square, and four stories high, and is very beautiful being made of mosaics and has the appearance of open work at the top.

*Tuesday, March 24th, Florence.*
Went today to the Pitti Palace. It is a large massive structure erected by one of the Pitti family to rival the Strozzi. The Grand Duke resides here. The gallery contains five hundred pictures, none bad, and many fine. Of course I cannot mention all, but only those which struck me most. First was the Madonna della Sedia, by Raphael, of which we see so many copies. His Madonna of the Baldaquin is in a rather unfinished state, two cherubs are in front of the enthroned Madonna, and saints on either side. In the Madonna dell' impannata two women worship the infant Saviour, and John is seen a sweet-faced child in a corner of the pic-ture. There was a copy by Giulio Romano of Raphael's *Madonna of the Lizard* or *Under the Oak*. In this, John is presenting a roll, with "ecce agnus Dei" upon it, to the Saviour. Titian's *Magdalen* I did not admire. A Holy Family by Rubens, with his peculiar pink flesh tinge. Also a group of himself, and brothers. By Carlo Dolci, there was a sweet John the Baptist, as a child, asleep, his mother looks at him, and thanks God, and Zechariah is reading. Also Peter seated, and bitterly weeping, after he has heard the cock crow. St. Mark by Fra Bartolommeo a grand majestic fig-ure. The Three Fates probably by Michael Angelo, of which Uncle has a copy at home. By C. Allori - Judith with the head of Holofernes, said to be his likeness, and Judith's that of his mistress, and The Sacrifice of Isaac, when Abraham's hand is stayed by an angel; in the face of the for-mer, submission is expressed, though with a death like pallor, as of fear. There were two of Salvator Rosa's battle scenes, and the conspiracy of Cataline. One of Murillo's Madonnas. By Guido, Cleopatra placing the asp to her breast. A full length portrait of Philip II in a rich dress by Titian. Portraits by Raphael, at the age of 22, of Maddalena and Angelo Doui. His *Vision of Ezekiel* a small thing but very grand. The *Ancient of Days* is upborne by cherubs, and stands upon an ox, an eagle, and a lion and is surrounded by cherub heads and the glory of the sun. We left after this feast of beauties, with greater desire to come again.

We then went to the government manufactory of mosaic work. There were some elegant works: perfectly beautiful fruit, flowers, and

shells also landscapes, but less striking. Some were for the chapel of the
Medici. The monument to the late Grand Duchess was there, to be
placed in the chapel. It was a porphyry base, which took twenty men, five
years to cut; upon this was another kind of marble with coats of arms in
mosaic upon it and above all a rich crown. We saw part of the process of
making the mosaics. One man paints the desired picture, then draws in
outline, the separate parts, and gives to each workman the stones which
are needed, for the shades of color. They cut these the required shape,
then with the greatest care, glue them together; when all is done they are
laid upon the marble slab and a corresponding piece being cut out from
it, are inserted in the slab; at least so I understand it. After a certain age,
these workmen have a pension as it injures their health. Afterwards we
went to some mosaic stores, and saw some very beautiful things. A
superb table purchased by Mr. Stewart Murray of Scotland. In the centre is a dove, upon an olive branch, bees are flying around, and it is
enclosed by a rich wreath of grapes and leaves. Around the whole is a
border of figured work, and little vases holding fruit, the grapes are
amethysts, the pomegranate seeds garnets, the currants are cornelians
and emeralds adorn the vases, it cost $10,000. We visited Bartolini's stu-
dio, but saw nothing very remarkable. Wm. Tell's son was pretty. There
was a copy in marble of the Madonna of the Goldfinch.

*Wednesday, March 25th, Florence.*

Went to the Church of the Annunziata, to see mass performed in the
presence of the Grand Duke, but hearing he was unwell, and would not
be present, we came away, and drove and walked again in the Cascina.
Went to the Church of Santa Croce, it is quite old, and very plain exter-
nally. The square in front was the scene of the inauguration of the republic of Florence in 1450. The church has been called the Westminster
Abbey of Florence, because of the illustrious dead, who repose within it.
The first object that attracted us was the tomb of Michael Angelo
Buonarotti. At the top is a fine bust of him and, resting against a marble
pedestal, figures of lifesize of Sculpture, Painting, and Architecture, the
sister arts mourning his loss; they are fine figures, the first holds a small
statue in her hands, the second a brush and manifests the most sorrow,
architecture has a plan, and pair of compasses.

Next is Dante's monument. His body rests at Ravenna, but this is to
his memory with the injunction "onorate l'altissimo pöeta." Dante is
seated above, with a lyre and trumpet by his side. Florence, as a female

with a civic crown is pointing to him, and Poetry rests her head in sorrow upon his monument. There is a monument by Canova, to Alfieri, a tragic poet, and Florence is again personified. In the monument to Machiavelli, a female figure holds a bas relief, with his likeness upon it. Raphael Morghen the celebrated engraver is also buried here and there is a full length reclining statue of him. There is a monument to Galileo who lies buried here. It represents him holding a telescope; on one side is a female figure holding a geometrical plan, another holding a map of the moon. On a dark colored stone was represented some of the heavenly bodies, in allusion to his discoveries. We saw also the tomb of the wife and daughter of Joseph Bonaparte.

We saw some good frescos by Taddeo Gaddi, a scholar of Giotto; they are scenes from the life of the Virgin. One is her presentation in the temple, another her marriage. They are quite easy and naturel in the grouping, and free from the old Byzantine stiffness. They are in the Baroncelli Chapel, where is also an altar picture on wood, by Giotto, but very dark, and in a bad light. In a chapel near by is a monument to the wife of the young Pretender Charles Edward. In the sacristy was a crucifixion by Cimabue, and one by Giotto, both very painful figures. We saw a very sweet Madonna by Gaddi, though the fingers were long and stiff. In another chapel, we saw some interesting frescos, by Giotto, scenes from the life of St. Francis. The death scene is quite impressive. The monks surround the lifeless body, mourning, kissing him, and gazing at the stigmata in his hands. The complexions are pale, but not the old olive green. Another is the removal of his body to Assisi. Over the altar is a portrait of the Saint by Cimabue.

### Thursday, March 26th, Florence.

Visited today the Gallery of the Uffizi, and first the hall of Niobe. In this, are Niobe and her children, seventeen statues in all, and separate, except that the youngest child clings to her mother. They are being killed by the arrows of Diana and Apollo, because Niobe boasted that she had more children, than their mother Latona. They are all in various attitudes, expressing horror, fear, death, and expectation of the event. One is lying down dead, another seems ready to fall. Many of them are very fine; they were found at the gate of S. Paolo at Rome. We saw two pictures by Rubens, one the battle of Ivry, and the other Henry IV's entry into Paris. In the hall of the bronzes, we saw the celebrated Mercury by John of Bologna. It is full size, and seems blown along by the breath of

the wind, light, airy, and graceful. There was a little David, with his shepherd's hat and Goliath's sword. The shield of Francis I, and his helmet,
with many other little objects. Among the ancient bronzes was a chimera,
from Etruria, with a serpent's goat's and lion's head. There were six small
niellos engraved on silver, from which came the first idea of taking
engravings. St. Peter's ship, used as a lamp, was interesting as a Christian
relic. In the room of gems, were some very valuable objects. Little pillars
of rock-crystal, and precious marbles. A casket of rock-crystal, with
scenes cut in it, from the life of Christ. It was a present from Clement
VII to Frances I on the marriage of Catherine de Medici his niece to
Henry II. It is very beautiful. There is also a vase of sardonyx with the
initials of Lorenzo de Medici. I can not enumerate all the costly objects
to be seen here, in the greatest profusion; one was a little figure, whose
body was three great pearls.

We have visited the Sta. Annunziata this afternoon, and went in
through the large cloister. Over the door of the church, in a lunette, is
Andrea del Sarto's *Madonna of the Sack*. It is rather pleasing, Joseph is
leaning on a sack and reading a book, which the infant is stretching forward to reach. The church contains a fine crucifixion in bronze, by John
of Bologna and behind it, is his own tomb. In one chapel is one of
Perugino's finest works at Florence. It is the assumption of the virgin
who is surrounded by angels, and saints are adoring below. The first
chapel to the left, on entering the middle door is very rich indeed. The
altar, lamps etc. are of sliver, and part is pearl, with gems inlaid, in rich
profusion. In the centre is a sweet head of our Saviour, by Andrea del
Sarto, set in a gold frame. In the oratory is a picture of the virgin, kept
covered, except on state occasions, but according to the popular belief,
painted by angels. The walls are inlaid with mosaics pearl etc. and the
whole effect is exceedingly splendid. The small cloisters, adjoining the
entrance contain fine frescoes of Andrea del Sarto who is buried in the
church. They begin with scenes from the life of St. Philip, representing
him taking the dress of a mink and clothing the naked. The others are,
lightening killing some card players whose companions fly in terror. The
birth of the Virgin. Her marriage is painted by his friend Franciabigio,
who struck his picture with a hammer, because the monks uncovered it
before he was ready and the faces of the two figures are spoilt to this day.
The Assumption of the Virgin is by Il Rosso and not very agreeable. It
has rained much today and we could not go about very much.

*Friday, March 27th, Florence.*

We have been again to the Pitti Palace. And saw an "ecce homo" by Cizoli; a Pharisee and a coarse man exhibit the suffering Saviour. Two marine views by Salvator Rosa, the shores are like Amalfi, and Salerno, near which places he was born. Two of Rubens' landscapes the *Return From the Fields,* and Ulysses in the island of the Phaeacians. The colors are light and brilliant. A fine portrait of Oliver Cromwell, by Sir Peter Lely, presented by the Protector himself, to one of the Grand Dukes. A fruit piece by Rachel Ruysch 1664. The grapes peaches, plums, and flowers, were excellent and looked luscious. Titian's portrait of Charles V. There were many other pictures by inferior artists. Canovav's *Venus* a fine statue, stands in the centre of one room. There were some handsome marble tables, one was of malachite.

After this we went into the Museum of Natural History and saw minerals, shells, insects, birds, fishes, crustacea, and every variety of such things. There were also wax models of the internal structure of plants, the spiral coils, air vessels, epidermis, etc. all magnified. The wax plants were most perfect in their resemblance to nature, among them were lilies, a camellia, a tuberose, calcialaria, in pots. I never saw any so beautiful. There were wax models of the human heart and other internal parts, also those of animals; and a fine collection of stuffed birds of beautiful plumage. Connected with the Museum, is the Temple of Galileo, constructed by Leopold II the present Grand Duke. At the end of the little tribune is a statue of Galileo, in a glass case behind, are his telescopes, a lens made by him for his own use, his loaded magnet, a finger taken from his skeleton!! and busts of his scholars Viviani and others. In other cases were instruments used by the Academy of Cimento, of which he was the founder. The arches are ornamented with bas reliefs of his discoveries, and gilding on a blue ground. On the walls were frescoes representing Leonardo da Vinci showing a plan, as the precursor of Galileo. Then Galileo as a youth watching the chandelier at Pisa, which suggested the pendulum, in another, at the same place, he is demonstrating the velocity of falling bodies, some experiments with ice, and a mirror, a loaded magnet and galvanism. We afterwards went for a while to the Cascine.

*Saturday, March 28th, Florence.*

We have had a most magnificent day, really delightful after the rain, and we improved it, by a ride to Fiesole. It is not very far distant, but in an elevated position, overlooking Florence, of which it is the parent city. On going up, we saw a part of the old Etruscan wall, for it was an old town of that nation. Behind the Duomo which has a tower, like many in Florence, of mediaeval times, is another large portion of the wall of large irregular stones and in very good preservation. But the great attraction of Fiesole is the view. We walked up to a high point of the town, and there, the view of the valley of the Arno, Florence with its towers and cupolas, villas scattered over hill and valley, the Cascine its green fields and woods and a soft haze resting upon all, was exquisite. Just below us was Boccaccio's villa. But we could not enjoy the prospect in peace for we were beset by women, wearing large Leghorn hats, who urged us to buy their plats of straw. On descending we turned off to visit the Villa Buoninsegni, which was the favorite villa of Lorenzo the Magnificent, and was built by his father Cosmo il Vecchio. The terrace was his chosen promenade, whence his eye could stretch over the enchanting view. The house is plain with a tuscan roof and square. The rooms airy, but not very comfortable, with their brick floors. The garden was full of sweet flowers and the gardener was picking violets, to send to Florence to scent tobacco with. Went this afternoon to the Church of San Lorenzo, but saw little, as the principal chapel was closed. Before the front altar Cosmo il Vecchio is buried, and in the sacristy, Giovanni di Averado and his wife Picarda, father and mother of Cosmo, and founders of the greatness, of the family. The color of the church within, is grey and it is in mourning on account of Lent.

*Sunday, March 29th, Florence.*

Went all day to the English chapel which is at quite a distance, in a very pleasant part of the town. Saw there for the first time the Wheelers and Mr. T. Dwight.

*Monday, March 30th, Florence.*

Went to the Uffizi again, in some little rooms on each side of the tribune and saw a beautiful sea view by Claude, with his peculiar softness. Mary visiting Elizabeth, by Albertinelli a scholar of Fra Bartolommeo, the figures are large and fine, and the coloring quite rich. Some little pictures by Lorenzo di Credi, a pupil of L. da Vinci they are: Christ with the woman of Samaria, Mary Magdalen, and John; and Mary with the Saviour after his resurrection, very exquisitely finished and soft like miniatures. Medusa's head by L. da Vinci when very young; he is said to have studied reptiles for it, and has succeeded in making it frightful enough. Hunters drinking from a cup presented by a woman by Wouvermans. A little infant lying upon a cross, by C. Allori. There were several little pictures by Fra Angelico da Fiesole. Two small ones by Pontorno, a scholar of Andrea del Sarto, who was jealous of his success. One is Joseph carried to prison by Potiphar, the other, the same presenting Jacob to Pharaoh. Entering the tribune again we looked at Titian's two Venuses, they are entirely naked and very unpleasing to me. We also went into the Hall of Baroccio. His picture was a Madonna interceding for the poor, a large picture, with many figures, some very good. There were besides, Carlo Dolci's Magdalen of which Uncle has a copy. (In another room is a Sta. Lucia, with a wound in her neck, much like it.) A portrait of Philip IV of Spain by Velasquez, and A Man With a Monkey on His Back by Annibal Carraci. We went for a few minutes into the Etruscan room, but there was not much to see, besides vases.

In the afternoon we made an excursion to the Poggio Imperiale, one of the Villas of the Grand Duke. The Wheelers accompanied us, and we girls rode in one carriage, and the elders in another. It is not far from the gate, and is approached by a long avenue of cypresses. There is nothing remarkable about the house; it contains long suites of rooms adorned with frescoes. We saw an Apollo, supposed to be the work of Phidias, playing on a lyre which rests on his knee, it is a beautiful little thing, and Canova considered it the finest piece of sculpture in Florence. Also a miniature Moses, like the one at Rome, found, they say, in Michael Angelo's studio. There were a number of Charles' beauties, some of the faces were very pretty. The garden was full of flowers, and the view of Florence from this point was lovely.

We then went on somewhat farther to Galileo's tower, a low tower where he made his discoveries and took observations. Here also is a fine view; a perfect circuit, Florence which lies just below, the hills and mountains covered with snow, behind, and around, the Prato di Pistoja and the green fields and villas. Near by is the house where Galileo lived, and died, and where he received Milton as a guest. It has a tower on one side and is simple in structure. There is a bust of him, and an inscription, on one side of the house. We enjoyed the whole excursion very much. Antonio has gone to Paris on some business, and we have in his place for the time Giovanni Amato.

*Tuesday, March 31st, Florence.*

Went to the Medicean Chapel entering through the crypt. It is to connect with the Church of San Lorenzo, but is not yet finished. The interior is octagonal, and covered with rich marbles, in squares, urn shapes, and coats of arms of the cities of Tuscany. We saw the monuments to Cosimo I, to Francis, Ferdinand I, Cosimo II, Ferdinand II, and Cosimo III in the form of rich sarcophagi, in niches in the wall. The effect of the whole is rather sombre, the marbles being dark; the roof is frescoed. In the sacristy connected with San Lorenzo is a monument to Lorenzo and one to Julian, the first a grandson, the second a son of Lorenzo the Magnificent. They are by Michael Angelo. Lorenzo is seated, in a contemplative attitude, below are two figures Evening and Morning; the former a female with a sleepy look, as if just risen from her bed, the latter an old man, leaning on his elbow, weary with the labors of the day. Julian's monument was adorned by Night and Day, the first, a female overcome with sleep, an owl and poppies by her side. Day was an old man, but still unfinished. Michael Angelo built the sacristy, and the Madonna and Child over the altar, are by him, though incomplete.

We went next into the Laurentian Library. It is entered by a beautiful though unfinished vestibule, by Michael Angelo, of a dark stone grave and elegant. The library which is one large hall, consists mostly of manuscripts, arranged on slanting shelves, in pews as they seem, and are easily examined, though they are all chained. We were shown the Pandects of Justinian of the VIth century and the oldest in Europe; it was taken from Amalfi by the Pisans and regarded with great veneration. A Virgil of the IV cent. and regarded as very unique. A beautifully illuminated missal of the 14th cent., with arabesques from the life of the Saviour and other scenes. Two likenesses, of Petrarch and Laura, in a manuscript. The collection is numbered at 9,000, in all languages, and is very valuable. In a circular room adjoining is a collection of first editions, of Italian books, in print. The most ancient is one of 1468. The ceiling of the library is of carved wood, and the stained windows are designed by Giovanni da Udine.

After these we visited the Palazzo Vecchio, near the Uffizi, where the priors, and gonfaloniers of the republic, lived, the former, during their term, of office, were not allowed to leave the house. The interior court has a number of large columns around it, ornamented with stucco work. The building is rather gloomy, and strong enough for a fortress. We entered one splendid large hall. In this is a statue of Leo X, and one of

Clement VII crowning Charles V, both popes of the Medici family, besides statues and frescoes of no great merit. The Palazzo is now used for court purposes. We saw a chapel of the Medici time, and in one hall some curious objects of amber, and ivory ornaments, a crucifixion in ivory by John of Bologna, and St. Sebastian by Benvenuto Cellini. We mounted up and up, to the top of the square tower, at one corner of the building; it is very high and we had a splendid view of the city, the Duomo, various churches, and the adjacent country. We saw the communication of the Palazzo with the Uffizi, and there is one under the Arno, to the Pitti, and thence to a fortress on the hill. Twelve o'clock struck while we were in e tower, and it sounded finely, just above our heads. Along the upper stairs are cells for prisoners. In the highest one, where three people can hardly stand together, Savanarola was imprisoned, for two years and three months, and then hung and burnt in the Square, because he tried to reform some of the abuses of the time. In another more comfortable one, Cosimo II was imprisoned. After lunch we went to the suppressed Convent of St. Onofrio, to see a picture discovered 12 years ago, called Raphael's, but somewhat questioned. It is a Cenacolo or Last Supper and is in the old refectory. The grouping is not as fine as that of L. da Vinci's I think, but some of the heads are excellent. It seems to represent the moment when Jesus says to Judas "what thou doest do quickly." Most of the disciples are looking at him, who is seated opposite the Saviour some with suspicion, others as not seeming to understand and some indifferently. John has thrown himself on his face, overcome, and pale with emotion. It is a very interesting picture. In the same building is a small Egyptian museum. Here was saw a Scythian car found in a tomb; it is all of wood, with ivory lynch pins, and leather seat and is very light. Besides the usual mummy cases, there was a picture of an Egyptian beauty.

We then visited the Church of the Carmine to see in the chapel, some frescoes by Masaccio and Filippino Lippi. Peter and John laying their hands on the believers in the presence of Simon Magus, The Tribute Money, Peter and John healing the cripple and distributing alms are by Masaccio, done before the age of 26, when he died and show much talent, and a great progress, in the display of form, and expression. The work is continued by Lippi, in the Fall of Adam and Eve, Peter in prison, his liberation, and martyrdom. We were glad to come home and rest, after our fatiguing day.

*Wednesday, April 1st, Florence.*

We spent a short time at the Pitti Palace looking at our favorite pictures. It closes soon for repairs, and Holy Week. It has rained hard all day. Mr. T. Dwight called to see us.

*Thursday, April 2nd, Florence.*

This is the only day in the week for the Palazzo Buonarotti, Michael Angelo's house, so we improved the opportunity. In a sort of ante room, into which we were at first shown, were engravings of his pictures and a large marble cherub etc. In the saloon were pictures around the walls illustrative of scenes in his life. In one, he is sent for in haste by Julius II. In another some Turks are asking him to build a bridge at Constantinople. His plan of defense for Rome. His presentation to Leo X of the model of St. Peter's and another represents him seated confidentially by the side of the pontiff. He is received by the Grand Duke Francis, who makes him sit, while he stands, uncovered to do him a signal honor. He gives instruction in his own house, when quite old, to some young nobles. Finally the universal genius, seated in his study composing poetry. On the ceiling he is seen, being crowned by Poetry, Sculpture and Architecture. There was a Madonna painted by him, not at all pleasing to my mind; and below it, a bas relief of some naked figures, his earliest work. The next room was his bed-room. On the table were two pair of his slippers, one had iron heels. The room was furnished with old arm-chairs and in a little closet was the sword and canes that had once belonged to Michael Angelo. There were a number of studies for the Last Judgement and several heads. A room opening into this was a private chapel and here was a Madonna in bas relief by the great sculptor and busts, of the present Mr. Buonarotti and his wife an English lady, the last of the name. Michael Angelo's study came next. It was a very pleasant room, the walls were wainscoted with dark wood and in the centre hung a handsome wooden chandelier, here were paint pots, and other things used by him. The house was plain, but well furnished and preserved as a memorial of its former illustrious owner.

*Friday, April 3rd, Florence.*

We have today made an external survey of several buildings. We saw the Palazzo Strozzi now the property of the government. The family was formerly a rival of the Pitti, who boasted that they would build a palace, which could contain the Strozzi in its court. The Riccardi Palace was the residence of the first Medici's. We went into a room filled with offices and saw a splendid carved and gilt ceiling a remnant of former magnificence. In a chapel are some good frescoes by Benozzo Gozzoli representing angels singing "Gloria in excelsis" and the adoration of the Magi, which appears like a hunting scene. This was one of the first attempts, to introduce landscape into a picture. The "Casa di Dante" which we visited next, shows no trace of antiquity; but here Dante was born. The inscription on the house is: "In questa casa degli Alghieri nacque il divin' Poeta."

Not far from here is the Hospital of San Giovanni di Dio which occupies the site of the house of Americo Vespucci. An inscription says "Americo Vespucci patricio Florentino, ob repertam Americam, sui et patriae nominis illustratori, amplificatori orbis terrarum, in hac olim Vespuccia domo, a tanto domino habitata, patris sancti Johannis adeo cultori, gratiae memoriae causa. P.C. A.S. C. 1010 . C.C.XIX. viz (1719)." We stopt at the Palazzo Pandolfini, which has a facade designed by Raphael. The garden though small is very pretty and the conservatory rich, in very large and exquisite camellias. This afternoon we drove up the hill of Bellosguardo, into the villa Albizi formerly occupied by Galileo. It commands a fine view of the city, looking directly down upon it, and it is a delightful situation, for a residence. Not far from the city gate, but within the walls is the Villa Torregiani now occupied by two foreign families of rank. The grounds are very beautifully laid out. The walks wind about among fine tall trees and pretty shrubbery. There were fine pansies, and climbing roses, and several conservatories. Two large and graceful muscovite pines called forth our admiration.

*Saturday, April 4th, Florence.*

Called in the doctor for Auntie. She has had a bad cold, and oppression of phlegm on her chest, but through Dr. Hardee's prescriptions is now better. We went this morning to the Palace of the Podesta, the foreign officer of justice. It resembles the many palaces here, made of projecting stones of large size, and is now used as a prison. The court into which one enters, is covered with the amorial bearings of Podestas, of every imaginable form. We ascended a flight of steps, and passed through several corridors, to a chapel where a portrait of Dante by Giotto, has been lately discovered, by some English and American gentlemen. It was covered over with whitewash to the depth of an inch. He is one of a crowd of persons, who seem to be adoring something; the defaced condition of the fresco does not allow us to tell what. The face is youthful, and the head dress is a singular peaked cap; his robe is red. Besides this, there was also a Madonna and child and St. Jerome adoring the cross which are I suppose works of Giotto.

Afterwards we went to the perfumery of the Church of Sta. Maria Novella, where the Dominican monks make excellent perfumes and essences. They have a fine place, and elegant rooms. We went in the afternoon, to Careggi, which is about three and a half miles from here. It was built by Cosimo "Pater patriae" and was one of the favorite residences of Lorenzo the Magnificent, and where he had quite a farm. It is now owned by Mr. Sloan, an English gentleman. We went over the house which is quite large, and into the room where Lorenzo died; in one room was a bed of richly carved wood with his coat of arms, six pills, upon it. A large saloon was ornamented with armour in fresco, and a table was formed of the coat of arms, of a Medici pope. The owner is collecting portraits of the Medici family, of which we saw a few. One of Cosimo, Lorenzo, Leo X and one of Pico Ficino and Savanarola a very monkish face. We went out upon a terrace; and a portico in the attic story of the house, and had most beautiful views of city, and country, hill and valley. The garden is upon high ground, and is laid out in beds, the land then slopes downward, in green fields, of grain, to quite a distance. We have had an exquisite day.

*Sunday, April 5th, Florence.*

We attended the English church in the morning and Mr. Hanna's in the afternoon. Mr. Dwight called in the evening to say good bye. He leaves on Monday for Rome. The Whitneys have not yet arrived.

*Monday, April 6th, Florence.*

We have had a quiet day, the first for some time. The Doctor has given his judgement against Auntie's going on Wednesday and the time is uncertain. She has taken a ride in the Cascine, and is improving I hope.

*Tuesday, April 7th, Florence.*

Went to the Academy and spent some time there. The pictures are arranged in the order of time, to illustrate the Tuscan school. First we examined one from the Italian Byzantine school; a Magdalen with mummy-like drapery and green and red face, surrounded by like figures. A Madonna with angels on each side, by Cimabue. One by Giotto more graceful in attitude; also scenes from the life of our Saviour, and that of St. Francis. The adoration of the Magi, by Gentile da Fabriano, a most gorgeous scene; the faces were soft and pleasant, the gold and ornaments in relief, and a long train of attendants filled the background. The descent from the cross by Fiesole in very light colors. The *Baptism of Christ* by Andrea Verocchio; an angel kneeling on the left side, was by Leonardo da Vinci and a scholar of his and so superior to the master's that the latter gave up painting. Perugino painted, Christ praying in the garden and the disciples asleep, and an *Assumption of the Virgin*, with the saints below, among whom was a cardinal and a figure much resembling Raphael. There were two pretty little cherubs, by Andrea del Sarto, singing and quite naked and several other pictures by the same artist. By Matteo Rosselli, a goldsmith; St. Eloi showing a sliver ornament to Clothaire II king of France who is richly adorned, in a robe covered with fleurs de lys. Olindo and Sophronia bound to the stake; by Lorenzo Lippi. In a little room adjoining the long hall were some small pictures on wood, thirty five were by Fiesole, of scenes from the life of our Saviour. There was also a portrait of the artist monk, in his cowl, the face was sober, and with deep shadows upon it. In the cloister of the Scalzo' (a suppressed convent) we saw some frescoes in a dead color, by Andrea del Sarto, Faith, Hope, and Charity, and scenes from the life of John the Baptist, they were much defaced. After this we took a delightful walk in the Cascine, and found many flowers, a woman brought us some lilies of the valley.

*Wednesday, April 8th, Florence.*

We went out to do a little shopping and met Mr. and Mrs. Whitney who arrived on Monday, the former has been sick. We went to the Corsini Palace, which is just below here, it is large, and built round a court We saw a number of very good pictures by Carlo Dolci. Poetry, of which Uncle has a copy, is beautiful and so finely finished, that it bears the closest scrutiny. St. John as a child, with a cross, and a little lamb. St. Sebastian pierced with arrows, and gazing upwards. John the Evangelist. An "Ecce Homo" the face pale and worn with suffering, but sweetly mild. Petrarch and Dante crowned with laurel, by Naldini. A number of Salvator Rosa's landscapes, two, were soft sea views, and one of Terracina with rocks, and goats clambering over them. Also, by Tintoretto, there was a portrait of a doge of Venice.

This afternoon we went to La Petraja di Castello, a villa of the Grand Duke's. It is three and a half miles from here. The view is splendid. The flowers were in great profusion: anemones, scarlet, purple and white; and ranunculus. The castle belonged to the Bruneleschi family, and was once besieged by Sir John Hawkswood, and the Pisans. We did not enter the house, but the avenues and walks were very pleasant. The sun was intensely hot.

*Thursday, April 9th, Florence.*

Early after breakfast this morning, M. and I accompanied the Wheelers to the Pitti Palace, to witness the ceremony, of the Grand Duke washing the feet of twelve poor pilgrims. There were many people already assembled about the door, trying to enter, we went in by a smaller door, and following some other people, mistook our way, and had to return. The hall, when we finally reached it, we found quite crowded, and the seats all occupied, the air was close. There were tables, covered with nicely prepared food, along one side of the room and ornamented with bouquets of flowers. We were pushed back by the crowd, and saw little, except the face of the Grand Duke, who stood at the head of the table. I believe he was distributing food to the poor men, who were seated on one side of the table; old women occupied the other side. There was no washing as far as we could see, probably it was done beforehand, by the servants. At a little balcony, stood the royal ladies as we thought the duchess and a little son and daughter and two other ladies of whom, one, was perhaps the bride of the young prince, a daughter of the king of Saxony.

We made our way out soon, almost stifled, and spent two or three hours in the Boboli Gardens, which adjoin the palace. They extend to a fortress, called Belvedere, from whence the view is very beautiful. There were shady avenues, and walks fountains, ponds, and flowers, and we enjoyed rambling about in them. The circumference is four miles. This afternoon we drove to the entrance of the Pitti, to witness the procession of the Grand Duke, on his way to offer up his prayers, in six or seven churches. First came lines of soldiers, and between them marched, first, the household servants, dressed in brown, with red breeches, white stockings, buckled shoes and cocked hats, then some pages in crimson silk, soldiers with muffled drums, several officers and the Duke himself, on foot, with a chapeau, and green plumes. He looks old, with white hair, and moustache, and a stern expression. A step behind him, walked Prince Corsini; and behind, the eldest son of the Duke, a young man of about 22, also with green plumes. Surrounding these were generals and a company of the noble guards in red uniform, brought up the rear, followed by a led horse and two elegant carriages for the Duke and his son, if they were much fatigued. We then rode to a bridge, and saw the whole procession pass again, and also when they entered the Church of Sta. Trinita, so that we were quite satisfied with our view of them. The Duchess and her ladies, we were told, made the tour last year.

*Friday, April 10th, Florence.*

No bells in the city ring today. It commemorates the crucifixion of our Lord. It has been a rainy day but we were able to visit Power's studio and were much interested in what we saw. There was the original model for the Greek Slave; her hands are chained together and she droops her head sadly, it is quite naked. The model of an Eve, was there also. *Il Pensieroso* was a beautiful statue, the embodiment of Milton's grand imaginations. It represents a female quite draped with a long train which she holds up with one of her beautiful arms, she holds one finger to her chin, and gazes upwards, the whole attitude is very graceful and she seems as if actually in motion. It is for Mr. Lennox of America. The model of the America is here, the original has gone home for exhibition; it is a fine thing. A woman leans with one arm upon rolls of parchment, probably the constitution, upon which rests a laurel wreath; she raises her other arm, and tramples upon chains, which have just fallen from her. There are stars upon her brow, and an expression of exultation in her face. We saw a model for a bust of the Duchess, a head of Proserpine, and a boy listening to a shell.

We have heard more about the ceremony yesterday, from some friends of the Wheelers, who had a position in front, and saw it all. They said that the Duchess took off the stocking of each old woman, a noble poured water over it, and she wiped, and kissed it, and the Duke went through the same, with the old men. They had however previously been well washed.

*Saturday, April 11th, Florence.*

Went to the cathedral to witness the last ceremony of Lent. We had excellent seats in the choir. Mine was just behind the bishop's chair, and we saw everything. The church was quite full. The service began by the entrance of several priests, who went through the usual genuflexions etc. The Archbishop, as we took him to be, sat at one end of the choir, and a bishop performed high mass. The organ played, the trumpets sounded and a choir of boys sang. When they came to the "gloria in excelsis" a dove, made of paper or wood, descended from a pillar at one end of the choir, along a string, to the open door of the church, where was placed a car of ornamented fire-works. We could see no shape to the dove, but fire, sparks and a loud noise, accompanied its course. It then returned and exploded, and this was succeeded by various thundering explosions in the car, which soon disappeared. If these fireworks do no succeed, the people expect a bad harvest. So the government ordered that if unsuccessful the men who arrange them, shall be imprisoned for two months, and they generally go off well. Two little boys with censers swung them back and forward, the priest then took the wafer, and three times drained the cup of wine, and the service ended. The coverings of the altar and chairs were taken off, as Lent had terminated.

In the afternoon we went to the Church of Sta. Maria Novella. It is quite complete, strange to say, and made of black and white marble, with a sun dial on the front. In the Spanish chapel which opened into the cloisters, were frescoes by Simone Memmi; the preaching of St. Domenic, and Peter opening the gates of heaven; Christ bearing the cross and his crucifixion. On the other side by Taddeo Gaddi were St. Thomas Aquinas, Faith, Hope and Charity; the canon and civil law, theology, arithmetic and Abraham as its inventor below!! under each, were the persons most distinguished in that branch of knowledge. In the Rucellai Chapel was the Madonna of Cimabue, it was quite good, especially the kneeling angels on each side. Before its completion, Charles of Anjou, passing through Florence, was taken to see it, and all the inhabitants followed, when finished, it was borne in a triumphal procession to the church. In another chapel was a carved wooden crucifixion by Bruneleschi. He is said to have shown it to Donatello, who had made a poor one, for Sta. Croce, the latter, who had his lap full of eggs and cheese for his dinner, dropt all and exclaimed "to you belongs the power of carving the figure of Christ, to me that of representing peasants." In another chapel were frescoes by Orcagna, but it was too dark to see much. In the sacristy were three little reliquaries by Fiesole. The first was a Madonna standing and holding the infant, and beautiful figures on each side of it. In the adoration of the Magi the Virgin is gracefully robed in purple, with a gold border. The third was a coronation of the Virgin. The church was richly adorned with flowers, and hanging, and some Dominicans were performing a service. We expect to leave here on Monday. The bells are ringing out Lent most lustily.

*Sunday, April 12th, Florence.*

Went to the English church in the morning, but on account of the violent rain stayed at home in the afternoon.

*Monday, April 13th, Coviliajo.*

We are nearly on the summit of the Apennines. We left Florence at nine and soon began to ascend. The views of hills and valleys were fine. It was quite showery, and poured hard most of the time, and the wind blew so fiercely as to shake the carriage. The road was good except in one place, where a bad hole had been filled with loose branches, over which we shook. The inn is quite good, for such a place, and we were glad of a bright fire. It was once the scene of horrible murders.

*Tuesday, April 14th, Hotel San Marco, Bologna.*

After a day's journey we arrived here. On the mountains we saw patches of snow, but the sky has been very blue and our view extended over hills and crags. Although at the foot of the mountains, our route today has not been all descent. Oxen have been required, a part of the time, to drag us up the hills. Bologna belongs to the pope and the Austrians hold it for him. We had considerable trouble at the Roman douane or custom house. They made all but Auntie get out of the carriage, and searched most particularly, even in the dressing cases, for three quarters of an hour. The chief man refused the fee which generally smoothes all difficulties.

*Wednesday, April 15th, Bologna.*

We visited the Academy of Painting, containing the peculiarly national school of the Caracci, Guido, Domenichino etc. Raphael's *St. Caecilia* is a beautiful thing. The saint is listening earnestly to a heavenly choir, St. John and St. Augustine gaze at her, and St. Paul regards the broken instruments on the ground. There is a fine crucifixion by Guido. Mary clings to the cross, the virgin weeps apart and John is gazing upon the dying Saviour, while all around is darkness. The Massacre of the Innocents was an early effort of this artist, one mother has lost two babes, and a fierce man seeks to kill her last, she has a face of agony. Samson drinking from the jaw bone of an ass, and treading on a dead Philistine, by the same. St. Bruno, the founder of the Carthusian order, praying in the wilderness, a Madonna and angels in the sky, by Guercino and one of his finest works. Domenichino's *Madonna of the Rosaries*, represents the

Madonna and infant Saviour in the sky, showering roses, upon saints who are being put to death, these hold rosaries in their hands, many of them. The Communion of St. Jerome by Augustino Caracci his finest work, and the original of Domenichino's picture on the same subject; the positions only being different. A Madonna by Ann. Caracci in imitation of Paul Veronese, the Saviour and John like Correggio, John the Evangelist like Titian, St. Catherine like Parmigianino. Count Ugolino of Pisa, a desperate looking man. The Baptism of Christ by Albani and larger than most of his. Opposite was a room containing old armour, Greek and Turkish guns and some horrible swords.

In the afternoon we went out to visit the cemetery which is very extensive. It is arranged in the form of rooms, with columbaria in the walls, and tombs in the pavements, open courts, and long halls. There were some very fine monuments. One to Matilda Tambroni professoress of Greek, in the University, a few years ago. Part of an old Carthusian convent, is now turned into a Pantheon and contains busts of the celebrities of Bologna. In its former state, Charles V once occupied it, when he came to Bologna to be crowned. Here is among others a bust of Cardinal Mezzofanti late professor of Greek. There is an arcade, of three miles length, joining this cemetery to the city, it also connects with St. Luke's Church on the hill. We then visited the old church of the Carthusians in the same enclosure, and saw a Crucifixion by Cesi much like that of Guido in the Academy, and from which the latter probably was taken. We afterwards went up to the Church of San Michele in Bosco. That was formerly a convent of the Olivetans, on the same hill the Cardinal Legate occupies as a villa. The view of Bologna from the garden is fine; it lies in a flat plain, which extends to the Adriatic Sea. In the house were pictures and engravings. As we again entered the city, we stopt to look at the two ancient leaning towers, one the Asinelli the other the Garisenda both square and made of brick. The latter leans eight feet, and Dante says that the giant Antarus when he stooped to pick up him, and his guide, resembled Garisenda, with clouds flying over it. We saw only the exterior of the celebrated University, it is now most celebrated for medical science. We went into the Pizza del Gigante, formerly the forum. On one side is the Palace of the Podesta, and opposite the Church of St. Petronio. Into this latter we entered. It is built in the Gothic style, and the pillars and arches are of a brick red color. Here Charles V was crowned for his Italian possessions. The chief characteristic of Bologna is its arches which are found in most of the streets. They form a pleasant walk, in hot or rainy weather.

*Thursday, April 16th, Ferrara.*

We stayed at Bologna till noon, thus having an opportunity to see again the finest pictures in the Academy. We took a lunch and started on our way to Ferrara, which is distant, about thirty miles. The road lay across a flat plain, we had, I believe, but one small hill to ascend. Poplar trees were quite abundant and fresh green fruit trees. The country looked fertile and flourishing. Ferrara is held for the pope by the Austrians.

*Friday, April 17th, "Corona Ferrata" Hotel, Rovigo.*

We spent the morning in Ferrara and taking a carriage went out to see the place. There were formerly 100,000 inhabitants, now not one third as many and they are gathered towards the centre of the city. I was much struck with the appearance of the streets. They are very wide and well paved with round stones but grass and weeds grow in the interstices and the sidewalks are often quite green. Few people are to be seen except in the busier streets, and the palaces and houses look deserted. I think I did not see more than a half dozen carriages during our stay, and we rode ourselves in a queer concern. People stared at us as if great curiosities, and as if they did not often see a stranger. It reminded us of Pompeii, to look up the streets so still and desolate were they. It was melancholy too. We visited first the castle, where the Dukes of Este lived, when they held sway over Ferrara. The last Duke was Alphonso II, and after his death, Clement VIII attached the duchy, to the states of the church, on plea of the illegitimacy of the next heir. It is a complete castle, standing in the midst of the city, with a deep and broad ditch still filled with water, a drawbridge, and walls with towers and battlements. We passed through the apartments now used by the papal legates. One hall of great size was ornamented by Dosso Dossi with frescoes of bacchanalian scenes; another called the Aurora saloon, contained four frescoes by the same artist, which were very beautiful. They were Early Morning, Aurora leading out the horses of the sun. Full daylight, the same flying before the chariot. Twilight, Phoebus steps out of the car, in which Aurora remains, a serpent bites one of the horses, and he is in the act of falling. In the last, Aurora too leaves the chariot, and joins Phoebus upon the grass. One room is shown as Leonora's sister of Alphonso II, and favorite of Tasso. It was in this palace that the pious Duchess Renée daughter of Louis XII, and wife of Duke Ercole I, lived and afforded an asylum to her persecuted country men. Calvin found an asylum at her court, under the name of

Charles Heppville, and she enjoyed his instructions. We were told that he had a room in the palace, but I think it is not known where; his memory would not be held very sacred. Olympia Morata lived with the Duchess. Her father was tutor to the two younger brothers, of the Duke. We went out upon the balcony whence Clement VIII blessed the Farrarese after he had taken possession of their city; a very satisfactory way of atoning for his injustice!!

Leaving the castle we went to the Hall of Magistrates and saw many interesting things. At the end of one of the halls of the library was Ariosto's monument removed together with his bones, from the Church of St. Benedetto. It is made of black and yellow marbles, with his bust in white marble on top and an inscription below. In another room is his arm chair, and a bronze inkstand designed by himself, and cast for him, by Duke Alphonso. It has Cupid enjoining silence on top, and female heads around the base. There was a manuscript copy by Ariosto himself, of some of his satires, it was very nicely written. We were much interested in seeing a page or two of the original *Gerusalemme Liberata* by Tasso. It was much corrected, one line was scratched out and written over in several ways, the writing was crooked and scrawly. Also a letter sent from his prison to a friend, with some shirts to be washed and mended, telling him not to mix them up with those he had sent before, and in the postscript begging his friend to come and see him. We saw also some choral books on parchment, with beautiful illuminations by Il Cosme of the 15th cent. The first printed edition of Orlando Furioso; and the last in Ariosto's time, dedicated to Card. Ippolito d'Este. Leo X gave him a patent for the exclusive printing of his own book.

Thence we went to Ariosto's house. The inscription, written by himself, is "Parva sed apta mihi, sed nulli obnoxia, sed non sordida, porta meo sed tamen aere domus." It is a simple brick house, We went in, and up stairs; his room opens into a hall in the second story. It is a square room of moderate size, the windows are of bull's eye glass, round panes. A table and four straight backed chairs are all his furniture remaining, with another bronze inkstand. The place has been bought by the government, and the poet's bust is placed here. The panelled door has been partly cut away by visitors. The woman who showed the house, said it was forbidden; but for a compensation, cut us off a tiny bit. Tasso's prison next engaged our attention. It is in the basement of the Hospital of St. Anna. The cell is a low dismal dark place, and very damp. There is much doubt whether it is the veritable prison. Byron's name is marked on the wall, and Lamartine's, as a testimony to the identity of the spot. The cause of Tasso's imprisonment is not clearly known. Alphonso II treated him very cruelly. We went afterwards to the palace, the finest in Ferrara, and built of projecting stones, not of brick like most. In the pinacotheca was a full length portrait of Alphonso II, the face is rather disagreeable. A picture representing John in the island of Patmos seeing the vision of the woman clothed in scarlet, quite a fine picture by Dosso Dossi. Christ praying in the garden and the disciples sleeping, John's face is exquisite, by Palma il Vecchio. We then took a lunch and setting forth on our journey came soon to the Po a fine broad river, but so high above the country, as to make embankments necessary. We crossed by a ferry boat, and after passing through a custom house, found ourselves in Lombardy. The country appeared flat as before. Rovigo is a cheerful town, but not particularly interesting.

### Saturday, April 18th, Hotel Danaeli, Venice.

Here we are in Venice, the "Queen of the Adriatic" of which I have heard so much, and longed to see. But I must take up my story, where I left off. We left Rovigo at eight, and rode in the vetture until about twelve, when we reached Padua. It is a scattered city, with large open spots within the walls. St. Anthony is the patron saint. His church is quite fine the roof is covered with towers and cupolas, we only saw the outside. We took lunch at the hotel and then drove to the railway station. The cars were delightfully easy and we arrived at the station, outside the city of Venice, in less than two hours. Here we took a gondola, a rather small one for four persons, it was painted black, as all the closed ones are, and looked like a hearse. We glided along the Grand Canal by palaces, all old, and some deserted and grass grown, then turning just before we reached the Rialto, and passing through the small rii we came to this place. We are upon the Giudecca, and looking out upon sailors, ships, a broad expanse of water and the isle of St. George opposite. I was in ecstasies with Venice, but letters that greeted us, turned our thoughts for a while.

### Sunday, April 19th, Venice.

We attended church in a palace, where one room is filled up for the English services. We rowed in a gondola. The congregation was very small, and the room had an alcove, in which were the desks and altar, inlaid with pearl and gilt. We had a juggler and musicians and a crowd of people amusing themselves, on the quay in front of our hotel. Sunday is the holiday here.

*Monday, April 20th, Venice.*

We sent for a gondola to row up the Grand Canal. The boat we had today, had merely an awning to shield us from the sun, and we could see easily from under it. The motion is luxurious, and very delightful. Each side of the canal is lined with old palaces, some of them exceedingly rich in open-work of stone. Their architecture is Gothic, or Oriental, with highly ornamented arches. One is the Foscari Palace, owned by a doge of that name. There are several old factories, or depositories of merchandise, in a ruined state, grass grew in the crevices. One belonged to the Turks, one to the Germans, and one to the Jews. For Venice in its days of prosperity carried on commerce with all nations. We visited the Manfrini Palace on one side of the Grand Canal. There has been a fine gallery here, but the best pictures were sold. We saw one by Georgone, an astrologer with disk and compass, and a young man and woman looking on. The Entombment by Titian. Mary supports the weeping virgin and two men bear the body. John is at one side. A cartoon of Noah's ark, it is said by Raphael, a huge thing and unattractive. A pretty little shepherd boy by Murillo, the only one by him in Venice. We met here the Whitney's Mrs. Stowe and Mrs. Perkins. I was rather disappointed in the collection.

In returning we stopped on the island of Rialto, the first part of Venice that was settled upon. Here is a square surrounded by arcades, the site of the old exchange, and where the scene was laid by Shakespeare of Shylock's meeting with Antonio. The Rialto is a bridge crossing the Grand Canal and lined with shops. We crossed it, and passing through several streets, came into the Piazza St. Marco. These streets are very curious, they are only as wide as a common sidewalk, and of course there are no carts or horses to be seen, but throngs of people, and stores on each side.

After lunch we took a survey of the piazza, which is but a short way from here. Just at the entrance to it, by the water's edge, are two columns brought from Constantinople, upon one is a lion, upon the other St. Theodore, stepping upon a lizard, the protecting saint of the city. To the right of the square as one enters from this side, is the Dodge's Palace, and beyond that the Church of St. Mark's, on the left is the Library, and a brick campanile stands in the middle. The other sides of the square are occupied by the Clock Tower, and the Imperial Palace, and arcades with shops opening upon them. The Clock Tower is crowned with a large bell and two hammer men. We heard the clock strike, and one of these men gave four strokes to the bell, and the other did the same. Below, is a small balcony and on certain days, three wise men appear from a small door, walk across, and out at another door. Venice is celebrated for its glass works, and gold chains of great fineness. The streets are very intricate, and in one part, a narrow line of white marble is let into the pavement by following which, one will come out at the Rialto sooner or later. The water carrier women are peculiar they wear small steeple hats, and carry two iron buckets, one at each end of a stick, over their shoulders.

We have been into the Church of St. Mark, and it is the most gorgeous I ever saw. To give a complete description is impossible. We entered first a vestibule, which surrounds two sides, and whose ceiling is ornamented with mosaics of different ages. The shape of the church is a Greek Cross and there are five cupolas. Near the door hangs a brass chandelier, in the form of a double cross, and the effect when lighted is very splendid. A silver one has colored glass around the lights, and looks as if studded with gems. Mosaics cover the cupolas, arches, wagon roofs, and floor, and marbles of every variety the walls. The mosaic date from the Byzantine age to beyond Titian and Tintoretto. Among them is a genealogical tree of the Virgin; and scenes from her life by an artist of the 16th cent. Upon one of the pulpits, was a ball of agate, the largest piece known. Of the 500 pillars in the church the most valuable as regards the marble, is a black and white porphyry. The capitals of the columns were of varied forms, but all gilded. Another pulpit was of Arabic character, and had a little gilded dome supported by marble pillars. The high altar is divided off by a rich screen of Grecian marble, sculptured with figures. The altar itself, rests upon four elaborately carved pillars brought from the Mosque of St. Sophia, Constantinople. From the same place, also was brought a bronze door with arabesques upon it. All countries contributed for the adornment of the church; at one time no ship could leave the place without engaging to bring something for St. Mark's. The base of one of the holy water basins came from a temple of Greece, and four pillars in the vestibule were from Solomon's Temple at Jerusalem. There were also in the vestibule, the tombs of several doges. The facade is extremely rich, in a balcony over the entrance, are four bronze gilt horses from Constantinople. There are mosaics upon the outside also.

This afternoon we visited the Church of Sta. Maria dei Frari. The interior is quite rich. We saw the monument to Canova, from designs by himself. It is a pyramid, into the open door of which, a female mourner followed by two young girls, is about to enter. On the other side are two genii, an angel with torch reversed, and a lion. Over the door is written Canova. Opposite is a splendid monument to Titian, erected by the Emperor Ferdinand I. Titian, a very old man, is seated under a splendidly decorated Corinthian canopy, on one side is a figure of Venice, on the other, an angel. Below, are beautiful figures representing the arts. Near by is the old tablet with the inscription "Qui giace il gran' Tiziano dei Vecelli, Emulator di Zeuxi e degli Apelli." Over the entrance is an immense monument to the Doge Giovanni Pesaro it is supported by Negroes, in allusion to his conquests. The tomb of Doge Foscari is here also. In the church, is a picture by Titian, called *Pala dei Pescari*. The Virgin is upon an elevated seat and St. Peter below her, St. George holds a banner. Five members of the Pesaro family are introduced in the picture. The colors are very rich indeed.

*Tuesday, April 21st, Venice.*

We visited today the Academy, which contains several fine large rooms of paintings. In the first was Titian's *Assumption of the Virgin* a splendid thing. Above is the Father, the virgin beneath is upheld by clouds and cherubs of great beauty. The disciples stand below in various attitudes in astonishment and rapture. The coloring is very rich. By Giorgone, is a picture representing St. Mark, St. George, and St. Nicholas in a stormy sea, stopping the demons who are about to overwhelm Venice. The marriage at Cana, by Padovanino, a large picture, and finely executed. The delivery of a Venetian slave by St. Mark, Tintoretto. A large picture, the presentation of the Virgin, by Titian was very fine. She, a little girl ascends the steps to the high priest and a crowd of people are looking on, near by, sits a woman selling eggs. A fisherman presenting to the doge a ring, which St. Mark had given him, exhibiting the doge and his council in their rich dresses, by Paris Bordone. In the afternoon we took a gondola and sailed over to the other side of the city, to the island of Murano to visit the glass works. We passed the cemetery on our way; there was much wind, and the water was rough. At the glass works, we saw them melt the composition in the fire, roll it, and draw it out into very long thin tubes, for beads. These they then cut into bits, of the requisite size and filling the holes with sand to prevent them from melting together, placed with sand in the fire. This is to round them, by melting slightly. They then cleaned them and polished with bread crust dust and they were finished. The very nicest beads were made by dropping the melted material, upon an iron wire, which being whirled around, they hardened quickly. They make bottles and other objects by blowing through the iron tube which contains the composition, and forming whatever shape their fancy directs. They made us a little plate of red and white, alternate colors. To do this, they laid a number of glass tubes on a brick, in the fire, and when they melted, joined them together, and blew them out into the right shape.

### Wednesday, April 22nd, Venice.

We went this morning to St. Mark's again for a few minutes, it was draped in black, for the archbishop whose funeral is tomorrow. Afterwards to the Doge's Palace. This is an irregular square. There are two rows of arcades on the outside, towards the sea, and on the piazza, and the same round three sides of the interior court. On the fourth side, the Giant's Staircase leads to the state rooms of the palace. It is a rich entrance, at the top are figures of Mars and Neptune, one on each side. Upon this staircase, the doges were crowned. We entered first the ante room of the "Council of Ten"; in the wall is a hole called the lion's mouth, into which, secret accusations were dropt, and by means of them, people were arrested and tried. In the Council Room is a picture by Bassano, it represents the Doge Ziani returning from his victory over Frederic Barbarossa and his meeting with Pope Alexander III, Bassano himself holds the canopy over his head. From another ante room we passed to the Hall of Audience. It is a very handsome room, about the walls are gilded pilasters and there are seats for the doges and counsellors. The ceiling is very rich gilded, and there are paintings by Paul Veronese representing the triumphs of Venice, and doges introduced into the pictures of Madonnas In the "hall of the four doors" is a large work of Titian: A doge kneeling before a figure of faith, in the clouds, with a cross. Another is the reception by a doge, of the Persian ambassadors, who are taking presents from their chests.

We went into the hall of the Pregadi or Senate Chamber, a large room. There were many paintings, one, by Palma Giovane, The Siege of Cambrai, represents Venice as a lion challenging Europe a bull. The ceiling was magnificently gilded. The Sala del Scrutinio faces the interior court. Upon one side, is Palma Giovane's *Last Judgement*, and opposite a painted triumphal arch, in honor of the doge who conquered the

Morea, and destroyed the Parthenon. In this hall the forty one nobles were elected, who after many ceremonies chose a doge. The "Hall of the Great Council" is now a library. In it is Tintoretto's *Paradise* a very uninteresting picture, eighty feet long and 34 high, all on canvas with oil paint. The walls have been adorned by various artists, with pictures, illustrative of the history of Venice. They are the Doge Dandolo in the Church of St. Mark holding a conference with some crusaders. The election of Baldwin, Count of Flanders, as Emperor of Constantinople. The same receiving the crown from Dandolo. The Doge Contarini returning in triumph after a victory over the Genoese at Chioggia. The Emperor Frederic II met by Venetian ambassadors, who supplicate peace, but are answered, that unless they deliver up the Pope, Alexander III, he will plant his banner on the portal of St. Mark's. The pope delivering a consecrated sword to the doge, on his embarking to fight. The great naval battle, in which the Emperor's son Otho was taken prisoner, and brought before the pope, but this is a piece of Venetian boasting, Frederic II allowing the pope to set his foot upon his head saying "Thou shalt tread upon the lion and the adder" a scene in the vestibule of St. Mark's. The portraits of the doges are arranged as a frieze to the wall. They begin in 809 and number 72. One vacant spot has a black curtain, for Marin Falier a traitor and unworthy of a place in the honorable ranks. The private apartments of the doges were not notable, except for the gilded panels of the ceilings.

We went into the prisons beneath the palace, they were horrible places, without light or air; in one, the unfortunate beings were secretly strangled. Then we went to the "Bridge of Sighs" a closely covered passage way, to the prisons on the other side of the canal. We thus finished quite a thorough survey, of three hours, of the palace. Afterwards we visited the Church of Sta. Maria della Saluta, erected after a plague, in which 60,000 persons perished. The church is of an octagon form. In the sacristy was a large painting by Tintoretto, *The Marriage at Cana*, it has no great beauty. St. Mark and other saints is an early picture by Titian. And the Descent of the Holy Ghost a fine piece. Luca Giordano painted, the nativity, presentation, and assumption of the virgin. Others of no great celebrity. It has rained to day, and we have had to use a closed gondola. Venice is not the same under a rainy sky.

*Thursday, April 23rd, Venice.*

Mary and I visited to day the Arsenal, and because Giovanni was sick took a valet de place with us. We went in a black covered gondola. At the land entrance were two marble lions brought from Athens. The erect one was taken from a place in the Piraeus, to which it gave the name of Porta Leone, and was thought by some to have been a memorial of the battle of Marathon. Then we went into the museum, the only part to be visited, and saw various relics and curiosities. A flag taken from the Turks, by the Venetians at the battle of Lepanto. The shield and helmet of the Doge Ziani, much ornamented. The sword over five feet long, which Dandolo used, at the taking of Constantinople. Henry IV of France's armour given to him in 1603, by the republic. A model of the Bucentoro, in which, every year on Ascension Day, the doge went through the ceremony of marrying the sea. The model was quite large, all gilded and figures adorned the sides. The doge and his council sat at one end, in a lower part the nobles, and the sailors had places on the outside. Near the doge's seat was a small door, through which he threw a ring into the water. The old ship was burnt but we saw a few remains, parts of the gilded sides, and the doge's chair. A figure of Venice sat on the prow of the ship and a lion on the stern; it must have been very magnificent. There were specimens of ancient armour also to be seen.

In the afternoon, we again visited the Academy and besides the pictures we had examined before saw; the Piazza of St. Mark in the 15th cent., with a procession of priests, showing the costumes of the time. The feast of the Levite by Paul Veronese, a huge picture covering the whole of one end of a hall. It is a very lively scene, with many figures and is quite fine. On the stairs are halberdiers eating and drinking. Thence proceeding in our boat to the Church of San Giovanni e Paolo, we saw Titian's celebrated picture, *Peter Martyr*. The subject is not pleasing, but the execution is spirited. This church is the Westminster Abbey of Venice, and contains many monuments of doges. Here are two of the Falier family, the monument to Morosini, to Loredan whose prudence baffled the league of Cambrai, to Mocenigo and to Vendramin, the first, from the lately ennobled families, raised to the dignity of doge.

*Friday, April 24th, Verona.*

We left Venice this morning in the gondola, and took the cars. The scenery was attractive, the Alpine range snow clad, in the distance, and nearer to us, green hills. We passed through Padua again, and Vicenza and arriving here at about half-past three, lost no time in going out to see the city. The amphitheatre is a very perfect one not so large as the

Coliseum, but of about the same age, and much better preserved. The elipse is still covered with rows of seats, and used for shows even now. There are two entrances and each surmounted by a balcony in one of which, we were told, the allied sovereigns sat, at the Congress of Verona, to view some spectacle, and 60,000 people filled the other seats. We saw the Piazza d'Erbe" formerly the forum and the old Bourse at one end, also a column where stood the lion of St. Mark, when the Venetians held possession of Verona. The river Adige flows through the city and is crossed, by an arched bridge of brick, with turrets. The Castel Vecchio is also of brick; it is a large building, surrounded by a ditch, and erected by Can Grande II one of the later Scaligeri. We passed by the house where lives, Marshal Radetzky, Austrian governor of Verona, and hated by the Italians. An inn was pointed out to us as the old house of the Capulets, where Juliet lived. It is not very large, two or three windows are arched, and somewhat ornamented, but there are few traces of magnificence. In the churchyard of a suppressed convent, was, what is called the tomb of Juliet. It looks like a stone sarcophagus, or as it is in a wash house, it may be a wash trough. The man pointed out the hole for respiration. Another more probable tomb, has been destroyed. This will do, with the aid of a powerful imagination.

A part of the town wall was built of brick and small stones alternating, with turret work on the top, by the Visconti of Milan, when they held rule here. Upon one side of the Piazza dei Signori, is the Palazzo Consiglio with an ornamented façade, where the Scaligeri held their councils. Near by, in a small street is the Church of Sta. Maria Antica, in the churchyard of which are the tombs of the Scaligers. They ruled in Verona in the 13th and 14th centuries. Their names in order are, Mastino I, Alberto I, Bartolommeo in whose time Romeo and Juliet are supposed to have lived, Alboino I, Can Grande, Alberto II, Mastino II Can Grande II, Can Signorio. The first tomb, near the church door, is that of Can Grande I, below is his effigy reclining, with a crowned dog at each end, above is the same figure on horseback, with the helmet hanging off his head. At his court Dante found a refuge. A sarcophagus contained the remains of Mastino first, who was treacherously killed, in the Piazza dei Signori. In the corner is the rich tomb of Mastino II. It is two stories high, ornamented with figures from the *Old Testament*, and an equestrian statue on the top. In another corner of the small enclosure is the richest of all built by Can Signorio for himself at the cost of 10,000 florins. He lived in a house opposite. The tomb is marble and of Gothic architecture, ornamented with figures of warrior saints. Between the two last are Alberto I, Bartolommeo Alboino and Can Grande II who built the Castel Vecchio. Around all is a beautiful wrought iron grating with ladders on every figure. These, which were the family emblems appeared on all the monuments; the name means "bearers of the ladder." Verona is neat, and has a pleasant aspect. Soldiers abound. The streets are well paved and of good width. We saw in the travelers' book, Uncle's and Auntie's names of May 12th 1837.

*Saturday, April 25th, Hotel de la Ville, Milan.*

We left Verona in the cars at eight, and rode for three hours, passing through Brescia. The snow mountains looked finely. We passed the lake of Garda. It is very beautiful, extending north, among the Tyrolese Alps. One route to Tyrol, is by passing up the lake. We looked out upon the broad expanse of blue green water; in the background, were the mountains, lapping one over the other, more and more distant, and softened by the atmosphere into a delicate lilac, while the pure white snow glistened on the lofty peaks. On the shore were several old castles, one was built by the Scaligers. Near the lake is the plain of Rivoli, where Napoleon fought the battle of that name. We stopped at Cocaglio, and took a post carriage, for a few hours, as there is a break in the railroad. Then we waited some two hours for the cars, and arrived here about five.

*Sunday, April 26th, Milan.*

There is no English clergyman in town, so we had no service. Every other Sunday there is a French, and the remaining days, a German service. The latter unfortunately for us, was the case to day. Uncle only, profited by the occasion.

*Monday, April 27th, Milan.*

We have been to the Brera Gallery and saw there Raphael's celebrated *Marriage of the Virgin* painted when he was only twenty one. It is in his early style a little like Perugino, but soft, and delicate. Guercino's *Dismissal of Hagar* is a fine thing. The old patriarch's head is splendid, he wears a blue turban. Sarah stands behind, and the weeping Hagar and her son are going off, into the desert. The adoration of the Magi, by Paul Veronese. The virgin is sweet and young around her, kneel the wise men. He also painted the feast in the house of Simon, when Mary washed with tears the feet of her Lord. It is of very large size. St. Jerome praying in the desert, with a stone in his hand to beat his breast with, by Titian. A slightly colored design for our Saviour's head, in the Last Supper, by L. da Vinci. A Madonna with a saint on either side, and an angel playing below by Luini with many frescoes by the same. St. Mark preaching at Alexandria to an assembly of women in white, and Arabs, in black and red robes, a church is in the distance, and camels are also represented; by Gentile Bellini. This is but a small account of the hundreds of paintings in the gallery, but it must suffice for the present.

In the afternoon we visited the cathedral. We first ascended to the tower, upon the roof, to see the view, and examine the architectural details of the exterior, better than we could do from below. Our view was very interesting; the Jungfrau, the Splugen, St. Gothard, the Simplon all were in sight, with their snowy peaks. Monte Rosa can be seen in a clear day but the clouds prevented us from distinguishing it. The Tyrolese Alps we saw, the plains of Lombardy stretching out, a vast flat, and the plain of Marengo, where the famous battle was fought. All around us were the pinnacles turrets and flying buttresses of the roof, all in white marble, and ornamented in parts with a perfect garden of fruit and flow-ers. We saw a portion of the building erected in the 15th cent., a part fin-ished last year, and it is not yet complete, the oldest parts are already black with age. There are 6616 statues of all sorts of saints, and holy per-sonages on the exterior and interior. More than two hundred turrets beautifully ornamented have each of them twenty five statues. The high tower still rose above us, but our view would not be particularly improved by ascending it. The interior consists of five aisles, divided off by large clustered columns, with a canopy over each for a capital, and a vaulted roof, frescoed to imitate tracery, in wood or stone. The windows are of rich stained glass. On each side of the high altar were two gilded pulpits. The pavement is of mosaic in different patterns. A large lamp hangs in the choir, resembling a gilded pinnacle, and there is a cande-labrum of worked bronze, set with precious stones. We saw several mon-uments, one to St. Carlo Borromeo Archbishop of Milan. The effect of the whole was very fine, in fact more sublime than St. Peter's. It seemed more like an English cathedral than a Catholic church, the chapels and altars are not as prominent as usual. Milan is a pleasant city, the streets are clean and well paved. We have seen the Arch of Peace commenced by Napoleon. It is the entrance upon the Simplon road. Upon the top, is Peace in a chariot, and Fame at the four corners and there are bas reliefs representing various scenes. In the lapidary museum of the Brera is a bronze statue of Napoleon, which was intended for the top of this Arch but has never been raised to that position.

*Tuesday, April 28th, Como.*

In the morning, as we were not to leave till afternoon we paid another visit to the Brera. In one room is a bronze statue once gilded, of Bernabo Visconti, very stiff and clumsy, the first equestrian figure in Europe. He was a very cruel and tyrannical ruler. He is said to have had 5,000 hounds, and these he quartered on the citizens; if they were lean their hosts were fined, if too fat they were also fined, for feeding them overmuch, and if they died, the property of the unfortunate keepers, was confiscated. We saw a young Virgin with a lovely face by Albani, her father and mother and two saints are around her and she is looking up to heaven, where a door appears. A Madonna and child and kings adoring, by Ludovico Carracci, the shadows are dark, but the face of the child is exquisite. Peter the Hermit by a brook in the desert, by Salvator Rosa. There were also some modern landscapes of Alpine and woodland scenery. From here, we went to the Ambrosian Library. It was the first public library in Europe. Besides books and manuscripts, there were pictures and quite a collection of other things. Raphael's cartoon of the School of Athens is here; a few figures are wanting which were added in the fresco, but otherwise it is the same. Also part of the cartoon of the Battle of Constantine. A likeness of L. da Vinci by himself, done with red chalk, and many of his caricatures. Some of these are faces with every expression of grimace, or deformity, and legs bodies and various other studies. There were some small bas reliefs remains of the monument, to the French Duke, Gaston de Foix in whose army fought the Chevalier Bayard "sans peur et sans reproche." A bust of Conte Federigo Borromeo Archbishop of Milan, and founder of the library. The books are arranged on shelves, in the ordinary way. Among the manuscripts, we saw a letter by Lucretia Borgia, to Cardinal Bembo, with which was sent a lock of her flaxen hair, which we saw above. A book of drawings of machinery by Leonardo da Vinci. A copy of *Virgil* written by Petrarch, with a miniature in the beginning by Simone Memmi representing Virgil and a personification of Poetry. Two miniature Korans, and a palimsest of Cicero's oration on Scarus, with another subject written over it. Then we went to the Convent of Santa Maria delle Grazie, now used as soldier's barracks, to see L. da Vinci's *Last Supper*. It is in the refectory of the old convent, and has been much injured and repainted. It was done in oil, and hence in part its ruin. But there is much yet remaining to interest one, and the engravings make one familiar with it. We left Milan at three, and arrived here in an hour and a half. Como is a place of 20,000 inhabitants, the hotel is just at the foot of the lake.

*Wednesday, April 29th, Como.*

We set off at half-past eight this morning, for our sail up the lake. The steamboat was called the *Adda*, it was a little one, but comfortable. The views were extremely beautiful on either side, but my description will give little idea of them. Steep mountains rose up directly from the water's edge, some rough and rocky, others covered with verdure and one was of a soft green, like moss. Mist hung in wreaths upon their summits and when it became too heavy, it descended upon our heads, in a gentle rain. The lake of Como is thirty two miles long and in some parts two miles wide, and winds about like a river. Villages, and villas in beautiful situations, are dotted over the shores, and add to the picturesque effect. Upon the high peaks of the mountains, snow is to be seen, and it also lingers in streaks, in the deep gorges. The sunlight and shadows on the hills were fine.

When we came to a village, the passengers were carried off, or in, by means of little boats, that came out to meet us. In one of the deep bays is the Pliniaje, where Pliny, who they say was born at Como, used to resort. It looks like a pleasant retreat, near by is a large villa. The peculiarity of this lake, as compared with those at home lies in the snow-capped mountains, and the gay-colored villas and towns, that lined the shores, or were perched half-way up the hill-sides. We did not go more than half-way up the lake, but stopped at Cadenabbia, to see some fine villas. Here we found an excellent hotel, and it is said to be a great resort for the Milanese. We took a row-boat with one of the peculiar hoop-covered awnings and stopped first at the Villa Somariva not far distant. It is a pretty place and a path leads to the door through laures tinus, Portuguese laurel and a lemon arbour. The first saloon is furnished with handsome divans, and ornamented with works of art. In the centre is a Mars and Venus in white marble and life size. There is a Magdalen kneeling, with a cross and skull by Canova. Innocence, a beautiful boy, wreathed with flowers, and holding in his hand two doves. Around the room was a bas-relief by Thorwaldsen it was designed, for Napoleon, to place in the Quirinal Palace, but being left incomplete was carried on by

Prince Somariva. The villa was formerly owned by this prince, who was an advocate of Lodi and rose to rank and riches. It is now the property of the Princess Carlotta of Prussia, and called Villa Carlotta. The balconies in front were covered with exquisite little buff cluster roses, and below were pink roses. The grounds though not extensive were well arranged. We then crossed the lake to the Villa Melzi, a very fine one though less pleasing at a distance. Melzi was vice-president of the Cisalpine Republic, and we saw everywhere allusions to Napoleon. There was a portrait of him as consul. And a bust of the viceroy, Eugene Beauharnois. In the chapel near by is a monument to Melzi. The rain prevented our going to a villa higher up, to see the view and we retraced our way to Cadenabbia, and after waiting some time took the returning steamboat and sailed back in the rain to Como. Our fellow passengers were Irish and German gentlemen and ladies.

*Thursday, April 30th, Lago Maggiore, Arona.*
We left Como at half-past seven in a carriage, and drove for five hours, through a pleasant country. Near Como was the Badinello Tower, memorable in the history of the place, it has no door, but is entered by a subterranean passage. We passed several small lakes, and on reaching Laveno, after some delay, took a steamboat on Lake Maggiore. We went up the lake for a while, as far a peninsula, where is situated a large village, then curving into a deep bay, where were the islands Superiore, Madre, and Bella, we turned our course downwards to Arona. These islands are very small, the last is occupied by a hotel, and pleasant grounds, which are terraced on arches. The scenery is quite beautiful, here too snow mountains are visible, St. Gothard is at the head of this lake as the Splugen is at the head of Lake Como. It is a broader lake than the latter, and the views more soft, but I did not admire it as much. Near Arona is a colossal bronze statue of St. Carlo Borromeo. It is twenty two feet high and one can even climb into the nose. We are on the Piedmont side of the lake.

*Friday, May 1st, Hotel d' Europe, Turin.*
We left Arona this morning, and reached here in the cars in about five hours. We rode with a gentleman from Boston, Mr. Twin who lost his wife, last summer, in the Lake George accident. He seemed glad to meet fellow countrymen. We saw, though some clouds interfered, the Alps rising up loftily and clad in snow. The Po now quite a small river we crossed. Here, in Turin, we look out upon a large square, with the Old Castle, now the Madonna Palace directly opposite and the Royal Palace in sight.

The king of Sardinia, Victor Emmanuel, is a very liberal Catholic, and has therefore been excommunicated by the pope. He has aided the Waldenses in building a fine church here, and freely permits their worship. His country prospers, and Turin has improved much under his rule. We have taken already a ride about Turin, and find it a very pleasant city. The streets are wide and clean, the houses fresh looking, and there are arcades around the squares. There is a senate, and house of representatives, and also a written constitution. In the Piazza San Carlo, we saw an equestrian statue of Emanuel Philibert Duke of Savoy, from whose younger son the present line of kings descends. It is very spirited, he is in the act of drawing his sword. A granite obelisk in another piazza, commemorates the cessation of the civil power of the ecclesiastics.

*Saturday, May 2nd, Turin.*

We have been to the royal gallery of paintings in the Castello containing seventeen rooms. One picture represented the finding of Moses, by Pharaoh's daughter. She is splendidly dressed, in white satin and jewels, and several maidens are about her; one takes the child from the basket another calls Miriam who is in the distance. Another was the visit of the Queen of Sheba to Solomon. She kneels before the king, who is seated on his throne and servants bring the presents which she has brought with her all are richly dressed. Both of these, of large size, are by Paul Veronese. The supper at Emmaus by Titian, the face of our Saviour is mild and beautiful, one of the disciples expresses amazement, and the other folds his hands in awe. The Madonna della Tenda by Raphael, with some traces of a scholar's hand. It is very lovely. The infant leans backwards to listen to St. John, who whispers in his ear. By Spagnoletto is a blind fiddler and a man writing off his words; also some hermits. A pretty landscape by Salvator Rosa, the baptism of our Saviour in the foreground, and trees rocks and a stream of water to fill out the picture. Charles I's children by Van Dyck, and Cromwell and his wife by Peter Lely. A Jewish rabbi by Rembrandt. St. Francis Romaine by Guercino, an angel child stands by the saint, who holds the book of *Psalms*, a basket of bread is by his side, on the floor. Four very natural cows by Paul Potter. Then we went into a part of the royal palace, to see the armoury, which contains a fine collection. It is a very handsome room, with equestrian figures along each side. We saw the sword and baton of Alphonso Duke of Ferrara. Also the cuirass and helmet of Prince Eugene, worn when fighting with Louis XIV, at the battle of Turin. It has been deeply dented with bullet marks. The long broad-sword of Emanuel Philibert and a full suit of handsome armour, inlaid with gold, worn by him, at the battle of St. Quentin. He made his own armour, even to inlaying it. The saddle and bridle of the Emp. Charles V. Napoleon's sword used at the battle of Marengo. A Roman eagle made of iron, and two gilt French eagles, belonging formerly, to Napoleon's Italian guard. There were some guns splendidly decorated with precious stones, inlaying and chasing. Swords, daggers, and poignards, some of them Oriental, richly gilded, with pearl or malachite handles. There was some chain armour, and shields, one with a lantern and covering for the arm. Also suits of armour to protect both horse, and man. In the afternoon we visited the Egyptian museum, a remarkably fine one, and quite extensive. Here we saw a black granite statue of Rameses II he wears a helmet, and his face is pleasant. It is remarkably well done. Jupiter Ammon in the form of a crouching goat. A huge statue, of the son of the Pharaoh of Moses' time. Osiris, Isis, Ammon and many other statues of kings and gods. In an upper room were other objects, a fine large basalt sarcophagus. Two long papyrus rolls, one was the book of the kings, the other a funeral roll forty feet long; it represents a soul appearing before Osiris, a secretary writes, the actions are weighed, and 42 judges decide the cause. There were many mummy cases, and some mummies still unopened. Jewelry too, and other Egyptian curiosities and valuables. Scarabei were there to the number of 2000. We afterwards walked in a promenade, that extends for quite a distance round the city. The Alps are seen at the head of some streets, and look finely. The king has come to town today; he is still young, 37 they say.

*Sunday, May 3rd, Turin.*

We attended church at the new Vaudois Chapel, a very neat and pretty building. We heard a French service, and the sermon was very good indeed. The congregation consisted of gentlemen and ladies, poor men, and peasant women in their neat white caps, besides soldiers. In the afternoon there was an Italian service, conducted by one of the ministers that I saw in Nice. The singing was by children, led by a chorister.

*Monday, May 4th, Lanslebourg.*

We left Turin in the cars for Susa and there procured a carriage and six mules to take us over Mt. Cenis. We wound slowly up the mountain and found no snow till we had nearly reached the summit, and there, as well as on the north side, were drifts by the road sides, of five or six feet deep. The waterfalls looked very beautiful, pouring over the rocks, some were frozen and hung in long blue icicles. We found a few hairy white flowers, and large blue violets were given us. The descent was made in a short time and we were glad to see again trees and grass. The moon shone brightly through the mist. We reached Lanslebourg at a little after eight o'clock.

### Tuesday, May 5th, Chamberry.

Our road led us through wild and rocky scenery, still descending. The hills were covered with a kind of red heath or moss pink. At St. Jean de Murienne we took the cars. This is a neat little town with steep slated roofs, to the houses, which are quite pretty. The railroad passed through a charming valley of Savoy, with mountains on each side and green grass, and picturesque little towns, cleaner looking than we have seen for a long time. Chamberry was the capital of the duchy of Savoy. We again hear French spoken everywhere.

### Wednesday, May 6th, Lyons.

We left Chamberry at an early hour, and took a post-carriage for a long ride of eleven hours. We drove very fast and crossed the frontier of France. The country looked pleasant more so than we had seen in France before. We have our former rooms in the hotel.

### Thursday, May 7th, Hotel Westminster, Paris.

We have had a long hot and dusty ride in the cars of eleven hours. We find that Antonio has not yet returned from Greece.

### Friday, May 8th, Paris.

Mary and I went out shopping. We saw Dr. and Mrs. Beck. Afterwards we drove in the Bois de Boulogne, and found it very gay and pleasant. I caught a sight of the empress as the imperial carriage passed us. She was very pretty. Duke Constantine of Russia is here. The day we arrived there was a grand review of 50,000 troops in the Champs de Mars. I was sorry to miss it. We find the weather extremely mild.

### Saturday, May 9th, Paris.

We have rested today as we felt still fatigued after our journey. Dr. and Mrs. Beck dined with us.

### Sunday, May 10th, Paris.

Went to the Taitbout Chapel and as the service did not commence till twelve, were obliged to wait sometime. M. Fish preached a French sermon, on the account of Jesus walking on the sea. In the evening the imperial carriages passed here, on their way to the opera guarded by a troop of soldiers.

*Monday, May 11th, Paris.*

In the afternoon M. and I went to the Jardin des Plantes which is at quite a distance from here. We could not see the conservatories without a special permit, and therefore saw only the animals. Buffon had some part in the collection and arrangement of these and there were a great variety, but not I think so rare as those in London. It is a pretty place ornamented with trees shrubbery and flowers, and is much frequented by all kinds of people. We dined with Dr. and Mrs. Beck, in the Hotel Rivoli, whence they have a pleasant view of the Tuilleries.

*Tuesday, May 12th, Paris.*

We drove out to St. Cloud, but not being able to see the palace without a permit, we went on to Sevres. The ride for a part of the way was very pleasant with the Seine on one side, and the park of St. Cloud on the other. We saw some very exquisite pieces of Sevres porcelain; it was very expensive, four or five dollars for a small cup. Raphael's *St. Caecilia* was beautifully copied in porcelain, and other pictures; also a lovely portrait of the empress. The fruit and flower pieces were perfect, and we saw a cabinet that was to go to Queen Victoria when completed. We wished much to see the process of manufacture, but it is not allowed.

On our return we stopped at the Chapelle Expiatoire, erected by Louis XVIII to the memory of Louis XVI and Marie Antoinette. They were buried here in the churchyard of the Madeleine, and the ground converted into an orchard, by M. Descloseaux, to secure it from revolutionary fury. The bodies were afterwards removed to St. Denis, and the Chapelle erected on the spot of their first entombment. The ground is neatly laid out, and planted with ivy and cypresses and on each side of the garden, the Swiss guards were buried who fell at the time. The chapel itself contains, on one side a figure of Louis XVI kneeling and supported by an angel, on the pedestal is inscribed his last will. On the other side Marie Antoinette also kneeling, with Religion and a cross by her side. The guide told us that Madame Elizabeth personified religion and on the pedestal is Marie's last letter to her. In the crypt is an altar, on the precise spot where the king was laid, and near by the tombs of the royalists who perished on the Place de la Concorde. In the evening we accompanied Dr. and Mrs. Beck to the restaurant of the Trois Freres Palais Royal, to dine. This is considered one of the sights of Paris. We chose a small room, to be more private and had just what we ordered and no more.

*Wednesday, May 13th, Paris.*

M. and I took a walk in the Tuilleries and found it very pleasant under the shady groves of horse chestnuts and limes. We started for Gobelin, but just then receiving letters, we were too much occupied with them, to devote ourselves to anything but the Bois de Boulogne which we found very lively, with people and carriages. We saw here the cascade of Longchamp *built* last autumn it is a pretty place, though artificial. Some of the wood paths are quite delightful.

*Thursday, May 14th, Hotel Bristol, Paris.*

The mistress of the hotel came to us this morning, and requested us to leave the apartments as we had engaged them for only six days (which was not true) and another family were coming. It was very troublesome and we had a right to stay, but we thought it best to move, and we took snug little rooms in the Hotel Bristol for the night.

*Friday, May 15th, English Channel.*

We heard no news of Antonio, and concluded to wait no longer. Took the cars for Havre. The country was pleasant, principally along the Seine, We saw in the distance Gaillard Castle, perched on a crag above the Seine; built by Richard Coeur de Lion, against Philip Augustus. Here John was besieged in the conflict about Arthur of Bretagne. We passed through Poissy where a conference was held by the Calvinists and Catholics, Bera on the one hand and Card. Hippolito d'Este on the other in the presence of Charles IX and his mother. Mantes, set on fire by Wm. the Conqueror, was where he received the wound from his horse, of which he died at Rouen. We should have liked to stop at Rouen, but had not time. It is an ancient city, the capital of Normandy. We saw the Côte des deux amans, where a lover was to marry the king's daughter, if he carried her up the hill without resting, he died in the effort and she of grief soon after (Lai of Mary of France). We passed through Harfleur, and arrived at Havre in good season. The boat sailed at eleven. We established ourselves early in our berths, and passed a tolerably comfortable night.

*Saturday, May 16th, Pier Hotel, Ryde, Isle of Wight, England.*

We arrived this morning at Southampton, at nine and were glad of breakfast and a little rest. At two we took the boat for this place. Passing down the Southampton water, we touched at West Cowes, a pleasant little town, on the north side of the island. We saw Osborne House, the queen's marine residence, and where she now is. It is a fine place, and constantly improving. The shore of the island looked delightfully green, and fertile; it is well called the garden of England. Ryde is a pretty little town. We are directly upon the water. A long pier runs out for half a mile

*Brading Church*

into the sea and is a favorite promenade. We have a long twilight now, it is not dark till nearly nine.

*Sunday, May 17th, Ryde, Isle of Wight.*

We took a carriage and drove four miles to Brading, to attend church where Leigh Richmond used to preach. It is a lovely ride through roads lined with trees and green hedges and picturesque thatched cottages. The church is very ancient, though not anterior to the conquest. Upon its site were baptised the first converts in the island, by Wilfred, bishop of Selsea. The beams of the roof are bare, and the whole is rude in appearance. We had a good sermon from Mr. Heath, or a brother minister, the service was of course Episcopal. We sat in a square pew, near the pulpit. Behind the church is little Jane's grave. The verses upon it are,

> *Ye who the power of God delight to view*
> *And mark with joy each monument of grace*
> *Tread lightly o'er this grave, as ye explore*
> *The short and simple annals of the poor.*
>
> *A child reposes underneath this sod*
> *A child to memory dear and dear to God.*
> *Rejoice! but shed the sympathetic tear,*
> *Jane the young cottager lies buried here.*

Not far off were two inscriptions which she learnt one to Mrs. Ann Berry, at her teacher's request the other of her own accord. One of these is as follows,

> *It must be so our father Adam's fall, and disobedience brought this*
>     *lot on all*
> *All die in him, but hopeless should we be; blessed Revelation were it*
>     *not for thee*
> *Hail glorious Gospel heavenly light whereby, we live with comfort*
>     *and with comfort die*
> *And view beyond this gloomy scene the tomb, a life of endless happi*
>     *ness to come.*

The other is,

> *Forgive blest shade the tributary tear*
> *That mourns thy exit from a world like this,*
> *Forgive the wish that would have kept thee here,*
> *And stayed thy progress to the seats of bliss.*
>
> *No more confined to grov'ling scenes of night,*
> *No more a tenant pent in mortal clay,*
> *Now should we rather hail they glorious flight*
> *And trace thy journey to the realms of day.*

In the afternoon, Uncle, Mary and I walked over to Binstead Church. It is a pretty church, and we enjoyed the walk through pleasant roads and shady lanes. When we arrived the doors were not open, and we stood for a while, taking in the sweet scene around us. The green fields and cows pasturing upon them, the bright foliage, the concert of birds, and the soft balmy spring air, all united their soothing influences on this beautiful Sabbath day. The church is very small, with only one aisle. We heard another useful sermon. On our return we had a brilliant sunset, our view of Portsmouth and the sea was fine. We were disturbed at night by angry voices on the other side of the street and the cry of "murder" and "police" "every prospect pleases but only man is vile."

*Monday, May 18th, Shanrock Hotel, Niton, Isle of Wight.*
    We are snugly settled in a most charming little inn. A bow window extends into a porch, mantled inside and out with luxuriant ivy. A green bank slopes down to the road, and is terminated by a hedge, in the distance is the sea and a few pretty cottages are scattered about in the foreground. We have had a lovely day from beginning to end, full of excite-

*Little Jane's Cottage*

ment. Was there ever such a spot as the Isle of Wight? We left Ryde at nine in an open landau driven by a neat postillion. We passed first through St. Helen's. It is a pretty place, a village green, surrounded by thatched cottages. The scenery all along is quite enchanting, the hawthorn hedges line the roadside, and we saw growing wild, cowslips, purple hyacinths ,daisies, buttercups etc. We passed through Brading not, however having time to visit little Jane's Cottage. Brading Harbour runs, some distance into the land. A monument to Lord Sarborough, stands near by, on a grassy hill. From Brading we drove to Sandown on the sea shore, and turned off from thence, to visit the Culver Cliffs. Here we had a fine walk on the pebbly beach, the cliffs, of white and variegated colors, are lofty and look finely, jutting out into the sea. Our course then lay to Shaklin and we stopped there, at noon to take a lunch at the pretty inn, and then to visit the Chine, a chief object of interest in the place. It is a gorge, formed by the wearing of a little brook through soft rock. It is a sweet spot, a shady path winds along, following the course of the stream to the waterfall which is small, but very pretty. From Shanklin we went to Undercliff. Here are two long lines of perpendicular cliffs, one near the shore, the other higher up, with the downs beyond. They afford a

*Grave of the dairyman's Daughter,*
*Arreton, Isle of Wight*

complete shelter from the north winds and are much resorted to by invalids. Bonchurch is a sweet place, near by is Steep Hill Castle a modern edifice resembling the antique. Kentnor is quite a town, after that we came to St. Lawrence, where one of the horses lost his shoe, and had to be taken back to Ventnor. While waiting, M. and I sketched the very picturesque church of the place, one of the smallest in Great Britain. We had some talk with an old woman, who seemed interested in watching us, she was much astonished when we told her, that we came from America. After resuming our carriage, a short ride brought us to Niton, where we now are. The waiter told us that a nightingale sang here every evening, between eight and nine, but it is colder tonight, and I much fear we shall not be able to hear him.

*Tuesday, May 19th, Portsmouth, England.*

   We left Niton this morning and soon reached a place called Blackgang Chine which we descended to visit. We went down a long flight of rough steps, into the wild rocky gorge, on the sea shore. A sailor's cottage is placed on the beach. The man told us it was well nigh washed away last winter, he saw one wave 70 feet high. In 1836 the *Clarendon* was wrecked here in full view and only three persons could be saved. The sailor had some old cannon, washed up by the sea, one, a Spanish piece looked very ancient. The gorge is formed by a little brook, which has in the lapse of time worn out the rocks to the depth of 70 feet. It is said to have once been the resort of a gang of pirates and a fit place it is for such deeds, wild and savage, and close to the raging sea. From this point we could see the western extremity of the island, and the white peaks, called needles, terminating it, which are so dangerous to ships. Our ascent was quite fatiguing, but having at last reached the summit, we drove on to Godshill, where there is a pretty church. The road was now more inland and soft fields, bounded with green hedges, and fine elm trees made a pleasing landscape. We saw larks soaring up into the air, and heard them sing, as they mounted higher and higher, and then floated down again. It seemed like heavenly music. In Arreton we stopped at the "Dairyman's" house. It is a simple thatched cottage, with several fine trees in front. The room we entered was occupied by the nephew's wife and a grandniece of Elizabeth Woodbridge. They showed us her *Bible*, with her name written in it. A cupboard where the pewter used to be kept, and an engraving of Leigh Richmond over the fireplace remained as formerly. The bedroom where she died was in use and they objected to showing it but after some persuasion M. and I were allowed to go up. It is directly at the head of the stairs, and the room only remains the same. About a mile from here is the Church of Arreton and the churchyard where the Dairyman's daughters Hannah aged twenty-seven and Elizabeth aged thirty one are laid. The inscription on Elizabeth's grave is as follows,

> *Stranger if e'er the chance or feeling led*
> *Upon this hallowed turf they footsteps tread*
> *Turn from the contemplation of this sod,*
> *And think on her whose spirit rests with God.*
> *Lowly her lot on earth, but He who bore*
> *Tidings of grace and mercy to the poor*
> *Gave her his truth and faithfulness to prove.*
> *The choicest treasures of his boundless love;*
> *Faith, that dispelled affliction's darkest gloom,*
> *Hope, that could cheer the passage to the tomb,*
> *Peace, that not Hell's dark regions could destroy,*
> *And Love, that filled the soul with heavenly joy.*
> *Death of its sting disarmed, she knew no fear,*
> *But tasted heaven, e'en while she lingered here,*
> *O happy saint! my we like thee be blest*
> *In life be faithful, and in death find rest.*

The church is very old with something the appearance of a castle. We then went to Carisbrook Castle, one of the most interesting spots on the island. It was here that Charles I was imprisoned. It is a very picturesque ruin. The entrance is by a gateway, guarded by two towers. The walls are still standing, and we made the whole circuit, walking on top of them. Upon one side, we were shown the window of Charles I's room, and the bars through which he tried to escape, but was discovered in the act. At the north east angle is the keep, the most ancient part, and probably of Saxon times. It is reached by ascending a long flight of steep stairs. The walls are all overgrown with ivy, but from the summit is a fine view of the pretty village of Carisbrook just below, Newport the capital of the island, and the beautiful country round about. In the keep is a well 300 feet deep. Another well in the enclosure of the castle was 240 feet and 150 to the water. An ass turned the wheel, to bring up a bucket of water, and it was very delicious, a lamp was let down to show us the depth. The house, formerly occupied by the governors of the castle is being restored in the old style. A young lady who acted as our guide about the ruins, said she resided there. She showed us the room where, leaning on her *Bible* at the window, Lady Elizabeth daughter of Charles I died. The room where the king was at first confined was locked and we could not see it. We went on our way again and stopped at Newport for lunch. Then driving seven miles, we returned to Ryde where we took the boat for Portsmouth where we were shortly landed.

*Wednesday, May 20th, Southampton, Hampshire.*

    This morning before leaving Portsmouth, we took a boat, and rowed about the fine large harbour. We saw two men of war, that are to sail with troops at one o'clock for China. We landed at the dock but having no permit, and not being British subjects were not allowed to enter. The *Fairy*, the *Dolphin* and the *Victoria and Albert* were some of the queen's yachts. She embarks at Portsmouth for Osborne House. The *Fairy* is a pretty thing, its row boats are blue with gilt edges. We went on board the *Victory*, Nelson's ship, now used for training cadets. On the deck we saw the spot where he fell, and down in the cock-pit, as they call the lower part of the ship, below the guns, the place where he breathed his last. Nelson's motto "England expects every man to do his duty" was written up in a conspicuous place on the deck. We saw many other vessels but did not go on board of them.

    We took the noon train and after an hour's ride reached Southampton, whence without delay we set off in a fly for Netly Abbey which is only three or four miles distant. I was perfectly delighted with the ruins, they are so picturesque, and all covered with ivy. Large trees grew among the fallen blocks of stone, and stretched out their branches in all directions, while crows flew, cawing about the ruins. We wandered around seeking to identify some parts beside the church, and thought we found the refectory, kitchen, cloisters surrounding an open court, the abbots' apartments, and garden. The transept is the finest part, and still quite perfect. M. and I sat down under a tall tree to sketch a beautiful window; but I could not copy its beauty, and gave little idea of it. It was a Cisterian monastery, founded by the bishop of Winchester in the 13th cent. and was confiscated by Henry VIII.

*Thursday, May 21st, White Hart Hotel, Wiltshire, Salisbury.*
    It was a rainy day, or rather drizzly but notwithstanding we set off for the "New Forest," ten miles distant from Southampton. We passed through several villages in the forest, Lyndhurst the capital, where we saw "the merry Lyndhurst Hall" or king's house, a brick building with four gables in front, where the lord warden now resides. Minsted is another little town. Many of the thatched cottages are very pretty, with roofs curving over the windows, in a peculiar manner. Herds of horses, Spanish jennets, supposed to have descended from those wrecked, and cast ashore in the Spanish Armada, are found running wild in the forest, also deer and a species of wild boar in the more retired parts. The forest trees were very beautiful, old oaks, and birches sweeping the ground with graceful branches. The green glades and prespective views were lovely and the foliage is in its fresh green spring dress. We only went a short distance beyond Stony Cross, where is a triangular stone covered with iron to preserve it. This marks the position of the oak, from which Sir Walter Tyrrel's arrow, glancing aside killed Wm. Rufus who was hunting in the forest. His body was carried away in a cart, by one Perkess, and buried in Winchester Cathedral. They say, the Perkess family have always since, had a cart and horse, nothing more, and nothing less. The stone was put up in 1745 by Lord John Deleware who saw the oak still standing. We were interested in all we saw, though the rain was some drawback.
    On returning we took the train for Salisbury. We have already visited the cathedral, the chief object of interest in the place. It stands on a green and is in the form of a Latin cross with a spire at the intersection, a lady chapel, chapter house, and cloisters. The effect of the exterior is quite imposing, it is in the pointed arch style, and supported by many buttresses. The interior has been much injured; an organ placed at the entrance of the choir shuts off the rest of the church, it has also been whitewashed, and imitations substituted for the stained glass windows, of

which little remains in its original state. The groined roof has been filled in with plaster. The tower was added at a later period, and when it was found to be too heavy for the slender pillars to support, an inverted arch was thrown across the transepts, which injures their appearance. The pillars are clustered, and of fossil marble. They are not able to bear much weight, and have bent somewhat. The choir has richly carved stall or seats; there is a preacher for nearly every Sunday in the year. The monuments were interesting. There was one of Wm. Longspee Earl of Salisbury and son of Henry II and the *fair Rosamond*, his effigy is of wood, and somewhat mutilated. One, of a boy bishop. It was the practice among the choir boys to elect one of their number as bishop, for a few days near Christmas. If he died at that time, he had all the honors of a true bishop. The Somerset monument was of alabaster, and very handsome. Among others the Earl of Hertford and Lady Catherine Grey were buried beneath it. There is a tomb of Bishop Poore who commenced the church, that is, the present church, also that of Bishop Fisher, instructor to the Princess Charlotte. Side by side upon the floor, lie the two brass figures of a Catholic and Protestant bishop, also a Knight Templar. There is a tablet to the memory of Bowles the poet, and many of persons little known. The pew used by the royal family when present, resembles a cage, with a grating all around it. We saw a little Gothic chapel much ornamented; also many closets, used in Catholic times, for the scared vessels. We saw the old cope chest of circular form, and the table, where they say, the daily penny was counted out for the builders. The cloisters are very beautiful, and the interior court which they inclose, is covered with fresh green grass. From one side the chapter house opens out. It is now being restored in the old style. The floor is laid with bright colored tiles, and around the walls are scenes from the *Bible*, done in colored plaster. Some of the representations are really ludicrous. Cain deliberately places his foot on the back of the kneeling Abel, and with an axe chops open his head. Ham has a grin on his face, and Noah is about as large as the ark. The shafts are polished and branch out from the centre pillar, like a palm tree. It is hoped that the whole church will be also restored. Near by is the Bishop's Palace.

*Friday, May 22nd, The George Hotel, Winchester.*

This morning M. and I before leaving Salisbury, drove out 8 1/2 miles to visit Stonehenge. Most of our way led across the Salisbury plain, and the flocks of sheep grazing on the slopes, brought to our mind the old shepherd, and his little Molly. It is mostly unenclosed by fences and an undulating plain as far as one can see. We saw many larks, crows, and two little hares that flew swiftly over the ground. The strangeness and solitariness of Stonehenge impressed me much. It consists of huge stones, some upright with others resting on them, some are lying on the ground. It is considered to be a Druidical temple to the sun. Hundreds of years have passed over these stones, and as many more probably will; without bringing any more definite idea of their use.

We took a different route for returning, through pleasant scenery. Then we made another excursion to the Wilton house, the country seat, of the earls of Pembroke. It is now used by Sir Sidney Herbert, half-brother to the present earl. The entrance is by a triumphal arch, with a figure of Marcus Aurelius on the top. The grounds were very beautiful, what we could see from the windows, through the rain. A velvety lawn, with fine trees clustered in groups. Some of the finest "Cedars of Lebanon" in England are here, aged looking trees. The flower garden is in the Italian style. It was here that Sir Philip Sidney composed his *Arcadia*, for he was a brother of one of the countesses of Pembroke. In one room was a case containing a lock of Queen Elizabeth's hair, with the following, "This lock of Queen Elizabeth's hair was presented to Sir Philip Sidney, by her own fair hands, on which he made these verses and gave them to the queen, on his bended knee, anno domini 1573."

*Her inward worth all outward show transcends,*
*Among her merits regret commends,*
*Life, of sparkling gems her virtues draw the light*
*And in her conduct she is always bright,*
*When she imparts her thoughts, her words have force*
*And sense and wisdom flow in sweet discourse.*

The hair is light brown and very fine. The hall which we entered was adorned with the armour of the Earl of Pembroke who led the English, at the battle of St. Quentin, and armour that he brought thence. We went through a number of pretty rooms the views from the windows were very lovely, from one the cathedral appeared dimly through the mist and trees. The long room, called the "double cube," was very splendid, the paintings here were by Vandyke and considered very fine. One, was a family picture of one of the earls, his wife, five sons, and two daughters. The children of Charles I and others. In this room were elegant tortoise shell and brass tables, and some of wood mosaic. This part of the house was built by Inigo Jones, the walls were ornamented with gilded stucco. We saw the billiard room, and then the library, which is a fine long room, with the books arranged around on shelves; and here was a portrait of Wm. Herbert, first Earl of Pembroke in the time of Henry VIII, his little dog is by his side of which he was very fond and who died at his grave. This portrait was by Holbein. We took the 3 1/2 train for Winchester, and reached here by five.

*Saturday, May 23rd, "Golden Cross," London.*

At ten this morning, we went out to see the sights of Winchester, and first to St. Mary's college founded by Bishop Wickam. The chapel contains an old stained glass window, which had been saved from Cromwell's violence, dating from the time of Richard II and Bishop Wickam, who are represented upon it. The chapel is small for there are but seventy on the foundation as they call it, that is, maintained by the college funds, and seventy more pay for their tuition, and live with the master. The ceiling is of Spanish oak which is always free from worms and spiders. The cloisters are fine, but the boys are not allowed to go there much. In the dining room are only plain board tables and benches, and at breakfast and supper the boys eat off from trenchers which are square pieces of board. They have for breakfast, bread and butter, for dinner boiled and roast mutton and for supper cold beef. They drank ale with all meals. On Wednesday they have Yorkshire pudding and on Saturday and Sunday plum pudding. Whatever is left is put into a box and given to 24 poor people who each receive also, a loaf of bread and three quarts of ale. The bed rooms are well aired, and each student has a small bed, a case for clothes and books and a candle. Some of the beds are of wood 500 years old. Not far off is a hill where the scholars are required by law to go three or four times a week for exercise. The school is a building by itself, and behind is a piece of ground for playing cricket upon.

We next visited the Hospital of St. Cross. It was founded by Henry de Blois brother of King Stephen, and part of the building dates from his time. It maintains thirteen poor men, and their wives if they have any; over them is a master. Each one has three rooms, and a certain allowance of bread and ale. They wear a black cloak and silver cross. The porter who is one of the brothers conducted us round. Every poor person that comes to the door, to the number of twenty four, is entitled to receive a slice of bread, and horn of ale. On dole days much more is distributed. The chapel is a curious old building, with arches crossing one another and forming pointed arches, being one of the earliest instances in which this is seen. The master performs the service and a window is connected with infirmary, so that the sick can have the benefit of it. In the old dining room, was an altar piece a Madonna, supposed to be by Albert Durer, a remnant of Catholic times. The hospital surrounds a court and is a pretty building with ivy creeping over it. Chimneys were introduced here as quite a novelty, by Cardinal Beaufort, son of John of Gaunt.

We turned from here to the cathedral. This is not equal on the exterior to that at Salisbury, but the interior is very beautiful indeed. It was first built by Kinegils the first Saxon king who embraced Christianity. The Saxon foundation still appears, in the crypt. Over this the Normans built their church, and their work is seen in the transept, where there are three rows of round arches. Wyckam Bishop of Winchester, altered the nave, building over the Norman work, and here appear pointed arches, and very large columns, while the ceiling is groined in stone. The choir is splendid, made of richly carved oak and separated from the side aisles by glass. In another part altered by Bishop Fox the columns were gray colored stone. The screen, before the spot where once stood the high altar, was of rich stone work. The ceiling was ornamented with colored coats of arms. The monuments in the church were very interesting. On the top of the choir railing, were placed six chests, containing the bones of the Saxon kings Kinegil, his son Kenwalch, Egbert, Edmund Canute the Dane, his wife Emma, and son Hardicanute. In the choir itself is a gray marble tomb where Wm. Rufus was buried. In two rich chapels are laid the bodies of Bishop Fox and Bishop Gardiner the former is ornamented with very delicate stone work. In the nave is the alabaster effigy of Wickam lying in a little chapel with folded hands and three monks at his feet. There was also the tomb of Cardinal Beaufort Wickam's successor. Mary was married to Philip II in this cathedral and we saw her chair used at that time, which though comfortable as a seat, is by no means handsome. Near by the church are the ruins of the Bishop's Palace. Winchester was the capital of England until the time of Edward the Confessor. It was almost destroyed by Cromwell when he besieged the town. We took the London train and reached there in about three hours. Mr. Morse came in to see us in the evening.

*Sunday, May 24th, "Golden Cross," London.*

We went to hear Dr. Sumner bishop of Winchester, in St. Jude's Church, Southwark, on behalf of Sunday schools. It was a very excellent sermon, setting forth the importance of preparation, for the final state. In the afternoon we wished to hear Mr. Waddington of the Pilgrim's Church, but not being able to find it, we went into Rowland Hill's Chapel, a circular church, and heard a Mr. Deverden from the Crimea.

*Monday, May 25th, London.*

Called on Mrs. Boot, received letters from home again. We have heard nothing from Antonio and fear he has broken his engagement to return. Giovanni too is going. We went to see Mrs. Sidney Morse who is quite a sufferer from asthma, etc.

*Tuesday, May 26th, Thompson's Hotel, Berkley Square.*

We have moved into our old quarters, it is much pleasanter and far less noisy. We took a walk in Kensington Gardens and then to see a review in St. James' Park, but finding it just over, went into the National Gallery. We saw many modern paintings and some were very beautiful, though the crowd made it difficult to move about. There was *The Embarkation of the Pilgrims from Belgium.* Sir Roger de Coverly in church. Goldsmith's deserted village, representing a group on the sea shore, just leaving their beloved home. There were some beautiful drawings and some English landscape scenes.

In the afternoon M. and I visited the Polytecnic Institution where we saw a strange variety of objects, many of them new inventions and models. There were wax models of Indians, and Mexicans, also of the Siamese twins, and the Aztec children. Dried flowers and seaweeds, models of ships, a diving bell etc.

In the evening we drove out into the principal streets, to see the illumination in honor of the queen's birthday, which is tomorrow. She will be thirty eight. There were some very brilliant ones. "God save the queen and prince." "God preserve our gracious queen" "Victoria" "V. R." "V.A." were the prevailing mottoes, formed by gas lights, or oil in colored glass cups, which gave the effect of precious stones. There were also stars of light, and the rose, shamrock and thistle conjoined, and many other figures. It was a very fine illumination. The streets were as light as day and crowded with people.

*Wednesday, May 27th, London.*

We drove out to Greenwich Hospital this morning. It is eight miles distant. The oldest part of the building is what was built by Henry VIII as a manor house, Charles II added another building and William III devoted it with additions to its present use. It is a noble institution; we spent about two hours in going through parts of the buildings. There are 1,900 pensioners now here, sailors who have served the government faithfully, but are now disabled, or infirm. First we visited the library, where the men can freely go and read books or newspapers of all kinds, there is here, the *Bible* with raised letters, prepared for the blind. The kitchen is really amusing. It is a tea pot about four feet high, and requiring to fill it, about four pounds of tea, eighteen of sugar and twelve quarts of milk. They have tea in the evening, in the morning cocoa prepared in the same extensive manner. The pot of soup is huge, one might almost be drowned in it. The soup is drawn off by a cock and is very nourishing. The ovens are made with places for the meat in the upper row, and Yorkshire pudding below. The bread is not allowed to be eaten fresh. The dining room is arranged, with messes for four, at each table. They have a smoking room, with a fire in it. In the bedrooms are little departments like state rooms, and the owners adorn them with prints, or whatever ornaments they collect. One ward is for those who are helpless, and they have nurses. In the painted hall are many pictures, principally naval scenes. One was Nelson as a midshipman, in the Arctic regions, fighting with a white bear. The same at the battle of the Nile, with his arm shot off. And his death in the cockpit of the *Victory*. We saw also the coat and vest in which he was killed, stained with his life blood. There were several articles, found by Dr. Ray, in the search for Sir John Franklin, a fork, spoon, and medal ascertained to belong to him, and forks, spoons, and watches and a bit of coat sleeve, belonging to others of the company. There was a small model of a ship, all ready to be launched which was done by pulling a ring. We each tried it and down it slid most gracefully. The astrolobe of Sir Frances Drake used before the knowledge of compasses. There was a portrait of one of the pensioners who had lived to the great age of 111 and said he never paid a sixpence to a doctor, he preferred giving it to butchers and bakers. We saw the steward of the *Victory*, who gave Nelson his last cup of coffee, he is a fine old man. Wives are allowed to eat with their husbands and if there are widows they receive remains of the food.

In the afternoon we attended a concert, at the Havover Square rooms, given by the Cologne Choral Union. There were eighty singers. I was very much pleased with it. The voices were very sweet, and died away at times till scarcely a sound was heard, the harmony was beautiful. They sang a gondolier's song, a boat song, a serenade, Bohemian popular song and Lutzow's wild hunt etc. It was all in German, but we had translations in the programme.

*Thursday, May 28th, London.*

Today we attended an anniversary meeting of the charity schools of London in St. Paul's Cathedral. It was a very interesting sight. Stagings were erected in a circle just beneath the dome, upon which, row above row, the children were seated, divided off by cords into the different schools. The audience were in the centre, and down the nave. The girls were dressed in brown, green, or black dresses, with white caps, aprons, and capes. The boys wore suits of dark cloth. Several girls were frightened, and began to cry, they had to be taken out. The church service was performed, then the children sang, and Archbishop Campbell Lord Bishop of London preached on "Suffer little children to come unto me." We were near and able to hear him but many did not. The lord mayor and lady mayoress were present, he in a scarlet robe and fur collar, she a portly dame, much dressed. There were also some aldermen in scarlet. The service occupied about four hours. Mr. Morse dined with us; he is invited to the lord mayor's tomorrow.

*Friday, May 29th, London.*

We went this morning to the gallery of "the society of painters in water colors." There are about 300 pictures, in one room, mostly small. I was much pleased with what I saw. Among them was, 'Jennie Caxon returning disappointed from the post office'; a scene from the Antiquary. A beautiful bag piper, upon whose face, are shining the setting rays of the sun. Lady Jane Grey and Roger Ascham. Some beautiful scenes from the Isle of Wight, among them the little church of St. Lawrence. There were Scotch scenes Alpine and Venetian, Italian peasants, the old minstrel (in *The Lay of the Last Minstrel)* playing to the duchess, and her daughter. Stonehenge, Tintern Abbey, and the Gateway of Kenilworth. There were also fruit pieces, wonderfully well done, and flowers, primroses, camellias, azaleas, etc. Many were already sold.

In the afternoon I went with Uncle to St. Giles' Church Cripplegate. It is very unpleasant to ride in the city, that is, within Temple Bar, for the streets are crowded and very slippery. Our carriage became locked in with another and we got out till it could be unloosed. St. Giles is in the neighborhood of the worst quarter of London, though it was once the court end and near by was Queen Elizabeth's theatre. The church is 500 years old and the pulpit and pews 200. The chief attraction is Milton's monument. It is a bust fastened to a pillar in the centre aisle, underneath is carved a flaming sword, and a serpent holding in his mouth an apple. He and his father are buried under a pew close by. We saw also two marble monuments varnished and resembling wood, to the daughter and granddaughter of Sir Thomas Lucy of Charlecote, whose deer Shakespeare is said to have stolen. There was a tablet to Fox the martyrologist and one to Glover the heraldist. Oliver Cromwell was married in this church, and so was Ben Johnson. We returned home through Smithfield Market, and High Holborn.

*Saturday, May 30th, London.*

We spent a quiet morning in doors, and in the afternoon went out to Lewisham to see Mr. and Mrs. Ropes. They were very cordial and invited us to dine with them on Saturday next.

*Sunday, May 31st, London.*

Went in the morning to the Way House Chapel, to hear Mr. Binney, one of the best, of the Independent preachers. He was away, and we heard an old man, Mr. Massey. In the afternoon we stopt at Baptist Noel's church, but found he had gone on to the Mount, to preach in the open air, the other churches also were mostly closed, so we went into St. George's, Bloomsbury, and heard a young man.

*Monday, June 1st, London.*

Went again into the city, to the Bunhill Field Burying Ground. Milton lived in Bunhill Row and died there, but we could not ascertain the house. A queer old woman acted as our guide in the cemetery. In Bunhill Field was the great pit, where the bodies of the dead were thrown in the great plague of London. John Bunyan's tomb, was an oblong monument, the first part of the inscription was obliterated the latter part was "Mr. John Bunyan, the author of *Pilgrim's Progress.*" We saw John Owens' tomb and Gills' the commentator, and Baxter's which has sunk into the ground. Stotdard who has illustrated some of Turner's poems is buried here, and Fleetwood the son-in-law of Cromwell. We saw the grave of Isaac Watts in a good state of preservation. I noticed besides all these a number of familiar names, as Thomas Buxton, perhaps of the family of Sir Fowell. It was a large piece of ground and full of graves, some of which were in a very dilapidated condition. Opposite, is a chapel where Wesley used to preach.

After this we went to the Church of the Knights of Templars. It has been restored in the old style. The circular part first entered, is in imitation of the Holy Sepulchre at Jerusalem. The pillars are of Purbeck marble and clustered. Upon the floor are ten effigies of knights. Those who had been in the Holy War had their right foot crossed over the left, those who had only the intention to join in it, vice versâ. There as a monument to the earl of Pembroke, marshal protector in the reign of Henry VIII, another of Brian de bois Gilbert, one of the heroes of Ivanhoe, also of De Lucy, premier baron in the reign of John. The inner part of the church is much ornamented with arabesque letters of various kinds on the ceiling, and colored tiles on the floor. It was first the Church of the Templars, and was afterwards leased to the lawyers by whom it is now used. Thence we went into the Temple Gardens, which lie on the bank of the Thames, and are very pleasant. It was here that the red and white roses were picked, as the designation of the York and Lancaster parties. We saw the

Middle and Inner Temple, now entirely occupied by lawyers and students, they are divided by a lane. In the Inner Temple Lane is a staircase called Johnson's, which leads to rooms, where he once lived. In the afternoon we drove about Hyde Park and Kensington Gardens, and saw the exterior of Kensington Palace, which is of brick. The park was very gay, as it was the fashionable hour. There were many handsome liveries. We saw the two princes of Oude, who rode in a showy carriage, the footman and all, dressed in Indian costume.

*Tuesday, June 2nd, London.*

We went to the Gallery of Female Artists in Oxford St. There were several oil landscapes by Eliza Irving. Several flower pieces, a number of portraits, *We Are Seven* and other pictures of children. Some things were quite pretty. We then spent some time in the Soho Bazaar. In the afternoon we visited Hampton Court. It is a ride of about twelve miles, and our road led us through Richmond, and a pleasant region of the country till we arrived at Bushy Park. This seems to form an entrance to Hampton Court, and the road is lined with fine horse-chestnut trees. We went first into the "maze," a labyrinth, made by hedge lined paths. We became completely bewildered when trying to find our way out, and a man called to us to take the left hand path, everywhere following which direction, we soon emerged.

Hampton Court is built of brick, around several quadrangular courts. It was designed by Cardinal Wolsey, and he presented it to Henry VIII. It was the favorite residence of William and Mary who altered it in the Dutch style, especially the gardens which are adorned with canals, and straight walks, with stiff flower beds. It is an immense palace, we went through room after room. In the king's ante-room were weapons of war arranged to form figures on the wall. The throne room contains the red canopy of Wm. II with "Je main ty en drais" written upon it. In another room was the canopy of James II and we saw also Queen Mary's. There was in one room the funeral bier of the Duke of Wellington most magnificently decorated. Queen Charlotte's bed was covered with very handsome brocade silk, and the furniture was to match. Another bed of red silk, belonged to Wm. and Mary. The walls were decorated with many fine paintings, some by Sir Geoffry Kneller, as the Georges and Wm. and Mary. There was a portrait of Henry VIII, and several of Queen Elizabeth, one also of Bloody Mary as a child. Sir Peter Lely painted the beauties of Charles II's court to the number of seven, the Duchess of Cleveland and Nell Gwyn were two of these. By Holbein was the *Field of the Cloth of Gold, Battle of the Spurs* and the embarkation of Henry VIII at Dover. In one hall particularly devoted to them are seven of Raphael's cartoons for tapestry, of which we saw the arras copies in Rome. The "Great Hall" built by Wolsey is entered by a separate staircase. It is very splendid, in the Gothic style, with stained glass windows, ornamented with Wolsey's arms, and various mottoes. We were rather annoyed in our visit, by crowds of rowdy people, that the Whitsuntide holidays had brought out, to wander over the palace and gardens. Six o'clock came, the hour for closing, and we were obliged to go, though we left much unseen.

_Wednesday, June 3rd, London._

We have been this afternoon to the Chiswick Fête. It is held, about six miles from here. I was much delighted with all I saw. There is quite a large extent of ground, laid out in walks, bordered with flowers. Tents are seen here and there, and a military band played through it all. The scene was also enlivened by a great multitude of ladies and gentlemen, the former, though it was a cool damp day, were dressed in tules laces and muslins more suitable for an evening party, but they looked very gay and pretty. We went into a number of the tents in which were placed pots of most exquisite flowers, and in others fruit. We saw huge strawberries more than two inches in diameter, peaches, nectarines, cherries, raspberries, and splendid grapes, of course raised under glass. We were ravished with the flowers, our exclamations of delight, expressed but feebly what we felt. There were azaleas, and rhododendrons of all shades even buff. The geraniums were of every variety of color and name, one was called "Agnes." The pansies were three times as large as any I ever saw, I should think and of very remarkable colors. There were a large number of heaths, and very splendid roses. The Orchidiae were exceedingly beautiful and delicate, and very rare, many of them. There was a pretty arrangement of flower stands, with a very small fountain in the centre, which kept the flowers arranged about it, continually moist. The Duke of Devonshire's grounds were near by, but we were weary and it was rather too late to explore them. So we returned from the Féte, literally having feasted our eyes.

_Thursday, June 4th, London._

Went today far down into the city. First to the mint. We were shown over the building and saw the various processes, which were quite interesting. We then visited the Thames Tunnel. We descended to it by long flights of steps. It is lighted with gas and occupied by sellers of small wares, of course only foot passengers can pass through it. One of the sides curves in, for greater strength, and it was built with great care. It is a strange thought that the Thames River is flowing over one's head. An immense sum of money was expended on it. On our ride, we passed "Johnson's Court" Fleet St. another of Dr. J.'s habitations.

*Friday, June 5th, London.*

Spent the greater part of the day at the Crystal Palace. We went to hear a concert, given by the Italian Opera Company. Having reserved seats we spent some time beforehand in the grounds. They look more beautiful than ever. The rhododendrons of all colors were very fine. The day has been very warm, and the palace was a little like a hot house. We heard Madame Grisi and Mesdames Bosio Didieé etc., Singors Mario and Gardoni and others with a chorus of male and female voices and a band of violinists. It was mostly in Italian. The singers were very affected in their manners, but some of the voices were quite sweet. On the whole I was not particularly delighted.

*Saturday, June 6th, London.*

Went out shopping in the morning, and in the afternoon to Lewisham to dine with Mr. and Mrs. Ropes. It rained most of the time. We enjoyed it very much, and found them as kind and pleasant as could be. There are eight children, Ellen, Mary, Emily, Louisa, Willie, Alice, Earnest and Charlie. They sang us some Russian songs which sounded strangely.

*Sunday, June 7th, London.*

Went again to the Way House Chapel and heard Dr. Binney. He was not well, in agony he said, so of course the sermon was not what it would otherwise have been. In the evening we heard a good discourse from Dr. Hamilton.

*Monday, June 8th.*

M. and I went to the National Gallery, but many of its pictures have been removed thence. We saw two beautiful pieces by Turner, one, a coast scene, with several ships lying off the shore, another the building of Carthage by Dido, with most brilliant coloring. There were several of Claude's landscapes. By Murillo was St. John as a child caressing a lamb. A virgin and Joseph with the young child standing between them on a step. And a Spanish peasant boy. Raphael was represented by a St. Margaret, and the vision of a knight a small drawing, partly finished in pin holes. There were also pictures by most of the Italian artists. Cornelia showing her jewels by Padovanino. *The Brazen Serpent* by Rubens.

Ganymede carried off by an eagle, by Titian. Misers with their money bags, by Teniers, and Views of Venice by Canaletto etc. In the room of modern sculpture we saw Miss Hosmer's *Beatrice*, and a bust of Mrs. Stowe.

At two o'clock we started for Albins to take dinner with Mr. and Mrs. Gellibrand. The distance is eighteen or twenty miles, and the coachman did not know the way very well so we were late in arriving and they had just given up expecting us. Miss Elizabeth Ropes was there, and Mr. and the Misses Gellibrand nephew and nieces of Mr. G., from Australia. The house is of brick, and 200 years old. It is built round a court, and the picture gallery is 100 feet long. It is owned by Sir Thomas Albins who is too poor to keep it up himself, and lives in France, it is entailed so he can only rent it. The furniture, books and ornaments remain, under certain restrictions, and one room is lined with family crests. The grounds are very pleasant, consisting of 120 acres. The rhododendrons were beautiful, there were fine oak trees, two cedars of Lebanon, a cork tree and an evergreen oak. We had dinner after six o'clock, and it was a very handsome one, of six or seven courses, served by three men. We walked a while, in the garden and before long finding it to be eight o'clock, we bade good bye and set off on our return not reaching here till eleven o'clock. I enjoyed the excursion very much our friends were so very kind and hospitable.

*Tuesday, June 9th, London.*

Went to the Marlborough House to see the Vernon Gallery and other pictures removed there, from the National Gallery. We saw a number of Turner's pictures. The *Bridge of Sighs* at Venice. The *Temeraire*, less injured than many of them were, and with fine coloring. Apollo and Daphne in a pretty, landscape. The Bath of Phryne, a group of gay figures dancing towards some magnificent building, in the misty distance. The decline of the Carthaginian Empire a fiery colored scene, that did not please me. Napoleon when an exile, and the rock limpet. It is of very brilliant coloring, but the appearance of Napoleon was unnaturally enlarged, from the reflection in the water. The *Sun of Venice* going to sea, it is a gay looking boat, and the city is seen in the distance. Lake Avernus, rather indistinct. Ulysses and the Cyclops, a highly colored picture, but rather confused. Agrippina landing at Rome with the ashes of Germanicus, a rich scene, with the river, and palaces of the city. Finally, Shadrach, Meschack and Abednego, in the fiery furnace, a queer thing, with some ladies reclining near by, as unconcerned as possible. We saw a series of six pictures by Hogarth, called *Profligacy in Married Life*. It was not at all agreeable to me. The portrait of Sir Joshua Reynolds was by himself, and his pictures were A Holy Family of large size. Little Samuel praying, a pretty thing.

The graces adoring a figure of Hymen with flower garlands. Also some pretty angel heads. Wilkie's were, *The Blind Fiddler*, *The Bag Piper*. A man reading the news, to several, who are gathered round to listen. A parish beadle taking off some vagrants to gaol. The *Peep o' day boy's* cabin. He is asleep with his head on his wife's lap, a girl whispers to her, and danger is at hand. The village festival, a red-faced landlord is pouring out ale to several drunken men, among whom an old woman is shocked to find her son. By West was, Christ healing the sick, a lame man is brought to him, and behind, is an old woman held by two soldiers. Also, Orestes and Pylades brought before Iphigenia at Tauris. There was an excellent *Dame's School* by Webster, I have seen an engraving of it before. The return from the market by Calcott. It is a very pretty scene, a woman on horseback is fording a stream another holds a child on a horse, and a third is seen in front. *Happy as a King* by Collins represents children swinging on a gate. *The Cornfield* by Constable is a pleasant scene, a boy is drinking from a brook, near by, is a flock of sheep and a dog watching them. Sir Charles Eastlake painted *Haidee*, a handsome Greek girl, and the escape of the Carrara family, from Duke Galeazzo of Milan, the lord of Carrara, with his wife on a mule, are hastening off. The *Market Cart* by Gainsborough. A loaded cart with two girls on top is about to ford a pool of water two boys drive the horses, and another is gathering sticks. Sir Edwin Landseer painted two allegorical pictures called *Peace* and *War*. Two of Mr. Vernon's pretty spaniels. *Highland Music* a bag-piper playing before some hungry dogs and interrupting their dinner. *Low Life* and *High Life* are represented by two dogs, in their respective conditions. There was a fine portrait of West by Lawrence. Sancho Panza Before the Duchess by Leslie, and Uncle Toby and Widow Wadman in the sentry box, when he looks to see what is in her eye. *The Last In* was by Wm. Mulready. It is a truant boy coming into school, the master makes him an ironical bow, the others are busy with their lessons. Also *Crossing The Ford* two brothers carrying their sister over a brook, on a lady's chair. Edward M. Ward painted Dr. Johnson in Lord Chesterfield's anteroom, waiting for an audience. And the *South Sea Bubble* a confused scene, every one seems to be crying out, and holding up papers.

In the afternoon we went to Dulwich College Gallery. And saw there three Murillos: *Flower Girl* and two paintings of Spanish peasant boys, in one eating bread, in the other playing. A Madonna much like one in the Pitti Palace, and *The Good Shepherd* a small thing. An old woman eating soup, Gerard Dow. Several of Claude's landscapes. Cows by Paul Potter, and many other pictures, which made less impression on me.

*Wednesday, June 10th, London.*

We leave here tomorrow for Bristol. Took a last drive in Hyde Park. Mr. S. Morse called on us, his wife is better.

*Thursday, June 11th, Bristol.*

We left London at about one, after waiting an hour or two at the station which is a very fine one with a glass roof. We passed through a pretty, green country, noticed some scarlet flowers in the fields probably anemones. Bath was the largest place through which we passed, it is built partly on high ground, and is a large and fashionable town. Bristol is not particularly pleasant many smoky chimneys are prominent, we are staying at Clifton, in the suburbs, which is more agreeable. Robert Hall and John Forster preached here.

*Friday, June 12th, Bristol.*

We took a pretty drive along the Avon, where the scenery was quite wild, on either bank high rocks, some bare, others covered with trees. They are the St. Vincent rocks. On the hill above were some fine residences, the grounds were terraced. We stopped before No. 4 Windsor Terrace, Clifton. It was where Hannah More spent her last days, it commanded a beautiful prospect, Bristol lay in the valley below. We then visited the Elbridge Charity School; founded in 1738 by the Mr. John Elbridge, from whom Uncle takes his middle name. It educates about seventy girls in simple useful branches, among them sewing, and making out bills. Uncle has been busy all day in searching for records of this same gentleman, whose portrait hangs in the infirmary, of which he was treasurer. He has not been very successful.

We then drove out to Barley Wood, the residence of Hannah More, about fourteen miles hence. The ride was very pleasant, with a fertile valley lying below us. We saw in the distance Ashton Court, the property of Sir John Smythe, also a connection of the Elbridges. We drove up to the house at Barley Wood and found the family were absent. It is now owned by Mr. Harford. The servant was prevailed upon to show us up stairs, into Miss More's room, which is but little changed since her time. In it, is a large bay window, and another looking in the opposite direction, from one, there is a view of the grounds, full of flower beds, and green trees; from the other the eye rests upon the sweet valley below. The house is rather small and has a thatched roof. Flowers grow all about in beds, and a green lawn slopes down to the hedge, which divides it from the road. We took a walk in the grounds, through pretty wood paths, where wild flowers grew, and coming now and then on some rustic arbour. In one place was a monumental urn, with an inscription, saying that it was erected to the memory of John Locke, born in the village, (Wrington) by Mrs. Montague, and presented by her to Hannah More. A little farther on is another similar urn and on it is inscribed, "To Belby Porteus late Bishop of London, in grateful memory, of long and faithful friendship. H.M." We returned to Clifton again at about seven o'clock and only regretted that we had not continued our ride to Wrington, where Hannah More and her four sisters lie buried.

*Saturday, June 14th, Bell Inn, Gloucester.*

We stayed at Bristol till four o'clock, and took the opportunity in the morning, of driving out to Wrington church, by a different road, which was also very pleasant. We found Hannah More's tomb, which is a square flat tablet, surrounded bymvggfff an iron grating, where she and her four sisters lie together, the inscription is, "Beneath are deposited the mortal remains of five sisters."

| | | | |
|---|---|---|---|
| *Mary More* | *died 18th April* | *1813* | *aged 75 years* |
| *Elizabeth More* | " *14th June* | *1816* | " *76* " |
| *Sarah More* | " *17th May* | *1817* | " *4* " |
| *Martha More* | " *14th September* | *1819* | " *69* " |
| *Hannah More* | " *17th September* | *1833* | " *89* " |

*These all died in faith accepted in the beloved*
*Hebrews Chap. II, 5, 13.* Ephesians *Chap. I, 5, 6.*

The church is 400 years old and quite a handsome one. A woman was cleaning it, she told us, she remembered Miss More well, she showed us the new pew where the old lady sat, it was near the pulpit. She told us also about the affair with the servants, which affected her so much, that it injured her heath. It seems she had a box in which she put money for the poor, and her servants stole it. There is an inscription in the church to the memory of Hannah More, it is as follows, "Sacred to the memory of Hannah More. She was born in the parish of Stapleton, near Bristol A.D. 1745 and died at Clifton Sept. 7th, 1833. Endowed with great intellectual powers, and early distinguished by the success of her literary labors, she entered the world, under circumstances tending to fix her affections on its vanities. But instructed in the school of Christ, to form a just estimate of the real end of human existence, she chose the better part and consecrated her time and talents to the glory of God and the good of her fellow creatures, in a life of practical piety and universal beneficence. Her numerous writings in support of religion and order, at a time when both were rudely assailed, were generally edifying to readers of all classes, at once delighting the wise, and instructing the ignorant and simple. In the 89th year of her age, beloved by her friends and venerated by the public, she closed her career of usefulness, in humble reliance on the mercies of God, through faith in the mercies of her Redeemer. Her mortal remains are deposited in a vault in this churchyard, which also contains those of her four sisters, who resided with her at Barley Wood, in this parish, her favorite abode, who actively cooperated in her unwearied acts of Christian beneficence (then followed the names as above). This monument is erected out of a public subscription, for a public memorial of Hannah More, of which the greater proportion is devoted to the erection of a school, in the populous and destitute district of St. Philip and Jude in Bristol, to the better endowment of whose district churches, she bequeathed the rest of her property."

In a cottage adjoining the churchyard, was born John Locke. It was then an inn. We went up a narrow flight of stairs into the room. He was baptised at the font in the church. We returned to Bristol and took an afternoon train for Gloucester, which we reached in an hour or two. In this, the Bell Inn, Whitefield was born. It is an old town, we went out for a little walk and into the cathedral. It is quite a fine one, the foundation is Saxon and also several rude columns, somewhat of an oval shape. Along the nave are Norman pillars, and the rest of the building dates from Edward II's time. In the choir is a groined ceiling and some fine carved work. The monuments are interesting. That of Edward II under a Gothic canopy. He was murdered at Berkeley Castle near by and the offerings made at his tomb, furnished the money to improve the church. On the pillars around the tomb are painted white harts, with some reference to Edward. Osric king of Northumberland, viceroy of Ethelred, who founded the Saxon Abbey, also lies here, and there is an effigy of Robert of Normandy, made of painted bog wood. His legs are crossed and hand on his sword. In the church is a statue of Jenner, who introduced vaccination; he was born in Gloucester. The window of the choir is one of the largest in England. The exterior of the church is black with age, it is partly Norman partly English lancet in style. It is situated in a square entered by several old gateways; in an enclosure near by is a statue of Queen Ann.

*Sunday, June 14th, Gloucester.*

Went to a chapel of Lady Huntingdon's connection in St. Mary's square, founded by her in 1788. We heard a good sermon. A book of hymns was used, collected by the good countess. In the afternoon we went to St. Mary's church which is quite an old one, in the churchyard

Bishop Hooper was burned, tied to an elm tree.

*Monday, June 15th, Beaufort Arms Inn, Chepstow, Wales.*

We reached here in an hour or two from Gloucester, and after a lunch set off for a drive. We alighted after driving some distance, at a wood path that led to Windcliff which is the name given to a precipitous ledge of rocks, whence is a very beautiful view. After following the path for some time, we came upon the spot. We looked down upon a green meadow, round which, and at the foot of the cliff where we stood ran the Wye. We could see in the distance, the junction of the Severn and the Wye both being of a red mud color. Beyond this was a low range of very blue hills. We descended the cliff by a very winding path, down stone steps, and through the woods, until we reached "the moss cottage," thatched with straw, quite hidden by trees from the road below it, and having in the grounds about it, rustic arbors seats and tables. It is inhabited by a family and people often take refreshments here. The interior consisting of two rooms is all lined with moss, and groined as it were, with branches of trees. It is certainly a sweet spot, though the woman who lived there, said it was very cold and snowy in winter.

We joined our carriage here and drove on to Tintern Abbey, about five miles from Chepstow. We followed the course of the Wye, on which the Abbey is situated and as we approached it, the view was very fine. It is an enchanting ruin, far surpassing, even Netley. The walls are entire, in most parts hung with rich festoons of ivy, and the interior is carpeted with velvety grass of an exquisite green; as we saw it, the sun's rays were falling through the Gothic windows, and the crows were cawing about the ruin, as if in mockery of the rich strains of music that had once echoed through its aisles. It was built in 1287 by Roger Bigod Earl of Norfolk. The west window is almost entire, the extent of the aisles can still be traced and there are some of the roof tiles still remaining. Many broken pieces of sculpture and arches also and very massive bosses from the ceiling. We saw part of a figure of the Virgin and a monument of a knight that our guide told us was the earl of Pembroke but I do not know with how much probability. We went into the cloisters now partly filled up with earth, several slabs covered the remains of monks; adjoining, on the right, was the chapter house and sacristy, at the further end the guest chamber where distinguished persons were lodged. At one side was a large refectory, with a pantry adjoining, of which the roof groined in stone still remains. In the refectory was a pulpit for the reader, and between it and the kitchen a window through which the dishes were to be received. We ascended a narrow spiral staircase that led to the top of the wall, it is a

*Tintern Abbey, Monmouthshire, from the Wye.*

dizzy height. Four arches which supported a tower still remain. The steps and column about which they wind are all of one piece, that is, each step forms a piece of the column. We were exceedingly interested, and delighted with our explorations.

*Tuesday, June 16th, Chepstow.*

Uncle has gone to Swansea to make some investigations about the Salisbury genealogy. We have been to Chepstow Castle, which is but a few minutes walk from here. It is owned by the duke of Beaufort, as are also Tintern Abbey and Raglan Castle. It is upon a steep cliff overhanging the Wye. We entered by a gate, between two towers, which has still some of the iron bands that once fastened it. This leads into a large court where a huge tree is now growing. From some of the windows we looked down upon the river below, and saw the place where provisions or other articles were drawn up in case of need. Beyond the court is the chapel, with Gothic windows, and one wall standing, and farther on is another outlet across a bridge and by a tower. We were told that there were eleven towers in all to the castle. The old banqueting hall is occupied by the custodian. We went upon the top of the ruins, and into the keep, which is in one of the towers. In the second story of this, Henry Martyn one of the regicides was imprisoned for twenty years, he had his wife, children and servants with him, and in the same rooms Jeremy Taylor was confined a little while before. This castle was first in the hands of Charles I, then gained by the parliament forces, and lost again, at which Cromwell was much chagrined as he considered it the key of that part of Wales. The ruined walls are mantled with ivy. In the afternoon we had a drive to "Double View" where we saw the Wye below us, Windcliff and Piercefield Park, with the river Severn in the distance, and the valley where Tintern lies. Farther on was another fine view from a platform of rocks, we had a pleasant drive, but a storm came on as we returned. The railroad bridge at Chepstow is a tube, from which the tracks hang. It resembles the one at Menai Straits, but is not very ornamental. Uncle returned in the evening.

*Wednesday, June 17th, Ross, Wales.*

    We left Chepstow in a carriage, and drove 13 miles to Raglan. It is a fine old castle. Two towers guard the entrance; a moat surrounded the whole, but within that, and encircled by a separate mote, is the keep or Yellow Tower. We went up to the top of this, from whence there is a beautiful view. A pair of stairs led down to the water of the moat, through a little door in the wall. We entered the large court of the castle and went into the kitchen, where there is a huge fireplace and a smaller one with a place for a boiler. On another side and in the second story was the library. We went into the banqueting hall, where was a coat of arms of the Beaufort family. A beautiful bay window, hung with ivy as a curtain, projected from the central court and on the other side was the "fountain court" where, our guide told us, was once a fountain in the shape of a horse. From the chapel a flight of steps led to an upper story. We wandered into the towers, in one of which was a dungeon, and upon the walls, where we had some fine views. While here, a young man seated himself under a tree outside the gate, and played on a harp some Welsh tunes, he looked quite picturesque and reminded us of the Welsh bards of old. We walked partly round the castle, the circumference of which is a third of a mile, and saw loop holes to shoot through and larger holes for pouring melted lead upon enemies below. I believe it was a Norman castle, as most of the old ones in England are. It was held by Richard Strongbow Earl of Pembroke and has descended to the Beaufort family. It was besieged in the civil wars, and we saw a breach in the wall, made by the marquis of Worcester. The ruin is very picturesque and not very well preserved.

    We then drove on to Monmouth, and stopped there for dinner. We had to wait for it a long time, and we were rather vexed and yet amused, by the landlord, who acted as head waiter he was so very bland, and trying in every way to bring us back there for the night, after taking a beautiful drive that he described. But we were determined to go on, and then he was in a worry lest the bill should not be paid. Henry V was born in Monmouth and a square adorned by his statue is called *Agincourt*. Leaving the town we rode on a steep bank above the Wye, and had a charming view of the river and of Monmouth itself. Continuing on, we ascended the Kymin an elevated plateau whence we had fine views of the Welsh mountains. The path to it leads through a pretty wood, and there is a monument on the hill, erected to British naval heroes. Then we went to another "Double view" and saw below us the forest of Dean and Malvern hills and valley. We passed through a part of the Dean Forest, but most of the old trees are gone. Descending then, we followed the Wye again, along a charming road. We saw in the distance Courtfield, where Henry V was nursed by the Countess of Salisbury, father on we saw Goodrich Castle and Court and reached Ross at about eight o'clock. We are in a good hotel on a hill, with a sweet view of the hills and trees and the river Wye encircling a green meadow and making five distinct curves. The setting sun threw its yellow rays upon the water making a charming scene. It set at half-past eight, and we could read easily at half-past nine.

*June 18th, Thursday, Lion Inn, Shrewsbury.*

Before leaving Ross this morning we walked into the garden behind the hotel and thence into the old church where is a monument to John Kyrle the "Man of Ross," who died in 1724. He had an income of 500 pounds and with this he built an orphan asylum, an alms house, a bridge, gave portions to poor damsels, arranged the grounds about the church, built a spire, gave bread to the poor weekly and relieved the sick. Pope celebrates him in his essay on *The Use of Riches*. The monument is set in the wall and was I believe erected by the heir of his grand-niece. We saw a book on mathematics, with his name written in it and his pew close to the reading desk. An elm grew out of the pew floor close by a window, its leaves were green and fresh and turned towards the light. It was a sprout from a tree planted by the "Man of Ross," and now cut down. The effect was very singular. We took the cars at Ross, changed at Hereford and arrived here after a ride of several hours.

*Friday, June 19th, Owen Glendower Arms Inn, Corwen, Wales.*

Before leaving Shrewsbury this morning M. and I took a fly, for a short time, to see the city. It is very old indeed, the streets are steep and some of the houses very peculiar. They have their gable ends to the street, and are made of stripes of white bricks, and black rafters, alternating.

One, belonging to a Mr. Whitney was large, with several bay windows and much ornament. We saw the market place, an open arcade upon which (though changed since then) stood a clock, to which Shakespeare refers in his *Merry Wives of Windsor*. We saw also the old and new St. Chad churches.

Then taking the cars we arrived in about an hour at Llangollen Station. Here we left the railroad and entered a Welsh fly which is an open vehicle like a cart, with the seats facing one another, and a capital thing for seeing the country. Thus we wended our way towards the much talked of Vale of Llangollen (pronounced Clangothlen). It was about three miles through a pleasant valley watered by the Dee. After reaching the town of Llangollen we took a lunch and then made an excursion to the little Abbey of Vallecrucis. It dates from the latter part of the 12th cent. and is a good deal ruined. One end has three windows, in a transition state from the Norman, very simple in form, and older than the others. There were several tombs in one of which the founder is supposed to be buried. It is a very lovely little ruin, by its side stand several large trees. It is kept by a lady who lives just behind, and takes the tenderest care of her beloved ruins; she trains ivy over some parts, and pulls it down from others, as seems to her best. Not far off is an antique pillar, from which the place is called Vallecrucis. There are remains of an inscription and it is considered to be a thousand years old, and to have been erected by Elisey to his great-grandfather.

On our return to the town, we mounted some donkeys, to ascend the mountain, near by, to the Crow Castle or Caer Dinas Bran literally Crow's Shelter. It is an old Welsh fortress, and used too I believe by Owen Glendower. To the top of the hill is a steep climb, of two miles, my donkey took a notion to stop at one place, and all my urging had no effect, but they said afterwards that the creature always stopped there to rest. The wind blew furiously on the summit and almost carried us away. The ruins are very shapeless, merely parts of walls and holes for windows, there was a cellar partly roofed over, and one bit of stone groining. The view all around was very fine. The vale extended far beyond us, we could see just out of the town Plas Newydd where Lady Eleanor Butler and Miss Ponsonby lived in strange retirement. Their dress was peculiar, a riding habit and short hair, as masculine as possible. Their successors Miss Lolly and Miss Andrews live there now. The descent was rather difficult we preferred to slide down on our feet over the slippery grass.

Then we joined our carriage and continued our journey. The views of the valley became lovely; we were on an elevated road, and looked down upon green meadows and woods and the river Dee winding among them.

*Welch costumes, Left to right: errand girl, farmer's daughter, market woman, winter costume, and llanarth girl.*

We passed "Owen Glendower's mount" a mound covered with trees from which, they say, he used to observe the signals on Dinas Bran. His palace was near by, and he fought battles in all the country around. The vale is eight miles long and certainly its loveliness has not been exaggerated. We reached Corwen about 15 miles distant, for the night. We heard Welsh spoken by all the country people. I should think it was a difficult language to learn. The women generally wear black bonnets tipped down over their eyes. I have seen one with a tall beaver hat. The young girls have felt hats like a boy's and look very healthy with their rosy cheeks.

*Saturday, June 20th, Penrin Arms Inn, Bangor, Wales.*
    We left Corwen this morning and rode fifteen miles first, to Pentre Voelas. The scenery was very attractive through the Vale of Endeirmion, we followed more than one little steam, and in one, was a sweet waterfall. It was cloudy all day and rained hard some of the time but cleared up in time to give us charming views of the hills and valleys. We stopped on our way at the Swallow Fall or Rhaiadr y Wennol as it is in Welsh. We were led to it by a woman (for every pretty spot has its exhibitor here.) It was a lovely romantic spot, and so like some scenes at home that I almost forgot I was in Wales. There were two falls, one above the other, and tum-

bling white with foam over the rocks, the banks were wild and woody. Our next stopping place was Capel Curig. The inn here was sweetly situated on a bank, above the Conway River. Pretty walks and beds of flowers attract one down to the riverside and when there, the view looking up the stream is very beautiful. The river widens into what seems a lake, and above it, in the distance rises the grand mist-wreathed peak of Snowdon. We waited at this place some time for Frances and our courier Ranzani, their horse broke his knee on the way and they came up in the stage. On leaving here the scenery began to be very wild. Immense fields of broken rocks appeared and we saw distant mountains, one of which was Mt. Llewellyn. Around us were peat bogs where were men cutting and drying peat. Then a beautiful lake Lynn Ogwen came into view, surrounded by mountains which rose up from it on either side in wild savageness, one especially, a rugged thing, towering precipitously above us, was covered with nothing but rocks. The pass through the mountains was very wild, and the views afterwards, fine. We then came out into softer scenery, first a flat plain, with still, mountains around, then a woody vale. We passed the Penrith slate quarries, it gives a singular appearance to the mountain, there is an immense quantity of it, enough to last for ages. We saw Penrith Castle a fine mansion, where Col. Douglas Pennant lives and soon entered Bangor. The hotel is upon Menai Straits and we can see the Isle of Anglesea. The grounds are very prettily laid out with flower beds, and edged on the water side with large trees.

*Sunday, June 21st, Bangor, Wales.*

Went to the cathedral to the morning service. It is a long low building with a tower and of some antiquity. In the afternoon to a Congregational chapel and a little out of the town and a new erection. There was no settled pastor but we had an excellent sermon from a Mr. Parsons.

*Monday, June 22, Rhyl, Wales.*

Before leaving Bangor we took a carriage and drove across the Menai Straits on the suspension bridge which is three miles from Bangor. It is formed of bands of iron from which the bridge is made to hang. Farther down is the celebrated railroad bridge. This consists of two tubes, about one third of a mile long and twenty feet high. They are made of plates of iron and fastened with two million rivets. They allow of the passage of a train of cars through each tube. We walked into one of them a little way, and saw the cars pass through afterwards, with a thundering noise. We were then in the Isle of Anglesea, and drove six miles to visit the site of

Owen Tudor's house. He was a Welsh gentleman who married the queen dowager of Henry VI and from whom descended Henry VII and the Tudor family. The place is called Penmynydd. In a house built near by was a stone taken from the old house with the initials R.O.T. and the date 1376 upon it. Another had a part of the coat of arms. Two miles nearer we stopped at a little country church, where were two effigies of persons of the Tudor family, and a tablet to the memory of Coningsley Williams, who married Mary, daughter of Richard Owen Tudor.

We then drove back to Bangor and had time to take a lunch before the cars started. We rode in these only half an hour and stopped at Conway. Here we went immediately to visit the castle built by Edward I. It has still seven or eight towers, and would be in a more perfect state, but that the Earl of Conway stripped it of all the lead and iron it contained. We entered as usual a large court but by an ascent of many steps for the castle is much higher than the town. At the right is the banquet hall, with three groined arches still remaining, and festooned with ivy. We were shown King Edward's room and after passing through another court, Queen Eleanor's also. The position of this was fine, three windows looked out upon a terrace, and over the water of the Straits, and one into the castle court. In an adjoining tower was her private chapel, lighted only by an oriel window. The ladies in waiting had a room near the queen's, on the lower floor, so they say. We walked out on the terrace; below us were two bridges much like those at Bangor, one a tubular bridge for the railroad the other a suspension bridge. They are too near to produce a good effect. The piers supporting them are in character with the castle above. In another direction we looked out upon the town, and a pretty valley beyond. The town is inclosed by a wall with towers at intervals. It is 50 acres in extent and shaped like a triangle, and we were told that formerly it was a part of the castle, used for the accommodation of troops, and having gradually grown into a town. Poor King Richard II lived in this castle and here give himself up to Northumberland. The interior is very picturesque. Formerly it was a very strong place, and surrounded by a moat where the sea did not protect it. From here we went to an old house in the town called Plas Mawye. It was built by a Robert Wynne and is a good example of a house of Queen Elizabeth's time. The porters' rooms are on either side of the door, then a court, and beyond, the house proper. The rooms had carved ceilings, and huge fireplaces, adorned with the English arms, and the initials E.R. R.W. and in other rooms which we did not see R.D. Robert Dudley, coupled with "Elizabeth Regina" for he is believed to have had the house at one time. A school for little children is now kept there. In one room was a long table, and seats around the wall, also an old press. We took the cars again and after a short ride, arrived at this place. We have had a poor blind Welsh harper playing for us in the hall. He in not old, but lost his sight by an explosion in a mine. He played and sang several Welsh songs, one was the *Pewhon*. The words sounded very strangely, to our ears. We have seen more of the beaver hats on the women today. They are taller than steeple hats, and taper a little. We have not had very pleasant weather for a day or two; it has been cloudy and showery.

*Tuesday, June 23rd, Chester, England.*

We took an early departure from Rhyl and after about an hour's ride reached Chester. Soon after we started off to visit Eaton Hall, and entered the gateway, which is a fine entrance in the castellated style. For two or three miles we drove through the grounds, and for a part of the way it was very shady and pleasant. We saw herds of deer which fled at our approach, and after passing a lodge, arrived at the house. It is a long building in the Gothic style, adorned with towers, turrets, and pinnacles. The marquis of Westminster to whom it belongs is one of the richest nobles in the kingdom, and has spared no expense to adorn his elegant palace. It was begun by the late marquis and finished by the present one. The plan for each of the three stories, is, a long corridor running through the middle and rooms on either side. We entered by a square hall with very perfect imitations of marble upon the walls knights in armour stood in niches, and there were hat stands of deer horns. The corridor through which we next passed has a groined ceiling and is adorned with portraits of the family and their favorite horses. Touchstone is still living the fastest horse in England, we were told, and the late marquis had him brought up every morning for him to see. Hugh Earl Grosvenor, is the eldest son, and his son is Lord Belgrave. We went into the dining hall. Its ceiling is ornamented with colored coats of arms, and statues are placed in canopied niches along the sides of the room. There is an air of richness and elegance about everything, and it is all in perfect order. The ante dining room is the one for constant use, its ceiling is green and gold, with a paper to match. Then comes the saloon, considered the most elegant room in Great Britain. It is square, but the fan like columns give it a circular appearance. The ceiling and walls are frescoed in the Alhambra style, crimson and white, green and gold, and inserted in the wall, are Spanish landscapes. The windows are of stained glass like those of a cathedral. The ante drawing room is next, a pretty room the windows also of stained glass with tracery above in cream color and gold. The drawing room is very splendid, upon the ceiling are colored heraldic bearings, the doors are arched and of carved mahogany costing each 500 dollars. There is a gilded card table, eight ebony chairs, paintings and a Florentine mosaic cabinet and table. The library is a spacious apartment filled with book cases it has windows on three sides and here were several marble statues. The chapel has stained glass windows and paintings and the wood work of the room is oak richly carved.

The grounds in front are laid out in elaborate beds of flowers, and marble vases placed everywhere. One parterre is adorned with statues, one, of a knight of the family, another a bishop and another a lady Joan of Eaton by marriage with whom this estate came to the Grosvenors. We walked about, in the grounds, they are adorned with fine shrubs and trees. The conservatories are very fine. One contains some choice orchidiae, among which a scarlet passion flower was very beautiful. There were grapes already ripe, pineapple and strawberries and other fine fruit. One of the conservatories, made of glass and iron resembled a miniature Crystal Palace. Everywhere pleasant paths invited us to explore but we were too wearied to go far. The marquis owns some thousands of acres and has lately made a road of three or four miles length to a railroad station on his own grounds. It is indeed a very magnificent place and the strangest fact about it is that the family come here only in the autumn and winter while in June, July and August when it is so beautiful here, they remain in London.

On our return to Chester we explored the town somewhat. It is a very old place and shows the marks of it. The walls are now used as a promenade, we walked upon them for some distance and saw the tower where Charles I stood and saw his army defeated at Rawton Moor four miles distant. The abbey church is near by, it is very ancient and built of red sandstone. We went into the Church of the Trinity and saw a brass tablet, to the memory of Matthew Henry. Parnell the poet is buried there also. We saw some very old houses, the oldest had the date 1562, they say that Charles I lived here once, and that it was the only one exempt from the plague; over the door is written "God's providence is mine inheritance." Another house called Bishop Lloyd's is ornamented with grotesque carvings. Many of the houses have their gable ends turned to the street and are ornamented with black and white figures some too have their beams painted black or brown. One peculiarity is the arcade forming a sheltered sidewalk, sometimes also there is one in the second story, with steps leading up to it, and shops there, as well as below. The castle is now used as a prison. Chester was a Roman town.

*Wednesday, June 24th, Lancaster, England.*

It has been a dusty hot oppressive day. After leaving Chester we changed cars at Warrington, where we had to wait for about an hour. At Preston we again changed. From here we had expected to visit the first seat of the Salisburys in England, at Rile Chester, but found it too far distant, so went on to Lancaster.

*Thursday, June 25th, Ambleside, Lake Country of England.*

Leaving Lancaster we changed cars at Kendal, and at Windemere the railroad came to an end. The hotel there is very prettily situated, with some glimpses of the lake. We took a carriage to drive down the west shore of Windemere Lake. We only rode as far as Bowness and returned by another road. It was all lovely, but at one point, there was an exquisite view. Nearby the whole of the lake lay spread out before us. It is eleven miles long and not more than one broad. The scenery was very soft. At the head rose high mountains, one behind another mantled in a thin mist, which lightly veiled without hiding their outlines. These mountains gradually diminished in size until at the foot of the lake there were only low hills, and on the side where we were it was mostly level ground. Nearly opposite us was Furness Fell a wooded hill rising from the water, to which Wordsworth refers in "bees that soar for bloom, high as the highest peak of Furness Fell." Among the mountains at the head of the lake were two pointed peaks called Langdale Pikes, then Scaw Fell in the distance, the highest mountain in England. Upon the water were little boats and we saw several islands. The road back to Windemere was shady which was very pleasant, it has been so warm a day. After dinner we took a carriage again, and drove over Elleray a wooded hill that used to belong to Prof. Wilson (Christopher North). A wood road winds over it from whence there were views of the lake and of the pretty valley below us. Prof. Wilson lived in a plain house at the foot of the hill. We passed many pretty villas, with roses climbing luxuriantly over their walls. Continuing on to Ambleside about five miles farther, along the head of the lake, we passed Mrs. Heman's house whence there were lovely views, it is called "Dove's Nest." In the distance Miss Martineau's house was pointed out to us. Another house is inhabited by a maiden lady, who is very fond of fishing and shooting, she goes out in her little boat upon the lake and shoots wild ducks. Passing through Ambleside we drove down the other side of the lake as far as Weay Castle a mansion of some pretension. A little pond lay on our road. The views were less striking on this side than on the other. We have little prospect from this hotel, except of a church with a large steeple and green fields and trees.

*Friday, June 26th, Keswick, Derwentwater.*

We left Ambleside this morning and drove to Rydall Mount, Wordsworth's place which is quite near. It is on a slight elevation above a shady road. The house is plain but quite embowered in vines. A beautiful bush of fuchsia grew in front and a border of other flowers. An old servant acted as our guide. He took us down some steps to a grassy circle, to which Wordsworth himself had taken Uncle when he was here before. From here there was a sweet view of Windemere enclosed by hills. Then passing through the garden we came into a field where the poet had had a pleasant walk made. Upon the fence and forming part of it was a huge stone upon which, on a metal plate, Wordsworth had written as follows,

> *In these fair vales hath many a tree*
> *At Wordsworth's suit been spared.*
> *And from the builder's hand, this stone,*
> *For some rude beauty of its own*
> *Was rescued by the Bard.*
> *So let it rest; and time will come*
> *When here the tender-hearted*
> *May heave a gentle sigh for him,*
> *As one of the departed. 1830*

A little farther on is seen Rydall Water, a sweet little pond, but the trees have grown up, so as to obstruct the view somewhat. Then returning, we met a Mr. Carter, a friend of the family. He takes care of Mrs. Wordsworth, who is eighty-seven, blind, and quite deaf. There are two sons but they are not at home. This gentleman led us by another path, through a little summer house lined with pine cones, to a spot where Rydall Water could be seen just below us and a glimpse of Windemere. In the distance, he pointed out a mountain, whence he said, the poet in *The Excursion*, is supposed to descend into the valley below where the Solitary lived. Langdale Pikes looked finely. The grounds are tastefully arranged, though left as much as possible in a state of nature.

We took our carriage again, and drove through a half private road, passing Fox Howe the residence of Dr. Arnold, and where his widow still lives. In descending a hill called Red Bank, we had a fine view of Grasmere. It is a small lake but very beautiful enclosed by hills and mountains, and with an island in its centre. On the opposite side of the lake, and behind the trees, was a house in which Wordsworth once lived, and to which he brought home his bride. We drove to the church were he always worshipped; it is three or four hundred years old. In a corner of the churchyard, under a hawthorn tree, lies Sarah Hutchinson, sister of

Mrs. Wordsworth. On one side of her grave is that of Dorothy sister of Mr. Wordsworth and on the other his own inscribed with the name alone. Next is the grave of his daughter Dora with a lamb carved upon it, after hers that of her husband, and near by two young children and a grandchild of the poet. In the same corner is the grave of Hartley Coleridge who died in 1849, the eldest son of S.T. Coleridge. His mother was a sister of Southey. Within the church upon a pillar in the family pew is a monument to Wordsworth, a profile head and two sculptured flowers and the following inscription, "To the memory of William Wordsworth, a true Philosopher and Poet, Who by the special gift and calling of Almighty God, whether he discoursed on man or nature, failed not to lift up the heart to holy things, tired not of maintaining the cause of the poor and simple, and so in perilous times was raised up to be a chief minister, not only of noblest poetry but of high and sacred truth. This monument is placed here by his friends and neighbors in testimony of respect, affection and gratitude. anno MDCCCLI" He was about 81 when he died. The church is simple, with bare rafters.

After leaving Grasmere the views looking back were very lovely. Thirlmere next came in sight, a long and pretty lake. Then riding considerably farther we reached Keswick on the shore of Derwentwater. Here we rested, during the heat of the day and at half-past four started off for a drive of twelve miles round the lake. We went up the lake on the west shore and the road was very beautiful, close to the water and partly through woods. We stopt to look at the Borrow Falls in the grounds of a Mr. Langton, there was not much water, but they were pretty. In a bay which we passed is seen every three years the curious phenomenon of a floating island, covered with vegetation. It has now been under water for two years. Southey refers to it, in his *Madoc* in Wales. Near by descending through a deep notch in the wooded rocks is, usually, the "Cataract of Lodore," but it is now dry. Our road led us through part of the Borroughdale Valley through which the Derwent flows, behind are high hills, and in front, stands out, the Castle Hill a peculiar wooded point. We turned aside a little to look at a boulder stone 36 feet high it can not now be moved, though it stands on a sharp end. We climbed to the top by means of ladders. "Upon a semicirque of turf clad ground. Right at the foot of that moist precipice A mass of rock resembling as it lay, A stranded ship with keel upturned that rests, Careless of winds and waves." Wordsworth. Continuing on to the other side of the lake we rode under the shadow of a hill. The view behind us was fine. The mountains with their jagged outlines in sunlight in the foreground the Castle Crag in shade, then the lake spread out before us with its Herbert's, Vicar's and

Lord's Isles. It was all as calm and sweet as possible in the approaching twilight. On nearing this end of the lake we passed Greta Hall Southey's residence. From it there is a fine view of lake and hills. Keswick is not a very pleasant town, we have no view of the water.

*Saturday, June 27th, Carlisle.*

Before leaving Keswick we drove out a mile to see the old church where Southey lies buried. His tomb is a slate slab, he died in 1843. Beside him lies his wife Edith. In the church is a full length marble effigy with a calm placid expression on the face, though it is not very well done. Returning we passed Southey's house again and crossed the river Greta. We had a long ride before us, it was very warm at first, but a cool breeze sprung up. We rode over Matterdale Moor, the scenery was more tame until we reached Ulleswater Lake, and rode six miles by its side. It is not equal to the other lakes, though the hills at one end are fine.

At Pooley's Bridge we took dinner. Then we drove on to Lowther Castle. A little girl rode on the step of our carriage to open gates for us after entering the castle grounds. This castle stands quite alone in the midst of 600 acres and is an imitation of an ancient one, with towers and a wall about it. The entrance hall is fine, decorated with suits of armour. The staircase is of a light stone with banisters of wood and bronze inlaid with brass. In an ante-chamber in the second story Dresden and other old china was placed in cases round the room. Here was also a chair worked by Mary Queen of Scots. The state bedroom had two splendid wardrobes of bronze and wood inlaid with brass, the bed was of black oak and the curtains of white embroidered satin though not put up. An old woman guided us about. It is the seat of the Earl of Lounsdale who is a bachelor and quite old, but has his brother's or sister's family with him usually. The dining room was handsome, the walls were of yew and brick making a pretty contrast. The library has oak cases with ornaments on the top in the castellated style. The towers formed small circular rooms, in the library one of these was used for old books. The drawing room was fine, in this wire tables of tortoise shell and brass, but curtains and furniture were all covered up, in the absence of the family. Another dining room was adorned with old paintings. One, a village festival by Teniers. In another room was a portrait of the earl and one of his brother Col. Lowther. We then went on our way to Penrith. Our driver did not seem quite sober, the trunk fell off behind and he had to put it on in front and ride with his feet hanging over the side. At Penrith we took the cars for Carlisle.

*Sunday, June 28th, Carlisle.*

Attended the old Presbyterian church and heard an excellent sermon from Mr. Drummond a fine looking young man. In the afternoon we went to the cathedral and heard the dean. Mary Queen of Scots attended church there when on her way into England. A stone tablet in the floor marks the tomb of Paley.

*Monday, June 29th, Glasgow, Scotland.*

The trains from Carlisle were at 6 and 7 in the morning, at which hours it is very difficult to get off in England, so we occupied the morning in writing letters, etc. and took the three o'clock train. The scenery was not remarkable. We followed the Clyde River and crossed the Esk. We saw a great deal of yellow broom. Glasgow is a large city. We stayed at the Prince's Hotel opposite the George Square, in which is a column with Sir Walter Scott's figure, on the top. A cold rainy day.

*Tuesday, June 30th, Tarbet, Loch Lomond, Scotland.*

Left Glasgow in a steamboat to sail up the Clyde, it was very cold and misty. After an hour or two we took the cars for a short ride to Baloch which is at the foot of Loch Lomond. Here we took a steamboat, and sailed for about two hours, to this place which is ten miles from the head of the lake. The scenery was fine; rugged mountains, green, sloping hills, wooded islands, and points of land jutting out. We saw old Ben Lomond. A rock near the water's edge on our right, is called Rob Roy's prison, there was a cave which was invisible to us, where he kept his prisoners. We are now in a quiet hotel on the lake shore and in full view of Ben Lomond's peak. This afternoon we drove and walked four or five miles up the shady road by the lake, the views were fine and the air fresh and invigorating. We gathered a large bunch of honeysuckle and heath. Saw some turf huts with shavings' roofs. We are now in the Highlands of Scotland, and here I spend my birthday. It is nearly 9 and broad daylight still.

*Wednesday, July 1st, Loch Awe, Dalmally.*

We commenced our journey this morning by walking from Tarbet along a pleasant road, across the narrow isthmus that divides Loch Lomond from Loch Long. We passed Arroquar a hamlet on the lake shore and then drove round the head of the lake, and for some distance on the other side. It is really an arm of the sea and has a tide. The view down the lake was pleasant. Then turning off we entered the wild, and savage pass or vale of Glencroe. High hills rose on either side rough with stones, and with no verdure but short grass. On our right Ben Arthur or the Cobble showed its cragged peaks. Not a tree was visible around us, and the only signs of life were a few lone sheep browsing on the steep hillside. A brook ran through the valley fed by the mountain rivulets, that descended from all sides. Our imaginations were busy in peopling this rugged scene with Highland warriors, and in picturing the events that might have taken place here. After six miles of such scenery we came upon Loch Restal, a pretty and very small lake, at the foot of the mountains. On the road side was a stone seat with "Rest and be thankful" marked upon it. Then we passed through Glen Kinglass another wild valley and soon reached the Caindow Inn situated on the shore of Lock Tyne, where we stopped to change horses. We rode round the head of this lake, and six miles on the other side. The views were pretty, the water reflected the bright blue of the sky and a few islands were scattered over its surface.

We stopt at Inverary to dine. Here is the Castle of Inverary, the country seat of the Duke of Argyle. It is a square building with four towers at the corners, and one in the middle. The trees in the grounds are beautiful, we approached the castle by a bridge over the Airy River. Inverary though a small place is the country town of Argyleshire. After dinner we had a ride of sixteen miles to Dalmally. The first part of the way was through some pleasant woods. Then old Ben Cruachan, with its three peaks rose up to view, and then Loch Awe came in sight, a beautiful lake with Cruachan and other mountains rising from its east side. From here we ascended to Dalmally which is at the entrance of the Vale of Glenorchie. Some of the hills today have been covered with purple heather. It has been Highland scenery in perfection, with such fine air and bright sunshine.

### Thursday, July 2nd, Loch Tay, Kenmore.

Leaving Dalmally we rode through Glenorchie and then Glen Dochat a wild and rugged valley between bare mountains. The hills were furrowed with rills and wild brooks tumbled over the rocks in many places. This is the general character of the scenery and it becomes almost oppressive after a while, one longs for softer views. We saw many poor miserable hovels with turf roofs the costume of the peasant is not peculiar except that the boys wear kilts, Scotch caps and their legs bare. We stopt at Killin to dine. The inn there is beautifully situated on the river Lochay, and the grounds slope to the water's edge. After dinner we took a boat, and rowed up the river some little distance to see the Finlarig Castle an ancient seat of the Breadalbanes of the Campbell Clan. It is a small river and quite shapeless, but prettily draped in ivy. Our guide who was a woman pointed out a sentry box and one or two places that have been identified, she talked in Gaelic to her father. Close by is a chapel, in which are vaults containing the remains of members of the family. We enjoyed the little sail on the river, the trees on either side bent down into the water, and the lights were beautiful.

Then taking a carriage we visited a waterfall in the Lochay, two or three miles from Killin. An old man of 85 acted as our guide. They belong to the Marquis of Breadalbane. Our path led us through the woods, till we came to the falls, which are in three parts flowing over a rocky bed. They are very lovely. Returning we pursued our way on the north side of Loch Tay. We saw Aukmore at the end of the lake, one of the seats of the marquis of Breadalbane. Our ride was charming, it was sixteen miles to Kenmore. Ben More rose up in the distance, in the direction of Killin. Before we had ended our journey, the sun had set behind Ben Lawers, a rainbow arched over its falling rays, and was a beautiful sight, but as the event proved an omen of rain. In the loch is a wooded island where Sibylla daughter of Henry I and wife of Alexander I of Scotland is buried. It was nearly nine when we arrived at our hotel, which is near the Gothic and ivy covered entrance, to Taymouth Castle.

*Friday, July 3rd, Loch Tay, Killin.*

This morning before leaving Kenmore, we drove into the grounds of Taymouth Castle, in the rain. We were accompanied by a guide in the Highland dress, a small cap, a black velvet jacket with silver buttons, the skirt was of the Breadalbane plaid green and blue with a narrow yellow stripe, bare knees, red stockings and leather shoes. The marquis is a very rich landed proprietor. His estate extends a hundred miles, to the Atlantic Ocean. We rode about a mile through the grounds, before reaching the castle. The park contains 900 fallow deer. There are some magnificent trees in it, maples, lindens etc., a brook winds about; crossed by pretty rustic bridges. The castle is of a grey color and surrounded on two sides by an arcade, which is covered with ivy and ornamented with deer horns. We went into a hall, also adorned with deer horns; on the left was a billiard room, hung with shields and warlike weapons. The dining room had window shutters and furniture of carved oak; it was very rich indeed. The baronial hall, the first of the kind, we have seen, was most magnificent. At one end was a large stained glass window. The wainscoting of the room was carved oak. The walls were decorated with the banners of sovereigns who had honored the castle by their presence. And the ceiling was carved with heraldic shields. The floor was mosaic wood, oak and laburnum. Here was also a beautiful table, made of two pieces of an oak root, polished.

The library gallery next claimed our admiration. It contains carved book cases and some paintings. Here was an elegantly carved cabinet, having spiral pillars of a light wood, in the curves a wreath of dark wood, carved into flowers, leaves and acorns. In this cabinet was preserved the sash of the young Pretender taken from him with his baggage after the battle of Culloden. The views from the windows in this room were beautiful, even in the rain, with the smooth lawn and fine trees. This gallery opens by a carved open work door into the library proper. Here were rich cases for books, over the fireplace was a boar's head the family crest. The drawing room appeared very handsome, even though the carpets were up and the curtains and window shutters covered lest the sun should injure the gilding. At one end was a stained glass window representing St. Caecilia. The ceiling was painted in bright colors. From the dining room a small cabinet opens called the Stuart Cabinet and containing miniature portraits of many of that family. As a whole I think it is the richest house we have yet seen. We saw a portrait of the marquis in a Highland dress, one of his wife and father, besides many paintings to which we paid little attention. The queen made a visit here some years ago. The housekeeper seemed to have no very agreeable recollections of it, she hoped she would not come again. I suppose she had all the labour and none of the honour. The men were displayed for her, in their Highland dress, Prince Albert stalked deer on Drummond Hill, to the right of the house, where there are not far from 1,000 red deer.

Returning then to our carriage we drove some distance and then walked through the barnyard and a field or two, to visit the dairy, not taking the usual path because of the rain. Around the dairy is a flower garden, we entered a little room adorned with shells and other curiosities, among which was the spade with which Queen Victoria planted a tree when here! This led to a circular room, with walls of buff tiles, columns of grey stone, a pavement of black and white marble, and a broad shelf of black marble around the room upon which were placed pans of milk!! It was all as neat as wax and very beautiful. The dairy maid showed us her cheeses; one kind was particularly for his lordship's table, and jars of salted butter, which they send to the family in London. From a room, above, where were sets of old china adorning the place, was a fine view of the loch and mountains. The marquis has the office of lord high chamberlain. Having closed our interesting survey, we returned to Kenmore and drove eighteen miles on the south side of the lake, to Killin again. On account of the rain we stay here overnight instead of pursuing our way to Callander.

*Saturday, July 4th, "The Trossachs," Loch Auchray.*
The clouds had not wholly broken away when we left Killin this

morning, and it has been showery all day. We drove through Glen Ogle another of those stern valleys or more rugged if possible and narrower. We saw the glen or Braes of Balquiddar, where Rob Roy McGregor was born and is buried. Loch Ogle is a small lake, set down in the valley. At the eighth mile we reached Earnhead where the lovely Earn stretches out its waters, with a background of hills somewhat reminding us of our own Saltonstall. While changing horses some of us walked on for a mile or two. We passed the poor and miserable huts of Strath Ire, where, in *The Lady of the Lake* the cross of fire to summon the clans "glanced like lightning up Strath Ire." Then we rode a long distance along the shore of Loch Lubnaig following the course of the bearer of "the cross" though reversed. This loch is very pretty. High hills rise up on all sides both soft and rugged. Benledi is one of these mountains. We passed by Ardhullary House a plain white dwelling, the residence of James Bruce the Abyssinian traveler. The Church of St. Bride was at the end of the lake, but we saw no traces of it.

We stopt at Callander for lunch and then took a carriage to the Trossachs. We passed the Ford of Coilantogle where Fitz James and Rhoderic Dhu fought, it is at the end of the pretty Loch Venochar, along which we rode for several miles. The country was rather level and under cultivation. Near the head of the lake, is a flat meadow called "Lanrick Mead" the muster place of Clan Alpine. We rode across the Brigg of Turc which spans a rapid stream, and then skirted Loch Achray, through a sweet wooded road. The Trossachs Inn is the castle form, it was full when we arrived, so we were placed in an opposite building. We have from here a lovely view of lake wooded hills rocks and old Benvenue, and here we are to pass our Sabbath. We are but a mile or two from Loch Katrine, and just at the entrance of the Trossachs Pass. We took a ramble on the hill behind our hotel, and had a pretty view and discovered a waterfall. So we spent our 4th of July.

*Sunday, July 5th, Trossachs Hotel.*

Not a pleasant day. It rained hard, part of the morning. We went to a small church about a quarter of a mile distant and heard a genuine Scotchman, with a strong accent. He gave us two short sermons, in this one service.

*Monday, July 6th, Stirling.*

Took a carriage this morning, and drove over to Loch Katrine through the Trossachs, a road shaded with trees and exhibiting several rocky wooded points. We took a little boat to go out upon the lake. The waves were rather high and the wind strong and cold. We passed first through an inlet with wooded shores and shut off from the rest of the lake by a peninsular. Our boatman seemed to be well read in the *Lady of the Lake* and repeated parts of it to us. He showed us a bay, where the stag was stopt in his fight and turned aside into a glade and in pursuing him, the "gallant horse exhausted fell." Ben An on our right was 1800 feet high, on the other side Benvenue, steep, rugged, and bare, though once covered with verdure. Upon its side, under the precipice, and among some loose stone was the "Goblin's Cave." Near by was the rocky pass of Bealnambo, where Rhoderick Dhu passing with his army stopt to hear Ellen's voice.

We had come to a broader part of the lake and yet the island was invisible, when, turning another point, it suddenly came in sight. We landed on its shore, close to an "aged oak" that overhung the water. We walked up the little path that leads over the isle, but found nothing of much interest, except its association with imaginary scenes. Lord and Lady Willoughby d'Eresby built an imitation of Ellen's house, but it was set on fire by a careless cigar. This island has, in reality, served as a shelter for the plunder, taken by the Highland Clans in their foraging parties. The rain came down quite fast on our return. Soon after reaching the inn, we retraced our journey past Loch Vennochar to Callander. After a lunch here, we took post horses for Stirling, which is 16 miles, and which we accomplished in two hours. The country, as we went on, grew more flat, and more under cultivation. We passed Doune, about half-way, and saw at a distance, Doune Castle.

Stirling Castle came in sight long before reaching it. It stands upon a hill, and the town on its slope. We soon set off to view the castle, after our arrival here. We rode up some very steep streets and entered the castle by a drawbridge. It is still in use, being garrisoned by 120 men, some of whom were in the Highland costume, and one soldier served us as a guide. We entered by a gateway, with two towers, that on the right, is called Rhoderick Dhu's prison. We saw the exterior of the palace built by James V; it is adorned by the most grotesque and horrible figures. Behind it, is the tower where Mary Queen of Scots was imprisoned. We entered by a court-yard, on one side of which was the Parliament House built by James III, and on the other the palace mentioned above. Opposite is the armory, formerly the Chapel Royal, built by James VI for the baptism of his son Henry. Here we saw several interesting things; a lochabre, a long pole with a blade on the end taken at the battle of Bannockburn, and swords from the field of Sheriffmuir. A drum belonging to the drummer of the 42nd Regiment at Waterloo, taken from him when dead, by the

French, and restored by them to the regiment. Our guide was a member of that body, and he said they always carried it with them, when on the march. A vast number of spiked poles, which were prepared, to arm the peasantry, against the expected invasion of Napoleon. John Knox's oak pulpit and a carved communion table which he used. Some wooden ornaments from a room now burnt down, in which Wm. Earl of Douglass was killed in a passion by James II, the wood is probably a thousand years old. The tilting lance of James V, and many other curiosities.

From the left of this building a path descends the castle hill, called Ballangerich, and whence James V took the name of "the good Man of Ballangerich." Upon the wall of the castle, passing on our way through "Mary Queen of Scot's garden" we had a fine view of the country. In the flat plain to our right, was the Abbey of Cambus Kenneth, where Robert Bruce was crowned, only one tower remains entire. Turning westward was still the plain, with a few wooded hills rising from it and in the distance Benvenue, Benledi, Lomond and Ben Voirloch. We continued our walk on the wall at different levels; at one corner, Victoria and Prince Albert stood, to review the troops, the only time the queen was ever at Stirling. Farther on, was a hole in the wall, through which poor Mary looked on the tournament below. We gazed down the precipice and saw, in a square, a series of raised beds of turf; upon inquiry we found it was the old tournament ground. Here are laid the scenes in *The Lady of the Lake*, where Douglass shows his skill. Looking southward we saw the position of the field of Bannockburn four or five miles distant.

*Tuesday, July 7th, Royal Hotel, Princess St., Edinburgh.*

Took the cars at Stirling and after a ride of about two hours, reached Edinburgh. On our way we passed Linlithgow, and saw the ruins of the palace, where the sovereigns of Scotland used, at times, to reside. We are upon Princess St., facing the old city from which a deep ravine separates us where the railroads are. On the bank are flower beds, and trees and pleasant walks and here also stands a fine monument to the memory of Sir Walter Scott. To our right on the hill we see the castle below us the national gallery and institution; opposite, the old city with its houses and churches and behind Arthur's Seat and Salisbury Crag. We spent the remainder of the day in shopping.

*Wednesday, July 8th, Edinburgh.*

Mary and I went out with a valet de place to see the city. We drove first to Calton Hill devoted to the monuments of great men. A tall tower is to the memory of Nelson; and a building in imitation of the Parthenon,

*The Scott Monument*

of which but 12 columns have as yet been put up, is to commemorate those who fell at Waterloo, then a little temple of Grecian style is to Dugald Stewart, a monument to Prof. Playfair, a square form with pillars, and the observatory is here also in an enclosure. The view from this hill is very fine, on the north lies the Firth of Forth with the town of Leith visible on its shore. Below us lay the city with its various buildings. The Martyr's Monument was quite conspicuous. It is a obelisk erected to the memory of the marquis of Argyle and many thousand others who were killed in the 17th cent. Descending the hill we passed Burns' monument, in the form of a temple ornamented with sculptured harps and griffins on the top supporting an hour glass.

We soon reached Holyrood Palace. It is a large grey building the front ornamented by a huge crown and two reclining figures. It is built round a court. On one side are Queen Victoria's apartments, for she makes this her Scotch country seat. We were first shown into a huge picture gallery, lined with 106 portraits of Scottish kings. Here were given balls by Prince Charles Edward in 1745. We then went into the audience room where, were also old paintings, one of Mary when 16, taken the year after her marriage with the dauphin, and a dark looking portrait of John Knox. A part of the palace was built by Charles II. Then returning to the other side of the audience room we saw Lord Darnley's bed-room,

*Holyrood Palace*

the walls were decorated with paintings. In a little turret adjoining, was shown the private staircase, by which the assassins mounted to Queen Mary's room to murder Rizzio. The broad staircase leads up from the audience room. Near the top we were shown a dark stain, said to be where the body of the poor Italian lay all night, upon the floor, covered with 56 wounds. Thence we entered Queen Mary's room. Here stands the bed of Charles I, once of a very rich silk and velvet, now mouldering away. A chair worked with a coat of arms by Mary herself and a toilet table and mirror, brought from France by her. The walls were hung with dark tapestry and ceiling low, and paneled. Adjoining is Mary's bed-room, much in the same style with tapestry brought from France. The bed was a piece of faded magnificence. Here was a work box made of wood and covered with silk embroidered by her when twelve years old. On one side is a little dressing room of irregular shape, also hung with tapestry. Answering to this, on the other side is the very small supper room, where Mary sat with three of four friends and Rizzio among them when Darnley and Ruthven came up and killed him. His body was dragged through the queen's room to the top of the stairs. In this room is the marble altar at which when in the Chapel Royal Mary knelt when married to Darnley. We went in the second story, into the apartments of the marquis of Breadalbane who is lord chamberlain, here was a chair or low seat which had belonged to Anne of Denmark queen of James I and some portraits by Lely and Vandyke.

We went by a lower door into the Chapel Royal or Holyrood Abbey now a ruin. It was founded in the 12 cent. by David I and now the nave alone remains of the whole Monastery of Holyrood. The ruin is very beautiful. There are tombs here and some of them quite recent. At the large window Queen Mary was married to Darnley. The latter was buried in a vault in one corner, but afterwards removed. On leaving the abbey we drove up Cannongate street and High which is the same continued. It was once the court end of the town now the abode of the lowest class of people. We passed the poor house formerly the duke of Queenbury's palace also a low building where the regent Murray had lived and the site of the old Tolbooth.

The "Heart of Mid Lothian" was pointed out to us. We saw John Knox's house a gabled building and very old. On a corner of the house, is placed his figure kneeling, and beneath, these words "Love God above all and yi neighbor as yi self." From these windows he used to preach to the people. We passed St. Giles, the Tron Church and High Church with a tower like crown. We drove then across the bridge and into the new part of the city, which is quite handsome. There were many squares and circuses ornamented with statues and fine blocks of houses around them. We stopt to look more particularly at the Scott Monument. It is a very beautiful Gothic structure and under the canopy a sitting figure of Sir Walter with a book in his hand and a dog by his side.

*Interior of Holyrood Abbey.*

*John Knox's house.*

In the afternoon we visited the castle which has a garrison of 800 or so men. After passing for a long distance through the castle we mounted a stairway that led to the crown jewels room. Here is the crown of Scotland adorned with diamonds, pearls, and various precious stones, said to have been Robert Bruce's, and hid away in 1707, in a great chest, until discovered by Sir W. Scott. Queen Mary lived here at one time, and we saw her portrait, and that of James VI, and the room where the latter was born. The view from the castle is very fine. In the battery is a huge cannon called "Mons Meg" used at the siege of Norham Castle in 1513 and made in 1486 at Mons, Brittany. It has now burst. We took a drive around Prince Arthur's seat called "The Queen's Drive," and had fine views. In a ravine between Arthur's seat and Salisbury crag are laid the scenes in the *Heart of Mid Lothian* and the chapel of St. Anthony is near by, in ruins. "Jennie Deans house" was pointed out to us, a small, tiled hut at the foot of the crags and on the edge of the city. We went to call at Mrs. John Scott Moncreif's and thus ended our busy day.

*Thursday, July 9th, Melrose, Scotland.*

We left Edinburgh in the half-past four train, and arrived here in two hours. Soon after we started out to see the abbey, which is not far distant. We entered it, at the west end of the nave. This part was walled up some years ago to serve as a parish church. The side aisles, are perfect, the groining of the roofs is entire and there are clustered columns with beautiful capitals of leaves and flowers. The east oriel window is in a very perfect state. It was here that the grand altar used to be. There are several tombs here, one of Alexander II, upon which the monk, and Wm. of Deloraine are represented as sitting in the *Lay of the Last Minstrel* until the cross of red should point to the fearful grave. Our guide showed us the grave, as they call it of Michael Scott the Wizard, a broken, flat stone with a cross upon it. In the chancel to the right of the altar is the "Lady Chapel." The transept is quite perfect and its windows beautiful. The capitals bosses and canopies were most delicately carved in stone. In one place a hand - holding a bunch of flowers made a corbel. From the left aisle we went into the cloisters, there is not much left of these but they are highly ornamented. The water spouts are most grotesque things, Negro heads, and animals of all sorts.

*South front of Melrose Abbey*

*South front of Melrose Abbey*

We went out into the burial ground and from hence the view of the east and transept windows was very fine. The south window too is very fine. Among the ornaments was a figure of St. John, of which the head, as our guide said (who was a funny old Scotchman) had been "hapt off." "There" he said "is a bonnie nun and monk on the other side laughing at her, there, is a monk telling his beads, and saying that he would rather loose his ear, than a bead, which I would not do, for all the bades that are made." He hated the remains of Catholicism, with his whole heart. We saw a beautiful canopy over the Virgin, it was of open-work, and a jackdaw always builds her nest in it. Over the east window is an image of David I, 1146, who founded the abbey. In one place we saw an image of Jupiter. Uncle asked the guide if it was a good likeness "wal says he I niver saw him but them's been in those heathen countries say it is." He said he had seen Sir Walter Scott "mony a time." He used to carry him grouse-cock, he never read any of his works he "niver saw no good of them, it did not help one to get salvation." Uncle told him that was not the only thing to be sought, though it was the chief thing. "Yes" he said "it is the only thing." He amused us highly by his queer talk and pronunciation.

*Friday, July 10th, Alnwick, England.*

We started off quite early this morning to visit the ruins of Dryburgh Abbey about four miles from Melrose. We crossed the Tweed in a boat and then walked some distance to the ruins. The nave is wanting except the entrance which is plain. The two ends of the transept are still standing; the one is a fine window, the other, called St. Mary's aisle, appears like a chapel, it is in the lancet style. In this aisle Sir Walter Scott and his wife lie buried and his son Colonel Scott. The monuments are of red granite. It was given the family as a burial place and other families are laid near by. We went into the chapter house which almost adjoins the transept. It still has a roof, and a seat all around it, within. In the centre is a circle which marks the grave of its founder, Hugh de Moreville, Lord of Lauderdale of 1150. There are other remains of the abbey, but much ruined. "St. Catherine's Wheel" is a beautiful window in an ivy-covered wall. It belonged at one time to the Erskine family. We were shown the house of Sir Ralph and Ebenezer Erskine, two divines, who separated from the Church of Scotland. I believe Grandpapa S. visited them when he was in Scotland.

We returned then to Melrose and took a different direction for Abbotsford, the house of Sir W. Scott, now owned by Mr. Hope Scott, whose wife was a daughter of Mrs. Lockhart. The present family live mostly in a new house, which they built to secure themselves from the annoyance of visitors. Abbotsford was built by Sir Walter Scott, and is a large pile of buildings, standing on a terrace, above the Tweed. We entered by a small room, where is a cabinet, called the Waverly Cabinet, where the unpublished novel lay before printing. Then we went up into

*Dryburg Abbey*

*North distant view of Abbotsford*

the study which is a little bit of a room, surrounded by books in cases, and with a light gallery, giving access to a higher row of books. In the centre of the room stood a secretary and his easy chair in front. In a small closet, were kept the clothes he last wore, a white beaver hat, coat, shoes, gaiters, vest and pantaloons. Adjoining was the library, a large room. The ceiling was ornamented, with imitations of the ornaments of Melrose Roslin and other ruins. In one part of this room was a case, filled with curiosities. Among these were the portfolio and case for pens of Napoleon, made of green velvet, with N. worked in gold upon them. Prince Charles' drinking cup. An oak cup lined with gold from Waterloo. "Rob Roy's purse made of leather. A silver seal of Mary Queen of Scots. In the room itself was an elegant ebony cabinet presented by George IV who also gave him two dozen ebony chairs. There was a portrait here of Sir Walter seated, with a dog by his side, and also a pleasing bust of him by Chantry. A little hall opens thence, covered with relics, old weapons etc. Rob Roy's gun Indian weapons, Scotch claymores with long blades and basket handles. Napoleon's pistols taken from his carriage. A candle stick, that had belonged to Robert Bruce. The next room was the drawing-room. Here over the mantel is a portrait of Colonel, Sir W. Scott, who died, at the Cape of Good Hope. A portrait of Miss Ann Scott, who died young, and one, of Mrs. Lockhart when a girl. There were eight of Turner's coloured sketches here, and some excellent wood carvings, of animals, done by a mill-wright who lives near, a self taught carver. We went thence into the chief entrance hall, which is paneled and has armour hanging on the walls. Above were the coats of arms of the Scots Elliots, Armstrongs, Kerrs etc. who kept the border in "auld tyme." Here was preserved the key of the old Tolbooth at Edinburgh, and the "skull of Michael the Wizard. We walked a little on the terrace behind the house, and saw the bay window of the room where Sir Walter died.

We took the railway cars again at a little after one. We crossed the Teviot River, and rode along it, some distance. Several castles border fortresses appeared at intervals. We changed at Berwick where we had to wait an hour. In the distance we saw where lay Flodden Field, at the foot of the Cheviot Hills. We took some trouble to come here to see Alnwick Castle, but find to our disappointment, that it is not open to visitors. It is the residence of the dukes of Northumberland, the Percys.

*Saturday, July 11th, York.*

Before leaving Alnwick we took a little walk in the grounds of the duke. The shrubbery and walks along the river Aln were pretty. The gateway is fine; it has towers and battlements with figures upon them. We took a noon train, and passed through Newcastle which is a smoky place. We stopt at Durham over one train to see the cathedral. It is a very fine example of the Norman style. The nave and one transept are of the round arch style, with huge massive pillars sculptured in squares, or spiral lines and having a curious effect. These alternated with clustered columns, to support the groined stone roof. The choir is of carved wood, beyond and terminating the church is a second transept, with windows of the lancet style and of a later period of architecture. On a platform protruding into this, is the tablet, under which lie the honored remains of St. Cuthbert. We saw that the stone was worn by the kneeling of pilgrims come to visit the shrine of the saint. At the west end of the church is the Galilee (the only one in England except that at Ely,) used as a lady's chapel, but differing from that, in being at the west, instead of east end. It is quite unique. There are four rows of clustered shafts supporting round and dentated arches. The ceiling is of paneled oak. The tomb of the Venerable Bede is here, his bones were stolen from Jarrow. There was an altar erected to him. Part of an old fresco remains. The cathedral was begun in the time of Wm. Rufus, and finished in that of Edward I. The church has an imposing effect. The exterior has a large square tower and two smaller ones. It stands on a high hill in the old city. The Bishop's Palace a large pile near by, is now used as a university. Durham is a very old town. We took dinner and then after a four hours ride reached York.

*Sunday, July 12th, York.*

We went to the cathedral service in the morning. The assises were soon to begin, so the high chief was present and other officials dressed in scarlet. Their chaplain preached a sermon on duty to magistrates. We were not very comfortable, sitting on bare benches, through all this long service. In the afternoon we added four to a thin congregation at St. Martin's.

*Monday, July 13th, Manchester.*

We took an early breakfast in York and went out to see the cathedral. The outside resembles Durham, with one large square tower and smaller ones at the extremities. This is of the early pointed or Edwardian style. The foundation (as seen in the crypt) is Norman but it is said to have been founded in 626, by the Saxon king Edwin. At one end of the transept were the celebrated "five sisters" simple lancet windows, tall and narrow but very beautiful, above, were five smaller ones. Over the door by which we entered was a fine wheel window. The columns are clustered and those which support the square tower, are twenty seven yards round. The arches are simple and painted. The nave is very broad for its length. The choir has been lately renewed. All the windows are of stained glass and even those in the clerestory, richer than in any other church in England. The chapter house has been restored, and is very beautiful. The floor is of tiles and the roof painted. We saw some old stone coffins of Roman times, for York is an ancient city. It was called Eboracum and is said to have been founded 938 years B.C. Here Serverus lived, and Caracalla killed his brother Geta.

We took the train at 9:45 and rode four hours through a manufacturing district to Manchester. It is a smoky place and as full of people as can be for the Art Treasures are exhibited here now. After dinner we went to the exhibition which is three miles off. It is in a building like the Crystal Palace and contains gems of various kinds, sent by the royalty nobility and gentry of England. We went into the halls of the ancient masters. Saw the *Good Shepherd*, a sweet thing, representing the child Saviour with his lambs, and a Madonna and child by Murillo. Several of Raphael's Madonnas. Landscapes by Salvator Rosa. One was the same as Uncle's mosaic picture. A portrait of Ariosto from Venice. A St. John by Domenichino like the one in Russia. An original of the Magdalen of Correggio. There were also, some good Dutch paintings. I can not attempt to enumerate or remember the myriad I saw and must stop with this for the present.

*Tuesday, July 14th, Manchester.*

We are in a very noisy hotel near to the cars. We spent from ten to half-past six at the exhibition, taking our lunch with us, and it has been an intensely fatiguing though interesting day. Among those by modern artists we saw, *The Letter of Introduction. The Jew's Harp, Blind Man's Bluff, The Rat Catcher.* Evangeline by Faed, in this the dress is brown and the cloak red. Another of Faed's was *The Recess At School.* There were several school scenes by Webster. Turner's packet ship at Cologne a bright soft scene and others by him. Johnson's black servant by Sir J. Reynolds. *Distraining for Rent*, and *Rent Day* by Sir D. Wilkie. Two dogs representing dignity and impudence and the dogs of St. Bernard drawing a man from the snow, by Landseer. *Uncle Toby and Widow Wadman* and Sir Roger de Coverly going to church by Leslie. The Palace of the Caesars and some boys playing cards in the foreground a scene of the 19th cent. by Hurlstone. The portraits are on either side of the nave. Among these were Scott, Pope, Gibbon, Lockhart, Southey and Byron. Busts of Wordsworth and Johnson and a small full length statue of Burns. We saw many water color drawings, some by Turner. Among those done in his early style was Tintern Abbey, a scene on the Thames, Vesuvius in repose, Eddystone Lighthouse in a storm and a beautiful view of Florence. *Grace Before Meat* a rough sketch by Wilkie and his autograph letter. Several by Stoddard, Ruth, a pretty thing and little cupid in various attitudes and disguises. Some fine drawings for chess men by Flackman.

There were in the nave some fine pieces of sculpture. Three little singing angels by Thorwaldsen. A Venus of Canova. A fisher boy by Powers. A beautiful figure in prayer. In the middle of the transept was Virgilius killing his daughter. We saw Archbishop Scroop's bowl of silver. Bishop Wickham's crosier, and that of Fox, which was gold. Miniature portraits of the family of the first Napoleon. And elegant gold dishes, tankards etc. In the Oriental court were some very rich articles, splendid shawls, Persian carpets, muslins and ginghams worked with gold. An East-Indian tent with articles of dress inside. Some exquisite bracelets, turban ornaments set in stones. Also some miniatures of Indian work. Altogether the objects were entirely too numerous to mention, and also to remember. Manchester is crowded with visitors. It is in itself so far as I have seen far from agreeable, nothing to be seen but smoking chimneys, and factories.

*Wednesday, July 15th, Bakewell, Derbyshire.*

We left Manchester in a post carriage and have traveled thirty four miles. We dined at Rexton. The country afterwards was quite attractive.

We rode along the Wye and through picturesque passes, or along sweet green meadows, where the hay-makers were busy at work.

*Thursday, July 16th, Matlock, Derbyshire.*

We took a carriage at Bakewell this morning and drove 4 or 5 miles to Chatsworth the Duke of Devonshire's place. It is situated in a park of 3,000 acres twelve miles in circumference. The part that we crossed was finely ornamented with trees. The Derwent flows through and cows and beautiful deer graze on the verdant meadows. We went first to visit the fruit houses. Five of these are filled with grape vines. Some of the fruit was already ripe. One was a pinery. In another there were two peach trees of great size. One of these covered 74 feet and bore 100 dozen peaches. There were several greenhouses filled with plants. One was a splendid water house erected by Sir J. Paxton and here was a Victoria Regia which he was the means of introducing into England. He lives on these grounds in a pretty house surrounded by beautiful shrubs and flowers.

After examining the flowers etc. we turned to the house itself. Prince Napoleon was, with several gentlemen, walking about at the same time with us. He was plainly attired, wore a white hat and looked much like the first Napoleon. He was quite delighted with the Victoria Regia using the expressions superbe, charmante, etc. The house is a large pile of buildings of yellowish color, the window frames are gilded. Around it are flower gardens laid out in continental style. We were shown into the hall where was a splendid slab of fossil marble. The walls were coated with Derbyshire marbles. We went up two pairs of stairs, to the old apartments. The building was finished in 1726 but the present duke added a wing. His right to the estates is not valid, but he only holds them for life. Lord Burlington is the next heir. We went into the dressing room; the walls were of embossed leather, as well as the state bedroom adjoining which were also ornamented with gilt. The window seats were of fossil marble, and from the windows was a beautiful view. In the distance was a square sheet of water whence a jet of 200 or 300 feet arose, one of the most splendid in Europe. There was another nearer the house and they played in compliment to the prince. To finish my account of this state chamber, the doors were of cedar, over the mantels were most exquisite carvings done by Gibbons of birds, fishes, and flowers. We were shown a black velvet canopy for a bed, in which George II died and the coronation chairs of George III and his queen Charlotte. The next room contained two splendid malachite vases and a clock a present from the late Emperor of Russia. The walls are hung with Gobelin tapestry copied from Raphael's cartoons. In the billiard room were several paintings including Landseer's *Bolton Abbey in Olden Times*, venison and other game are brought to the monks who peruse the letter accompanying the present. We did not see many of the rooms, but we heard that the library cost with the works of art in it more than 7 and 1/2 millions of dollars. The chapel is of carved cedar and adorned with frescoes from scenes in our Saviour's life. The hall of statuary was splendid and contained many fine works. Canova's last work, Endymion asleep and his dog gazing at him, full sized figures. Hebe by Canova in a graceful flying attitude, and holding in her hands a pitcher and a golden cup. A scene, or figures, from the song of the swan by Schwanthaler. There were also here beautiful vases and tables, altogether a very rich collection.

The hall opened upon the orangery and we passed through this and a flower garden, leaving on our left a line of conservatories till we reached the famous one built by Sir J. Paxton and the only one of the kind till the Crystal Palace was erected. It is more than 250 feet long by 123 wide with a gallery above. Three wide walks divide the lower space. It contains mostly tropical plants. A huge cocoanut palm had almost grown too large for the space allotted. We saw also a sago palm and a bamboo cane and many other choice things. On our way to this conservatory we passed through an artificial rockery, quite well made. There was an artificial weeping willow and by touching a spring, water spouted forth from the leaves in every direction. We returned by a different walk. This part of the country goes under the name of the "Peak" and Chatsworth is called the "Palace of the Peak." Often it is visited by 7 or 800 persons in one day.

We drove to the pretty little inn of Edensor at the entrance of the grounds, where we took a lunch and then rode a few miles to visit Haddon Hall. It is said that one of the Perverils resided here in the reign of Stephen, but little is known about it until 1425 when it was owned by Sir Richard Vernon. It came into the hands of the Manners by the marriage of Dorothy Vernon to Sir John Manners in the reign of Elizabeth. The duke of Rutland who is a Manners now owns it, though it has not been inhabited for upwards of a century. It is interesting as a sample of a manor house of long ago. It has the appearance of a castle. We entered through a door into the court-yard. On our right was a small room which was appropriated to the chaplain, and a small closet adjoining for a study, the whole arrangement was mean; and showed the position in which such a man was held in those days. A lady's maid was considered a good match for him. We then crossed the court and entered the kitchen. In it was a fireplace large enough to roast an ox whole, table also and larders. In the banquet hall was a dais which held benches and a much hacked table. Around two sides was a gallery for the musicians. At the door was an iron cuff where the arms were fastened, of those who had committed the grievous offense of not drinking their quantum of beer, and cold water was poured down the sleeves. Near by is the private dining room, the windows were all made with casements and had very small panes of glass. The ceiling was ornamented with the Vernon arms and over the mantel the words "Drede God honor the king." We went into the duke's bed chamber. It has old and faded tapestry upon the walls, worked by the ladies of the family, adjoining is a small dressing room, and connected with that, the page's room. The ball room is very large, it has three bay windows with carved seats for the spectators. Passing an anteroom we went into the state bedroom which Queen Elizabeth is said to have once occupied. It is hung with Gobelin tapestry, scenes from AEsop's fables. The bed is of red and green velvet, lined with white satin and with a worked coverlid, now all faded. There was here, a looking glass of brass and tortoise shell. From here one could ascend to the tower, the oldest part, even anterior to the Conquest, and called Perverils' tower. From the anteroom we passed out upon the terrace, where Dorothy Vernon eloped with her lover and by her marriage united the houses of Vernon and Manners. We drove thence eight miles, through a beautiful country, to Mattock.

*Friday, July 17th, Birmingham*

Before leaving Mattock we took a drive and rode through the Via Gelly lead mines. The view from our hotel was very fine crags and woods opposite and a river below. It is a great place for marbles of all kinds, and the shops are full of little objects, made from them. We took the cars and after a ride of three hours, and a long waiting at Derby, reached this place.

*Saturday, July 18th, Birmingham.*

At about ten this morning we took the cars for Warwick which we reached in about half an hour, and then drove about eight miles to Stratford upon Avon. We passed, on our way, Charlecote, an ancient-looking mansion, surrounded by extensive grounds, where, tradition says, Shakespeare stole deer, and was found out and carried to the hall for a reprimand or punishment. It is now, as then, inhabited by the Lacy family. Stratford is a small place and only interesting as the birth-place of Shakespeare. We visited the house first of all. It is an ancient looking place with small bay windows. The entrance room had the same old stone floor as when the poet was a child there. In the kitchen was a huge old fireplace, in which I stood up easily. We went up a steep staircase to the room where he was born, where the walls were covered with the names of visitors. Walter Scott's name was on a window pane. There is a portrait of

*Shakespeare's birth place*

the poet in the room quite a fine one. The house is owned by a Shakespearean society.

Thence we went to the town hall. We saw a fine full length and a seated figure of Shakespeare by Wilson. Garrick founded the hall, and there was a portrait of him by Gainsborough. We saw the place where Shakespeare's house stood after the marriage with Ann Hathaway, and where he died. Then the old room in the Grammar School where he was taught. Thence we drove to the church; passing from the gate through an avenue of lime trees. The church is upon the Avon and the view from the back of it was very lovely of river and green meadows beyond. The monument to the memory of Shakespeare is in the chancel. It consists of his bust and coat of arms, a spear and a falcon holding a spear and two genii with reversed torches. The inscription is:

*Indicio Pylium, genior Saceratum, arte Maronem.*
*Terra tegit, populus maeret, olympus habet.*"

----

*Stay passenger why goest thou by so fast.*
*Read, if thou canst, whom envious death hast plast,*
*Within this monument, Shakespeare, with whom*
*Quick nature died, whose name doth deck this tomb.*
*Far more than cost shall all that he hath writ*
*Leave living art but page to scribe his wit.*
          *Obit A.D. 1616.*          *aetatis 63.*

*Stratford Upon Avon Church*

His grave is under a slab below, upon which the inscription by himself is,

*Good friend for Jesus' sake forbear*
*To dig the bones enclosed here.*
*Blest be the man, that spares these stones*
*And cursed be he that moves my bones.*

We returned to Warwick in a shower, and then drove five miles in another direction to Kenilworth, to see the ruins of the wicked Liecester's castle. The old gateway is now a house, made such by Cromwell's soldiers. We went into one room, where was a rich marble mantel piece, taken from one of the castle rooms and above it oak carving, with Leicester's initials and E.R. and his arms and ragged staff. The room is paneled with wood taken from the ruins. Through this then splendid gateway of four towers Queen Elizabeth rode in state, when she went to visit her favorite. Beyond is a large court, and this leads to another, enclosed on all sides but the front by buildings. To the right is Caesar's Tower the oldest part of the castle and the walls were immensely thick. We stood in the lower part, and, looking up, saw remains of frescoes in the small tower. Behind this was the kitchen, now unmarked except by the remains of a fireplace. At the end of the court, and forming one side of it, is the banquet hall with fine large bay and Gothic windows. In one of the towers are windows belonging to what are called Queen Elizabeth's dressing room and sitting room but the walls and floor are gone. On the left is Leicester's Tower where were his private rooms the date is 1571. The ruins are much broken and draped in ivy and very picturesque. Looking from the windows we saw flat meadows where were the beautiful pleasure grounds and where now, a lake can be formed by letting on water over a part of them. We returned and took the cars again to this place. Between Kenilworth and Warwick we passed "Guy's Cliff," a house once the retreat of Guy of Warwick and his wife, and near which they are probably buried. Also near by is Blacklow Hill where is a pedestal and cross to the memory of Piers Gaveston Edward II's favorite beheaded here by Guy of Warwick.

*Sunday, July 19th, Birmingham.*

I did not go to church in the morning, having a headache but in the evening went to Dr. James' a Congregational chapel and heard him preach a sermon upon "giving" which was very good. He is a celebrated preacher having written some excellent works. He is 73 years old and has been settled here 50 years, but though grey-headed appears hale and active.

*Monday, July 20th, Oxford.*

Again we stopt at Warwick, and this time to see the castle. We entered the gateway and walked through a path cut in the solid rock shaded with trees and ivy vines. Passing through another gateway we entered the court of grass. Attached to the right wall of the gate is "Guy's Tower" a plain round tower built in 1394, to the left is Caesar's Tower the oldest portion of the buildings. Within the court, which is surrounded by a high stone wall is the present mansion of the earls of Warwick. We entered this and came first to the baronial hall. It is paved with red and white marble and the ceiling is of carved wood. Around the walls are hung arms among which was Oliver Cromwell's helmet. Adjoining this was the dining room where the most remarkable object was a carved sideboard ornamented with scenes from "Kenilworth," as Queen Elizabeth's entry into the gate, her discovery of Amy Robsart in the arbour, Leicester at the queen's feet, etc. it was very finely done. From here we went to a small drawing room, in which was a Florentine mosaic table, once owned by Marie Antoinette. From the large drawing room there were fine views of the river Avon far below and the park in the distance. In the state bedroom the bed and furniture had been Queen Ann's but was given to the

Warwick family by George III, it was partly of red velvet and embroidery. We returned by a long corridor at one end of which was the celebrated picture by Vandyke of Charles I on horseback and his armour bearer. It had no frame and stood out like life.

After leaving the castle, we walked in the park, and visited the house erected for the Warwick vase, by the grandfather of the present earl. This vase was found at Hadrian's villa Tivoli, and is 124 feet in circumference, the designs are heads of Hercules, and lion skins, in high relief; it is of white marble, and a huge thing. Near the outer gateway is a small room containing relics of the family. There was the immense porridge bowl where Guy of Warwick who was a giant of 9 feet ate his porridge, and eight soldiers with him. Also a thing like a pitchfork to fish meat from the pot. The bowl is now used for punch, and the woman who showed it, said she had twice seen it filled, when the present earl came of age. It takes 16 gallons of rum 18 of brandy 100 lbs. of sugar etc. Here was also Guy's shield of iron, an inch thick, his breast plate and helmet, two handed sword and walking staff a huge long pole. We saw also the marshal's rod of Ralph Neville "the king maker." Thence we visited a hospital, in which twelve poor soldiers are maintained. It was purchased by Robert Leicester in 1571 as a retreat for his poor servants and retainers, and is several hundred years older than that but well preserved. It is of the style so common in Chester carved beams and painted. The Leicester arms are scattered here and there. The master who is a descendant of the family has rooms at the end of the court. We went into a hall formerly the Guildhall, before used as a hospital. Up stairs we saw some of the soldiers rooms they were very nice. They are obliged to wear a cloak, with a silver badge of the bear and staff on pain of a fine if they do not, whenever they go out of the building. In one room we saw a richly carved wooden cabinet or bureau taken from Kenilworth and said to have been used there by Queen Elizabeth. Also a piece of needle work the bear and staff and coronet worked, as they say, by Amy Robsart.

From here we drove to St. Mary's Church a very ancient one. At the end of the church is the tomb of Thomas Beauchamp Earl of Warwick in Ed. III's reign and his wife with full length effigies of white marble. In an adjoining chapel is the tomb of Richard Beauchamp of Henry VI's reign it is a brass effigy representing him lying upon his helmet with his feet upon a bear he was the ancestor of the Dudleys. Near by is the tomb of Robert Dudley, and his third wife who survived him, it is of marble, with an ornamental canopy, and the arms. Also that of his brother Ambrose Dudley. We saw here the tomb of a young boy, son of Robert Dudley, called in the inscription "an imp," the old form of expression for a person of that age. We went to the hotel for some refreshment and then took the cars and in about an hour reached Oxford. We find that we can not see "Blenheim House", because of the recent death of the Duke of Marlborough. I am sorry for this.

*Tuesday, July 21st, Oxford, Eng.*

Today a member of Parliament is to be elected from here; the candidates are Mr. Cardwell and Mr. Thackeray and this hotel "the Star" is the gathering place for those of Mr. Cardwell's party so that it has been very noisy all day. We started off on our sightseeing, and visited first Christ Church College. It is like most of the colleges built around a square. We ascended the tower where "Great Tom" the great university bell is, and saw the view from there. Then we went into the hall where all the members of the college dine together. It was furnished with tables and benches, has a carved oak ceiling and portraits hung on the walls, of Queen Elizabeth, several bishops of Durham, and celebrated members of the college, in times past. Oxford Cathedral is the particular church of this college. Part of it is in the Norman style, and some of a later period. Prayers are read here morning and evening. Cardinal Wolsey commenced Christ Church College, but fell before its completion. We passed from here, down a broad walk with Christ Church meadow on one side and Merton fields on the other and behind these Corpus Christi and Merton Colleges. The walk was shaded by large beech trees and is called Addison's Walk. We came out at the Botanical Gardens. Prof. Danberry is the Prof. of this department, and he lives on the grounds. They are very beautifully laid out in flower beds and shrubbery. The plants have their botanical names and part are arranged on the natural and part on the Linnaean system. We went into several conservatories, saw a small banyan tree and a coffee tree also a cinnamon tree. In another were water plants, red, blue and white lilies, and a splendid lotus plant with large rich buff flowers, papyrus too with leaves like fennel growing on a long stalk. There was a grass garden with many species of that plant. Near by were two apple trees upon which the mistletoe was growing. It is propagated by merely rubbing a berry on the stem of a tree. The golden yew was a beautiful tree.

Nearly opposite these gardens was Magdalen College which we next visited. In an antechapel, was a large painted window, of the last judgement, it was fine, and the colors dark and rich. The chapel stalls were much carved and the screen too. We went through the cloisters, the buildings are quite attractive with some oriel windows, and ivy clambering over parts. Thence we visited the Bodleian Library. The room we first entered was very plain. There were bookcases of stone and pictures of eminent men on the walls, Archbishop Land, Philip Sidney in burnt wood, Pope, Addison, Wm. IV and his queen. Here also was a chair made from the ship, in which Drake sailed round the world. Guy Fawke's lantern, and a facsimile of the letter of warning written anonymously to Lord Montague. There were models of various buildings. One done by natives of a palace in India five stories high and all built under ground for the sake of coolness. In a lower room were more books and reading rooms. We saw an ornamented book of Queen Elizabeth's, a Saxon calendar consisting of a stick, with the days marked upon it. The library consists of 300,000 volumes. Looking from the windows we saw Braze Nose College and All Souls' and in front the Radcliffe Library. In the afternoon we went to see the "Martyr's Memorial" erected at the junction of two streets in imitation of the Waltham Cross to commemorate the death of Cranmer Latimer and Ridley. They are represented on each side of the monument. It is a very rich Gothic structure. Opposite Baliol College a cross in the street marks the spot where they were burnt.

From here we went to the Divinity School where they dispute on certain subjects, and where Cranmer used to dispute. The roof is very rich indeed. Here Charles I held once a parliament, when the plague was in London. Thence we went to the Radcliff Library. This contains only 20,000 books; it is a circular building and quite handsome. Returning through the court of the Bodleian Library, we saw the Clarendon building, built from the funds arising from the sale of Clarendon's *History of the Rebellion* and used as a printing office. Near by is the theatre or Great Hall, it is circular and so well arranged that it can accommodate 4,000 persons. Here the chancellor of the university has a seat. On opposite sides are two richly carved rostra, one for the Latin the other for the English orations and when these are delivered the pit and galleries are crowded. Once Bishop Herber made an oration here which was received with such applause, that his aged father was much overcome, and never fully recovered from it. Fellows are those who by a certain scholarship are entitled to quite a handsome allowance, and home in the college, and nothing in particular to do, some have clerical livings.

The Ashmolean Museum is near the theatre, it is rather out of repair and another building is being prepared to receive the curiosities. The principal ones were King Alfred's jewel found with his name upon it, near the place where he is said to have watched the cakes. It is of gold and has a figure in mosaic or painted under a crystal. Queen Elizabeth's watch a large thick one studded with turquoises. Oliver Cromwell's watch a clumsy thing of silver with a catgut spring and no minute hand. A ring of the Bishop of York son of the Pretender with a portrait of his father and mother on each side. A shoe of the Hermit of Dinden, made of bits of leather nailed together, as was also his whole dress. A lodestone so powerful as to hold up 100 pounds, and communicate magnetism by merely rubbing steel upon it. There were shells arranged according to the species, a head and foot of a Dodo bird now extinct, a stuffed sloth one of the peculiarities of which, I did not know before, that it can turn its head entirely round. We saw the new college chapel, it is something like Magdalen. In the antechapel is a fine painted window of the nativity, to which in looking from the interior the organ seems to form a frame. The carving and stone work is fine, and the cloisters attractive with ivy growing up over them.

We saw the garden of St. John's Chapel, it is very beautiful with smooth grass, shrubs and fine trees, a charming place to study. We afterwards visited the university press and first the part where Bibles are printed, one million and a half Bibles testaments and prayer books are printed yearly. One side is devoted to the university books. We saw several processes, pressing by hydraulic power to give gloss and smoothness etc. Returning after our day of pleasure-work, we found that the election was decided against Thackeray in favor of Cardwell that the opponents had broken windows of the hotel and rushed in with rude weapons to murder Cardwell if they could find him. We were very glad not to have been here. One poor man, being ill before nearly died from the excitement and weariness of his office of clerk.

*Wednesday, July 22nd, Windsor.*
We left Oxford in the twelve o'clock train for Windsor. The ride was short, we drove over to the town three miles, from the Slough Station and stopt at the "Castle Hotel" very near to the royal castle. We took a drive in the afternoon. We entered the castle gate, and drove down the long avenue, which extends from the front of the castle three miles in a straight line. On either side is a foot path lined with trees. At the farther end we walked up a hill to see the equestrian statue of George III put up, upon a pedestal of rocks, by his son George IV. Then we drove three miles more, through the park, and found it very pleasant indeed. The trees were fine. We passed by the royal lodge, or conservatory as it is now. It was the summer residence of George IV and larger then, he used to come there to rest. Prince Alfred, they say, came here last summer to study. Not far off was the hunting lodge, once the residence of the duke of Cumberland, and in sight of this, an obelisk erected in memory of the victory at Culloden, gained by the "Butcher Cumberland" as the Scotch called him.

We left the carriage, and took a charming walk along the Virginia water. It is a lake of considerable length, narrow, but winding almost like a river. We met several picnic parties and found it delightful, along the bank, on the soft turf, and among the trees. In one spot were some imitation ruins, and a waterfall was made in a small brook. A fishing temple stood on the opposite side of the lake, a pretty little building, red and buff like a Chinese pagoda. It is for the royal family and a little yacht is anchored there for their use. This park contains 1800 acres, and is open to the public, the home park near the castle is strictly private.

After meeting the carriage we drove on to see the Runnymeade made famous, in the time of King John, for the signing of the Magna Charta. It is a long flat smooth meadow, extending along the river Thames and just opposite, in the river is the "Magna Charta Island" where the barons took John from the press on the meadow to make him sign the Charta which he did on a table that is shown there. We wanted to go across but the people who live on the island refused us permission and we had no boat. We returned to Windsor and from the long avenue had a glimpse of Frogmore and saw the gardens, the property of K. R. K. the Duchess of Kent. Prince Albert's farm lands are near by.

### Thursday, July 23rd, Cambridge.

Windsor Castle could not be seen till eleven so we visited Eton College first. It was founded by Henry VI is of brick with oriel windows, except the chapel which is stone. There are seventy boys who are supported on the foundation, others board with the masters making in all 500. They wear gowns. The first quadrangle is quite large, the next smaller with cloisters around it, for the fellows. The Eton scholar's highest ambition is to have a fellowship in King's College Cambridge to which they are admitted to the number of five a year to fill up vacancies. It is rather singular, that the foundation boys generally have more of these than the ophidians, though so much fewer in number. We went into the dining hall. They have bread, meat and ale and a clean cloth every day. The library though small is quite valuable. It is for the masters and fellows only. The chapel is a fine Gothic building. In the ante-chapel is a marble statue of Henry VI and some stained glass windows. In the centre of a large court where many of the scholars were studying, talking or playing is a bronze figure of Henry VI. Eton Monteni has been abolished.

On returning we went to Windsor Castle. This covers a large surface of ground. In one tower near the chief court King John was imprisoned before being taken to Runnymeade. Another tower is called Queen Elizabeth's, and a row of buildings a little removed from the principal part of the castle, was the castle of her time. Windsor Castle was used by the Saxons, even long before the Conquest. The present building was begun by the Conqueror but altered by Ed. III and still later by George IV. The queen's private apartments at the farther end of the court are not shown except by very special permission. We saw only the state rooms. We were ushered first into a small audience room. Upon the wall was Gobelin tapestry, representing Esther fainting, her purification, and Haman leading the horse of Mordecai. The next room was quite large and called the Vandyke Drawing Room, being solely adorned on one side, with pictures by that master, and on the other side windows looked out upon the court. Among these paintings was Charles 1st Henrietta and a child also the children of Charles 1st etc. The furniture was gilt with green and buff silk damask. The next room contained paintings by Zuccherelli mostly landscapes. The way there led through a small dining room used as such for hundreds of years and ornamented with old Gobelin tapestry. Thence we passed through a hall lined with arms and banners, and then into the grand audience room. The ceiling is richly gilt, the walls covered with tapestry and the furniture of a rich crimson satin and velvet damask. From here we went into St. George's Hall. At one end of this was a throne with Edward III 1350 carved upon it. The ceiling is covered with the arms of those who have received the honor of Knights of the Garter which is here conferred by the sovereign. In larger size the arms of the sovereigns who have received the order, are also painted upon the wall. It is used as a banquet hall, and is of large size. In another hall were some curiosities, an Indian palanquin and lady's chair, and a piece of the mast of Nelson's ship. A chair from a tree on the field of Waterloo, a chair of Walter Scott's made from a tree near the scene of *Tam O'Shanter.*

After finishing our survey of the state apartments we mounted to the top of one of the larger towers, where we had a fine view of all the country around. We walked upon a terrace outside the castle and overhanging the home park. From a gateway we saw the church of Stoke Pogis, the scene of Gray's *Elegy on a Country Churchyard* and not far off a large house with a dome, where Wm. Penn, used to live. We were then going into the chapel but found that the Queen of Holland had just arrived to see the castle and other visitors must wait. So we went to take a lunch and then to the queen's stables or mews as they call them. When the queen is at the castle there are about 110 horses and 50 carriages in the stables. We saw several gray ponies and a beautiful white Arabian horse, also some little Spanish ponies for the children. The state carriages were not there. We saw one with four seats and an awning given by Louis Philippe, and a little pony carriage in which the queen drives herself out alone. One stable was for the prince's horses. It was all very neat and clean, quite luxurious quarters for horses.

We went then to St. George's Chapel. The Queen of Holland had not yet come out, so we waited, and had a good view of her as she got into her carriage. She is of a fair complexion and very pleasant expression, wearing small curls in front. The chapel is fine, the roof is of fan tracery work with circles in the centre. One window in a side aisle is very beautiful, the nativity from designs by West. In one corner is a little chapel with a monument to the Princess Charlotte, daughter of George IV and wife of Leopold of Belgium. It represents her body upon a bed, covered with drapery, four ladies-in-waiting kneeling by the side, and weeping, while her spirit ascends to heaven, and an angel carries her little infant. There is a gilded canopy above and stained glass windows of rich color. The choir is very rich. The queen's seat is a little carved window above. She seldom comes here but has a private chapel. In the floor is the vault of the George's and Wm. IV, opened only in that way. In the aisle surrounding the choir are buried on one side Henry VIII and Jane Seymour, Edward IV and Elizabeth Woodville, and on the other Henry VI and Charles Brandon Duke of Suffolk. Wolsey's chapel is not shown. We took the cars in the afternoon for London then rode three quarters of an hour through the city and took the cars again for Cambridge.

### Friday, July 24th, London.

We went out at an early hour this morning to make our survey of Cambridge. At first we visited Trinity College founded by Henry VIII. His statue is over the gate, which leads to a fine court in the centre of which was an ornamented well or fountain. We went into the dining hall, the ceiling is of oak beams with pendants, at one end are two oriel windows and the walls are ornamented with paintings, one, of Newton, who was educated here, and whose observatory was over the gateway. It is now vacation, so there were few about the colleges. We even went into the kitchen, the fireplace was huge and many spits stood before it, in a store room were 120 large stone jars of currant jelly. In another part of the buildings, is the combination room, where the fellows retire after dinner, to eat their dessert, which they alone have. We then went to the chapel. In the ante-chapel is a very fine statue of Newton by Roubillac. The folds of the gown are very well executed, he holds a prism in his hand, and his face has an earnest expression. He once stood for seventeen hours in that position, when he discovered the prismatic colors. Opposite is a seated figure of Lord Bacon, who was also of this college. In the

126.

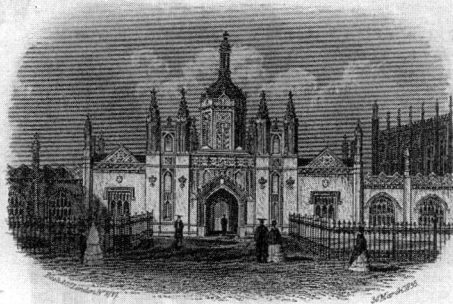

Entrance to Kings College, Cambridge.

There casts of King's a very The handsome of open- divides court ... were other models antiques &c. College is fine one gateway is & a sort- -work screen the first from the

street. The chief object of interest is the Chapel It is the finest we have seen & was begun by Henry VI & completed by Henry VIII The exterior is ornamented with crowns & roses. There are no less than 27 windows in the church, of stained glass. The screen & organ are carved with Henry VIII's & Anne Boleyn's arms. The floor of the choir is paved with black & white marble & upon the altar is a picture of the descent from the cross by Daniel da Volterra. The effect of the interior is very striking from

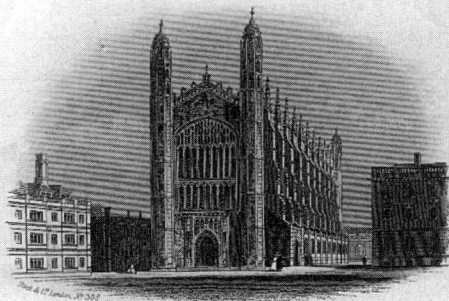

Chapel of Kings College, Cambridge.

the unusual comparison width. we went Observatory quite a A notice not admitted" sent in with ... height in with the From here to the which is at distance. said "Strangers But Uncle his card United States

*Journal page 126, a portion of the entry for July 24th when the travelers were in Cambridge.*

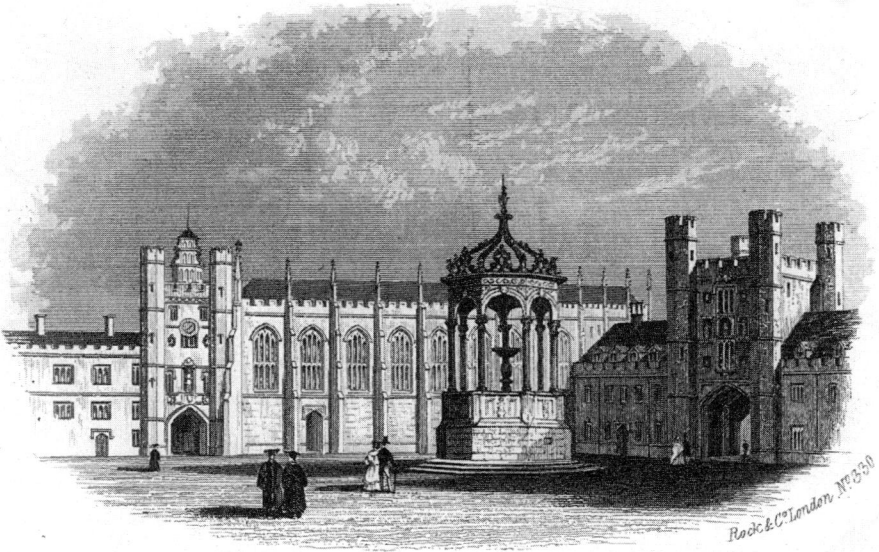

*Trinity College, Cambridge*

chapel is some handsome carving by Gibbons. The library is a very fine one & consists of one long room with windows at one end looking upon the grounds and alcoves along the sides with busts of celebrated men above them. We saw here a manuscript of Milton's a part of Lycidas, and part of *Paradise Lost* arranged as a drama, which was the original plan. Also a sheet of the Scotch Covenant with the names "Maitland Boyd" etc. signed to it, drawn up in the time of Charles 1st, when he tried to introduce episcopacy into Scotland. A pair of Queen Elizabeth's shoes large, gilded, pointed at the toes, and slip shod at the heels. We saw also Newton's mathematical instruments, and the telescope which he used in making his discoveries.

We then walked down a shady walk across the bridge of the Cam, and around into St. John's College grounds. The entrance and cloisters are of the fan tracery work. We passed by the modern buildings, and crossing a bridge made in imitation of the Bridge of Sighs in Venice came to the old part founded by the countess of Richmond. They are of brick, and look well, but we only entered the dining hall, in which there is nothing in particular.

We then visited the Church of the Holy Sepulchre built in imitation of the one at Jerusalem. It has no connection with the college, but is of early Norman style, round, with later additions. We saw then Jesus College. The chapel and cloisters belonged to a nunnery in the time of

*Trinity Walk, Cambridge*

*Church of the Holy Sepulchre, Cambridge*

Henry II. The tomb of the last abbess is in the ante chapel. The chapel has been restored, with its Norman arches, which had been covered up by Cromwell. The glass windows are of the lancet style narrow and high. We went to Christ College, to see a mulberry tree planted by Milton in the garden. It is a gnarly thing, but still bears fruit. When a branch falls, it is carefully divided among the fellows. The university library consisting of about 200,000 volumes, is not usually shown to visitors but as we were from the United States they allowed us to enter. This library is

*Chapel of King's College, Cambridge*

entitled to a copy of every book published in Great Britain. A new part is being added, to surround the old.

We also went to the Fitzwilliam Museum though it was not the hour of admission. It is a fine building and much ornamented. It contains paintings by the old masters though nothing very striking. We saw here a model of the palace tomb of Agra East Indies. It is made of ivory and very beautiful. The original is of white marble and precious stones and erected by the emperor who promised his wife when she was dying that she should have a tomb the most splendid ever made. There were other models casts of antiques etc.

King's College is a very fine one. The gateway is handsome and a sort of open-work screen divides the first court from the street. The chief object of interest is the chapel. It is the finest we have seen and was begun by Henry VI and completed by Henry VIII. The exterior is ornamented with crowns and roses. There are no less than 27 windows in the church, of stained glass. The screen and organ are carved with Henry VIII's and Anne Boleyn's arms. The floor of the choir is paved with black and white marble and upon the altar is a picture of the descent from the cross by Daniel da Volterra. The effect of the interior is very striking from the

*The Observatory, Cambridge*

unusual height in comparison with the width.

From here we went to the observatory which is at quite a distance. A notice said "Strangers not admitted" but Uncle sent in his card with United States upon it and soon, a young man the son of Mr. C. the astronomer came out and received us very pleasantly. He showed us the transit instrument and we went in and met his sister whom he introduced and afterwards his mother & another sister. They were quite pleasant and sociable, and showed us portraits of astronomers, about whom they seemed to know a great deal. Then the brother and first sister took us to the observatory proper, where we saw the large telescope given by the Duke of Northumberland, a very fine one. We came away, much pleased with our visit here. Then we went to All Saints' Church to see the grave of Henry Kirke White. It is a simple tablet but on the wall is a marble one erected by a brother of Dr. Boot who admired his poetry very much. The tablet is Henry Kirke White born March 21st 1785 died Oct. 19th 1806.

> *Warm with fond hope and learning's sacred flame*
> *To Granta's bowers the youthful poet came.*
> *Unconquered powers the immortal mind displayed*
> *But worn with anxious thought the frame decayed.*
> *Pale o'er his lamp, and in his cell retired,*

*The martyr student faded and expired.*
*O genius! taste! and piety sincere!*
*Too early lost midst duties too severe*
*Foremost to mourn was generous Southey seen*
*He told the tale and showed what White had been*
*Nor told in vain for o'er the Atlantic wave*
*A wanderer came, and sought the poet's grave,*
*On yon low stone he saw his lonely name*
*And raised this fond memorial to his fame.*

                                        *W.S.*

We took an afternoon train to London.

*Saturday, July 25th, Thomas Hotel, London*

We are in our old quarters again. Have spent the day in doing various business. We took a drive and walk in the park. The grass is really yellow from want of rain.

*Sunday, July 26th, London*

Heard Dr. Hamilton preach. His church is in Regent Square. In the evening we had an excellent sermon from Baptist Noel whose church is in John St. He is a thin man with grey hair and a delightfully sweet face.

*Monday, July 27th, Dover.*

The French signature was required to be put on our passports as we were going to Calais and we were delayed till nearly five o'clock, and were late in reaching Dover. The hotel was full, with a Scotch regiment the 42nd I believe about to embark for India.

*Tuesday, July 28th, Lille*

It was rather an unpropitious morning raining hard. We could see the white cliffs of Dover where Julius Caesar landed. We took the Calais steamer at eleven and made the passage in two hours, but it was very rough indeed. We shipped seas several times and most people were very sick. Auntie, M. and I managed to keep well by lying perfectly still, but poor Uncle was quite upset and so weak and sick, when we landed, that we had to go to the hotel in Calais, to let him rest two or three hours. We took the cars for Lille passed through St. Omer. The country was fertile, crops being just gathered in. Much flax is raised about Lille. Lille thread is the linen twisted.

*Anvers*

*Wednesday, July 29th, Antwerp, Belgium.*

We left Lille this morning at eleven and arrived here at half-past five. We entered Belgium at Mouscron and had a little delay at the custom-house. Belgium has now a king of its own, Leopold, whose first wife was the Princess Charlotte, his second a daughter of Louis Philippe. The country was once united to Holland under the name of the Netherlands, but the last French revolution separated them. We passed through Ghent and saw the cathedral from the cars. It has two towers, and a square belfry at some little distance. John of Gaunt was born here and hence named. Charles V was born here also. We passed through Alost and then Mechlin and reached Antwerp after changing five or six times. It was very hot and dusty.

We are in quite a good hotel, rather Frenchy in character and in full view of the cathedral the tower of which Napoleon compared to Mechlin lace for its delicate fret-work. Mary and I took a walk after dinner. In the centre of the square which is nearly opposite to us is a bronze statue of Rubens, some of whose best works are in this place. The left tower of the cathedral is fine, but the other is still unfinished. We saw many curious looking houses with gables facing the street. The women wear great muslin caps, with huge lappets and some large calico cloaks, with hoods, which they wear over the head like sunbonnets. Dog carts are much used

here. The cathedral has 97 bells for chiming. At each half hour there is
an air from Lucretia chimed and at each hour a romance or vice versâ. It
sounds well.

*Thursday, July 30th, Antwerp.*
    Mary and I went out this morning with a valet de place to see the
sights of Antwerp. We went first to the museum or academy. While there
a Persian ambassador to Belgium with his suite came in. He was dressed
in a high pointed cap of fur or beaver a cashmere figured coat with short
sleeves and pink cambric undersleeves, with white pantaloons. He had two
brooches or decorations on his breast. Two of his suite were dressed much
like him and two more in the military costume. In the entrance hall of the
academy was a black effigy of Isabella of Burgundy. The pictures were
mostly by Rubens and finer than we have before seen. *The Crucifixion*
represented the Saviour on the cross and a soldier piercing his side. On
either hand are the thieves and a soldier is breaking the legs of one of
them, with an iron bar, he is convulsed with agony and has torn one foot
from the nail. The Magdalen who kneels, is urging the one who pierces
the Saviour, to forbear and the Virgin, John and another Mary stand by
full of grief. It is a picture, almost too painful to look at, but shows great
power in the artist. A Madonna and child, and Joseph behind them shows
more beauty in the faces, than usual for Rubens. St. Theresa kneels in the
dress of a nun and two little angels are half drawing a poor creature from
the fires below. Thomas looking at the marks in the hands of our Lord, it
is not as fine as some, of this subject that we have seen. On the two wings
of this picture, are the portraits of the Burgomaster Rickkox and his wife.
His, is a very fine painting, and an interesting face. The adoration of the
Magi is a very large picture, the child is held by its mother, one king bows
with a censer before them, the others stand by. Anna teaching the virgin;
an angel is bringing to the latter a wreath of flowers. We saw a crucifixion
by Vandyke who is a scholar of Rubens. It is a dark scene, Sts. Catherine
and Domenick are near the cross, two little angels with reversed torches
stand near by. We saw a Pieta by Quentin Matsys a blacksmith, who
became a painter, because he fell in love with the daughter of one. It is of
an early age and stiff but some of the heads are soft and pleasing. A portrait of Otho Vennius a master of Rubens a fine picture and pleasant face.
    Leaving the academy we saw among other objects of interest Rubens'
house. It is quite a large one and handsomely ornamented. Vandyke's
also which is a handsome one of brown stone. The general appearance of
the city is pleasant. In general the streets are broad and clean, and the
houses cream color or white. We drove around the docks and along the
Scheldt in one part were two American ships. We passed the citadel which

*The Bourse of Antwerp*

was, in 1832, besieged by the French with over 64,000 men and went into the Bourse. This is a large square roofed with glass though former-ly open to the air. The merchants, used formerly to meet here to transact their business.

    Afterwards we visited the church of St. Jacques. This is much orna-mented with marbles, but the chief thing of interest in it is the chapel where Rubens lies buried with others of his family. The altar piece is by him. It represents himself, his two wives and children, his father and cousin, under the figures of St. George, Martha, and Mary Magdalen, angels, St. Jerome and his grandfather as Time. The coloring is fine and some of the faces beautiful. In this church was a fine piece of brown stone carving, the rising of the cross, in high relief, done by Vervoort. This afternoon we have been to the church of the Augustines it is very plain in itself. The altar piece contains more than twenty figures. It represents the marriage of St. Catherine, with the Virgin and child upon a pedestal Joseph, Peter and Paul, saints on the steps and below St. Augustine, St. Lawrence, and St. George. The Ecstasy of St. Augustine is by Vandyke, the light upon the face of the saint is fine, he is upheld by angels. The cathedral we saw last. It is plain within, of the Gothic pointed arch style, and has seven aisles. On the high altar is the Assumption of the Virgin painted in 16 days for 1600 florins. But the chief interests here are two pictures with wings by Rubens. One is the elevation of the cross, and the wings are women weeping and the Virgin and John standing apart and soldiers. The other painting the Descent From the Cross is very fine. Death is most wonderfully depicted in the lifeless body, and its contrast with the white sheet is striking, Joseph is a fat good looking man and all are assisting in the sacred office. The wings of this are the salutation of Elizabeth to Mary and the presentation in the temple. We have noticed today the queer caps of the women and besides these some of the ugliest bonnets conceivable, more like coal skuttles than anything else.

*Friday, July 31st, The Hague, Holland.*

We left Antwerp this morning at twelve. The cars were very good, in the English style and the country flat and uninteresting. We crossed the border into Holland at Roosendaal where the baggage was examined. After riding some distance further we took a steamboat on the river Meuse for Rotterdam and owing to head winds were two hours on the way. The scene was peculiar; Dutch craft heavy and ungraceful were sailing sluggishly along. We saw 50 or 60 windmills, 22 in one spot looking funny enough. Stopt a moment at Dort an island in the broad river or delta. There was an ecclesiastical council held here by the Dutch divines at one time. Passed one or two other small towns until we came to Rotterdam which is a large and very flourishing city. We drove along a canal which in many parts takes the place of streets. Many of the houses come almost down to the edge of the water. The canals are quite stagnant and covered with a green scum.

We took the cars again for three quarters of an hour. The level country was unbroken save by the canals which divided off the fields where black and white cattle were feeding. We saw storks, much venerated by the Dutch. Windmills and straight rows of trees made up the landscape. We passed through Delft Haven where the Pilgrim fathers first embarked in the *Mayflower*. We also passed through Ruyswick. Along the canals, we saw many tea houses, like little summer houses, where families or friends meet to drink tea together. La Haye is the capital of Holland. We are in a hotel fronting a park or the "Bosch", as it is called, belonging to the royal palace, where are deer. Canals are seen everywhere here also.

*Saturday, Aug. 1st, The Hague.*

We visited the museum first which contains many paintings of the Dutch school. A piece by Paul Potter and one of his finest works, a bull, cow, and sheep with one man. There were two other cattle pieces by him and very life-like. Flowers by Rachel Ruysch. Fruit by Heem. A piece by Gerard Dow which cost 5000 lbs a woman with a baby and older child.

Another of a woman holding a light. A large battle piece by Wouvermans. Portrait of Prince Maurice and of Prince Eugene of Savoy by Rembrandt. One by Bol of Admiral de Ruyter, a large coarse face. A pretty landscape by Both. The crow stript of the feathers it had taken from other birds by Hondekoeter. A grocery shop by M. Van Meiris very life-like. A cottage door with musicians and boors drinking by Ostade. A doctor feeling a girl's pulse by Steen. The alchemist in his kitchen surrounded by crucibles etc. by Teniers. Portraits by Albert Durer, brown and hard but good. There were also some Italian pictures.

From the windows we saw a pond with a green island in the middle made by Prince Maurice. Below, in the first story were many curiosities. The guns used on Admiral de Ruyter's ship, large, heavy things. The armour, chain and medal and rich sword that he wore. The coat breeches hat and pistols which Wm. of Orange had on when he was killed. And a large enameled watch once owned by him. A medal of the house of Peter the Great at Saardam. Chinese and Indian curiosities. A large model of the island of Desima in Japan where the Dutch reside, and many other curious objects.

We took somewhat of a survey of the city. Saw a square with a bronze statue of Wm. the Silent, and another square ornamented by a statue of the late king Wm. II. We stopt to look at the palace of the present king Wm. III. It is of brick and painted a light color and very simple. Opposite and in a garden is the late kings palace. We went into a square lined with houses, where is a Gothic building called the Binnenhof, the only remaining part, of the old Palace of the Counts of Holland. It is of brick and within is a hall the roof of which is of open beams something like that of Westminster Hall. It is the oldest house in the Hague. Opposite, the grand pensioner Barneveldt was executed. We saw over a gateway the prison where De Witt was imprisoned and it was near the museum on the border of the grand vivier that he was torn to pieces by the people who falsely suspected him of an attempt to assassinate the Prince of Orange in 1672. We saw the very modest houses or palaces of the king's brother and uncle. The houses are mostly of brick and the streets paved with the same. The city has a quiet pleasant appearance.

In the afternoon we took a drive in the Bosch which is really quite a wood intersected by canals which in one place widen into a lake. The "house in the Wood" is the queens palace. It is built mostly of brick, but the interior is quite unique. We were shown into a dining room with black and white Turkey carpet and blue and white chairs and all as neat and cool as could be. Then into a room papered with Chinese paper, another had satin embroidered chairs a present from the emperor of

China, as well as many rich pieces of silk embroidery which hung upon the walls. There were many articles corresponding, large jars, and pieces of lacquer work inserted in the walls, and one room was hung with white satin embroidered, another had curtains of the same. There were also glass or porcelain chandeliers in the shape of flowers etc. The ball room was a hall covered with paintings referring to Prince Frederick Henry of Orange, by his wife a princess of Solms. The ceiling is a small dome. The hall opens upon a balcony from whence steps lead down to the garden where are flowers, and, farther on, a walk by the canal. A broad paved drive leads to this palace through the Bosch.

We saw a church called the Kelooster Kirk, which was once a Dominican convent and to the cloisters of it many French Protestants fled after the revocation of the edict of Nantes. Probably our Huguenot ancestors were among them for they were at the Hague. In the evening we went to the vegetable market, they were crying their wares. They wear mostly small caps and often a coarse hat bent down at the ears. This is a very peculiar place, the canals if clear would be a pleasant feature in the city. The water here is bad so we have to drink seltzer water mostly.

### Sunday, Aug. 2nd, The Hague.

We attended church at the English embassy in an obscure place.

### Monday, Aug. 3rd, Amsterdam, Holland.

We took an early train for Leydon, which we reached in about half an hour, and stopped there for a while, to see Mr. Seabold's Japanese Museum, considered the finest collection yet made. He is really a German or Belgian, but obtained admittance into Japan by calling himself "Low Dutch." We saw a model of a temple several houses and a cemetery, idols, and shrines, china as thin as paper, lacquer work, cloth, coins, two gold ones worth 400 florins, and most of these, had a hole for a string through the middle of them, bronzes, vases of quite a Roman form, straw dresses, brooms of cocoanut fibre, musical instruments and numerous other articles.

We drove a little around the town, and passed the Stadthouse which is an ornamented building, with the date 1598. Our Pilgrim Fathers with their Pastor Robinson lived here for some time but no one here seemed to know anything about them. We took the cars again and passed through. The railroad was built on a wash and sustained at first by wicker rafts. Arriving at Amsterdam, we rode a long way to reach the hotel. It is a busy place, we look out upon two canals and some queer gabled houses. The city is semicircular and has three or four large canals parallel and also circular, and 95 smaller ones. After taking a lunch Uncle, Mary and I set off for Brock the far-famed city of neatness. We drove down to the wharf and then took a steamboat to cross the Ig or eye as it is pronounced. It is an arm of the Zuider Zee which extended far away to our right. In the other direction lay Saardam where Peter the Great once lived. On board with us were some market women, returning home. Their head-dress was very singular. They have a broad gold band over their foreheads a large square pin each side and little rosette of false hair, their own they shave or cut. They have also a most peculiar bonnet, a white lace cap with quilled ruffle behind, ear-rings and a necklace of coral beads with a large gold clasp. Their gown was common. Some have silver instead of gold plates, and the ladies have diamonds and other jewels set in theirs. Others have a gold plate to fit the whole head and which shines through the cap. On reaching the other shore we embarked upon a canal boat on the Grand Canal which leads to the North Sea and upon which the great East Indiamen sail. In winter these waters are all frozen over and the people of all kinds go about on skates or in ice boats.

We were not long on our boat, but landed and took a gay colored carriage and rode upon a broad dike, along the canal, and a meadow on the other side, six feet below the level of the sea. We stopt at a dairy-farm. The first thing we were shown was the stable and it was so nice and clean that you could hardly give it such a name. It is divided into stalls, neatly painted white-washed, and with a floor of fine saw dust. In each stall crockery silver tins or anything of the sort, was arranged about, to make a show and here the family take their meals so as to save the rest of the house. We saw the cheese room where the little round cheeses are placed, then the milk room where is separated the milk of 25 cows. In the front of the stalls is a brick drain. The cows are washed twice a week in soap and water and their tails tied up to the wall. We went through several of the rooms, in one was a Friesland clock, of a kind unfortunately not made now; it will run 30 years without repair. All the houses have a sacred door never opened except to carry out a corpse, or at a marriage. The best room was in perfect order, ornamented with pictures and crockery.

At the entrance to Brock we left our carriage for such things are not allowed in the town. The streets or rather pathways are paved with brick in a kind of mosaic, and sanded. We crossed many pretty little bridges over canals. The houses are very nice, painted mostly buff or green, and placed at a distance from each other with a bit of garden about them. At the doors are usually placed shoes, to replace the sabots which are taken off on entering. We looked into the church and school house, and into one very small dwelling house. The beds were like berths in the wall and covered with a curtain. It is certainly the neatest town I ever was in, but more like a play town, than a real one. We drove by to the Ig and rowed across in a small boat as the steamer had not yet come.

*Tuesday, Aug. 4th, Dusseldorf, Prussia.*

We took a carriage this morning and drove about Amsterdam for about an hour or two. It is all built upon piles, and in some parts is a fine city. The water is too bad to drink and it is hard for the poor, who have sometimes in winter, to pay 10 cts. a bucket for their water. Almost all the houses have a front porch with one or two pair of steps and benches to sit upon. The gables are very peaked sometimes, and all have a crane at the top to draw up supplies to the top story, which answers the purpose of a barn or cellar. People are not allowed to carry baggage on a cart or carriage, but on the head.

We stopped at the museum to look at one or two paintings. There were 25 portraits all very lifelike indeed, one or two were drinking wine, others eating. Portrait of Mary daughter of Charles I and mother of Wm. III of Orange. *The Night Watch* by Rembrandt, containing a great number of figures with the light shining upon them. Also five of the drapers company. *The Evening School* in which are five different lights all admirably arranged by Gerard Dow. A waterfall by Ruysdael. A bear hunt by Paul Potter. We went afterwards to see the docks. The dykes are kept in constant repair at great expense, without this the city and country would be submerged. The Jews are 1/10 of the population. We have had a long hot fatiguing ride of 8 hours in the cars. The country was diversified, and quite pleasant after the sameness of Dutch scenery.

*Wednesday, Aug. 5th, Cologne, Prussia.*

We did not leave Dusseldorf until three in the afternoon, and had time to visit two or three of the galleries of paintings, of the modern school, now on exhibition. This school was formed in 1828 by Cornelius. We saw a beautiful view of the Jungfrau, also a Swiss lake scene, and a night scene, men, fishing, with a lantern and moon light. The child's secret, a little one whispering to her mother who is mending a dress while another tries to hear. A pretty fruit and flower piece. Several scenes in Norway. Storm on a sea coast. Two peasant boys, of rather large size, one gives the other some pennies and in the background is a monkey eating a carrot. A snow scene and pond with boys skating upon it. Portraits of two children by a young lady. A child dancing before her grandmother who is much pleased, the father and mother look on.

We went to the city gallery which is not very large. Here among other things was a painting representing Tasso upon the ground writing while Leonora and another lady pass by unnoticed. In another place was a small martyrdom of Huss by Lessing and two or three of his landscapes. The golden wedding represented an aged couple walking in a procession, while their little grandchildren carry green wreaths by their side. The school: an old schoolmaster figures on the blackboard one child is crying, in the corner is another, and the floor is cluttered up with flowers. A ruined church by Lansing. Besides the pictures, there is nothing of particular interest in Dusseldorf. We were only about an hour coming here but during that time a thunder shower came on, and since we arrived there has been a very severe one. We are in Deutz a suburb of Cologne which is reached by a bridge of boats visible from our windows. We have a good view of the town and its cathedral. It is noted for its bad smells as well as for its Cologne water. It was an old Roman colony and traces of the ancient wall remains.

### Thursday, Aug. 6th, Bonn, Prussia

The Prince of Wales was in the hotel with us, but we did not see him. We went into the city of Cologne across the bridge of boats. First we went to get some of the genuine Cologne water, and then to the cathedral. This is still quite unfinished, the western facade is to have two high towers, one is half finished, and the other is going on. 400 workmen are constantly employed upon it. It has three aisles. We admired very much five stained glass windows, presented by the present King Lewis of Bavaria. The colors are very rich. The ceiling is of wood, but I believe a stone one is preparing. The choir is circular and very beautiful and its height would contain the Centre Church at New Haven. The capitals of the pillars are gilded. In the sacristy we saw some very valuable articles. A large cross and huge ring of diamonds and emeralds given I believe by the King of Prussia. And a vase for the holy wafer of rock crystal and gold and all covered with precious stones. The most curious thing was the shrine of the Wise Men of the East. For they actually believe, that it contains their bones brought from Milan by Frederic Barbarossa. The front is of gold the rest silver gilt. It was once all covered with cameos and precious stones, many of which have been replaced by imitations; what remains is valued at 6,000,000 francs. In front is a topaz larger than the palm of my hand. The names of the wise men Gaspar Melchior and Balthazar are set in rubies and their skulls were once crowned with diamonds. Near by is a painting thought to be by Master Stephen of Cologne, the Virgin and child surrounded by saints and the wise men in adoration. Some of the heads are quite soft and expressive.

Upon the tower of the cathedral is a crane for raising stones which has been there a long time; the superstitious are afraid to have it removed. We next went to the Church of St. Gereon an early example of the use of the pointed arch. The nave is circular the pillars twisted and of blue and gold. The pointed arch is used only now and then. A flight of steps leads to the choir. All around upon the walls, are the skulls of the martyred St. Gereon and his followers, a ghastly ornament.

We took the cars for Bonn which is a short ride. Saw in the distance the Siebengeberge or Seven Mountains. On entering the town we passed the university, it is a plain building. We are just out of the city opposite the Hofgarten a pretty grove of trees. In the evening we went to Prof. Blake's Uncle's old instructor and friend. He is a very kind man, short and stout. We saw three of his daughters, and one son, also a cousin, a young lady from Amsterdam. The cousin the son and younger daughters speak some English, the other one French and Dr. B. German. Mrs. Blake is at the sea-side with a sick son.

### Friday, Aug. 7th, Bonn.

The weather not very pleasant. We went to Mr. Webers where Uncle and Auntie boarded when in Bonn before. We saw Mrs. Weber. The sky grew brighter and we made an excursion we had planned to Rolandseck with the three Miss Blakes and their cousin Miss Sette. We drove out about two hours the road was through an avenue of trees with fields beyond. We passed by Godisberg a very picturesque ruined castle erected by the archbishop of Cologne and blown up by the Bavarians, because it upheld the Protestant archbishop. At Rolandseck we left the carriage and climbed up the hill. One ruined arch only remains. The legend says, that it was erected by Roland the nephew of Charlemagne, to overlook the island of Nonnenwerth, where, in a convent, his betrothed had taken the veil, thinking he was killed in the wars. He died soon after her burial. The view from here up and down the Rhine upon the bank of which this castle is, is very fine. On the opposite shore is the "castled crag" of Drachenfels so called from a dragon vanquished by Siegfried who built the castle. It is one of the Siebengeberge almost all of which have some castle upon them or legend connected with them. One is Petersberg with a convent upon it. On the isle of Nonnenwerth is still a convent, and a school. We enjoyed our excursion very much.

### Saturday, Aug. 8th, Coblentz.

Went to the Popolsdorf Alley a long avenue of trees leading to the university. We could not see the university itself, but looked in at the rooms of geological and mineralogical specimens. One room had shells arranged in patterns, all over the walls, there were cases with raised plans of Germany, or the valley of the Rhine etc. Behind are the botanical gardens. From the terrace is a fine view of the Drachenfels. We made a call on Mr. and Mrs. Hasser and found them pleasant people.

In the afternoon we took the boat up the Rhine. Mr. and Mrs. Weber and their daughter Sophie came to see us off. We passed Konigswinter where the Prince of Wales is staying. Near this is the Drachenfels which look finely for quite a distance. Opposite Lintz is Linzig where the tradition is that the cross appeared to Constantine. Upon a high hill on the left was Ahrenfels and opposite and farther on that of Rheineck restored and made into a modern dwelling by Prof. Bethman Hollweg of Bonn. On the left bank were the ruins of Hammerstein Castle where the Emperor Henry IV once took refuge from the persecutions of his son. It is quite an extensive ruin but crumbling away. Andernach is quite a picturesque old town. We saw Kenwied which was once an independent little kingdom but is now attached to Prussia. The darkness came on and shut off our farther view. It was nearly ten when we reached Coblentz and having had no dinner we took it at that late hour. Our hotel is on the river bank and facing the high hill where stands the Castle Ehrenbreitstein. A bridge of boats leads to it. It was besieged by the French in 1688 and taken after a long siege. It is now kept up as a strong fortification.

*Sunday, Aug. 9th, Coblentz.*

Went to church this morning and evening at the English chapel in the summer palace of the King of Prussia. We heard all day much noise from the steamboats, twelve of which leave each way during the day.

*Monday, Aug. 10th, Frankfort on the Mayn.*

We left Coblentz at eight and took our breakfast on the deck of the steamboat. We passed, on the right side Stotzenfels built by the archbishop of Treves. Isabella sister of Henry III of Eng. and bride of the Emperor Frederick II was lodged there. We found the sail very delightful and were in constant excitement from the ruined castles and picturesque scenery on either side of us, all the way. In the old town of Oberlanstein was the old red palace of the Electors of Mayence. Most of the towns looked very old with their walls and towers. Marksberg Castle farther on is said to be a complete specimen of an old knight's castle, with its cells and narrow passages. On the left side were the ruins of Sternberg and Liebenstein called "The Brothers" because, they say, two brothers lived here and fell in love with the same lady, the elder resigned his claims, the other went to war and came back with a Grecian lady, his former love was so heart-broken that she retired to a convent. Both the castles are much ruined. On the same side appears the "Mouse Castle" called so in contra distinction from the "Cat" a little farther off. The Mouse however was really the strongest. At St. Goar a pretty place on the right bank we saw the castle of Rheinfels the largest ruin on the Rhine.

Lurlei is a lofty crag projecting into the river; it is so called from a sorceress of that name who inhabits the rock and answers to all that call her for there is a fine echo. A cannon was fired as we passed and it reverberated among the hills. Not far from here are seven rocks called the seven countesses and changed into rocks by Lurlei because they were hard hearted towards their lovers. They lived in the Schonberg Castle perched upon a rock to the right. At Bacherack there is a rock which if seen above water is taken as a sign of a good grape harvest. A little ruin of St. Werner's Church in the Gothic style was quite pretty. Soneck Castle now restored was once a robber haunt. Beyond is a celebrated wine country. Rheinstein Castle is the country seat of the Prince of Prussia, it is being restored in the former style. Not far off is the Castle of Rudesheim the scene of the *Father's Vow*. The knight of the castle vowed to dedicate his daughter to Heaven if restored to his home in safety. She had meanwhile been betrothed, and her father returning, and hearing of it, cursed her, and she threw herself into the river. Farther on is Ehrenfels Castle where, as the story is, a stingy bishop who burned alive in his granary a number of poor people was attacked by mice. He built a tower on a little island in the river, which is near by, and called "the mouse tower"; where he took refuge, but the mice followed him here, and ate him up. They had picked his bones uncommonly clean, and eaten his very mitre. We came to Bingen soon after where the river is very wide. The banks became afterwards lower and the scenery more tame until we reached Castel, connected with Mayence by a bridge of boats. Here after we had dined, we took the cars for Frankfort. We found here a crowded hotel.

*Tuesday, Heidelberg, Würtemberg.*

We began the day in Frankfort, by going to a few shops, to where stag horn work, is sold, which is here very beautiful. We saw a bronze statue of Goethe, and opposite, in the same square those of the inventors of printing Faust and Guttenberg. Frankfort is a free city. The new part is quite handsome with broad streets and large well-built houses. The old part is very singular, with pointed, gable, projecting roofs. We saw Göethe's house, also that where Luther lived, on a corner, one story projecting over the other, and standing on a pillar. We drove through the Jews' quarter which is old and dirty, here is the birthplace of the Rothschilds from whom kings, now, borrow money. Their mother

*Heidelberg*

resided in the same house, until her death. We went into the town hall. Here in a room which is rhomboidal in shape, the emperors used to banquet after their coronation. It is now adorned with portraits of the German emperors by modern artists, some are by Lessing. In St. Peter's Church opposite, was held the diet of Frankfort.

We went into the cathedral which is very old. In this, 46 emperors have been crowned. The coronation chair kept in a side chapel, is of velvet. We drove a little out of the town to the house of a Mr. Betheman who has a small building, full of statuary, and plaster casts. We went to see the Ariadne by Dannecker a celebrated German sculptor. It is a naked figure riding on a lion. Red curtains and tapestry are arranged so as to throw a red light upon her to give the appearance of flesh. I do not like it. We again took the train and reached Heidelberg after dark.

*Wednesday, Aug. 12th, Baden-Baden.*

Heidelberg is beautifully situated on the river Neckar with wooded hills behind and the old castle overhanging the town. We drove first above that, to the Milkubure (?) the site, of the most ancient, electors castle; it is upon a hill, commanding a very fine view. First the old ruin below us, then the city, the river, hills, and far-off plain, with the Rhine scarcely visible. We then visited the Heidelberg Castle. It belonged to the Electors Palatine and was destroyed by the French under Louis XIV. Part is of very ancient date, and part was built by the elector Frederick V, who married Elizabeth of England daughter of James I, in honor of his wife. We drove through the gateway, across the moat, and into the large court. We visited the oldest part first. The grand banquet hall now a sort of stable looks down into the valley. From a passage way we saw the chapel where are still remaining some of the altar decorations. Here a heavy rain came on and impeded our full survey of the ruins. We went upon the terrace which overlooks the city at each end is an oriel summer house. Within one part of the buildings is a museum where are sold views of the town and castle, and a variety of objects are exhibited. Among other things was a ring of Luther's which had his wife Catherine's name upon it. The rain continued very severe with thunder and lightning and we were obliged to return to the town only half satisfied with what we had seen. After dinner we went to St. Peter's Church, where Olympia Morata lies buried. The monument is very simple. The University of Heidelberg is a plain building. The town has been often destroyed by enemies. We took several hours in the cars, to Baden Baden.

*Thursday, Aug. 13th, Basle, Switzerland.*

Before leaving Baden-Baden this morning Mary and I took a carriage to see a little of the town as a specimen of one of the German watering places. It is situated on the edge of the Black Forest. We went to the drinking house, a long building with pillared portico painted in frescoes. Inside, the water is drawn from a marble pillar by young girls and sold to those who wish, its properties I do not know. The conversation house is another long building; the ball room is very large, at one end is a gaming table, and again in another room. Two more ball rooms were ornamented with artificial flowers. The gambling runs very high. Near by, are avenues and a hill with walks upon it where people may amuse themselves. We saw the pump house also. Here was the curious bath of vapour; one sits in a box, with the head protruding from a hole at the top, there was an eye bath one for the ears, and one for the arms. We reached Basle about two and were much disappointed to receive no letters. We went after dinner to the Hitz's and saw the whole family, and Dr. and Mrs. Beck, and went with them all, to Dr. De Wette's where there was to be a small company. Miss DeW. (or Miss DeWette) is 16 and very tall, she talks French but not English. There is also a son of 18. There were several ladies and gentlemen present. We had a real German supper, meat, fish, salad, cakes and fruit.

*Friday, Aug. 14th, Bienne.*

Went again in the morning to Mrs. Hitzs and Mrs. De Wette's. We left at two, and Mrs. DeW., her daughter and a cousin met us at the cars. We rode an hour or two. The railway is new and a break occurred where there is to be a tunnel, where we had to ride in a carriage. Saw snow mountains on the edge of the horizon. Arrived at the railway, again, we waited quite a while for the cars, and reached Bienne about nine o'clock.

### Saturday, Aug. 15th, Lausanne.

Took the boat at 11 this morning on the Lake of Bienne which is ten miles long. It is not remarkable except for having an island, where Rousseau lived in exile. From this lake, we passed through a river, and came to Lake Neufchatel, where we changed boats. It rained so hard that we were obliged to stay in the cabin and saw little of the lake. At Loudon we took the cars for Lausanne.

### Sunday, Aug. 16th, Hotel Gibbon, Lausanne.

We look out upon the Lake of Geneva, but the rain which has continued all day much impeded our view. We went to the Church of St. Francis and heard an address to children in French. Close by here Gibbon wrote his history of the Roman Empire.

### Monday, Aug. 17th, Hotel des Bergues, Geneva.

Stayed at Lausanne until the two o'clock boat and then went down the lake for three hours, through rain again, to Geneva. We passed several towns the last of which was Coppet where M. Neckar, and his daughter Mme. de Staet lived, and are, I believe buried. Our hotel looks out upon the lake, facing a bridge which crosses the lake just where the Rhone pours in its swift indigo waters.

### Tuesday, Aug. 18th, Geneva.

We saw Antonio who has explained his conduct proving that the fault rested not with him but with a man who had an interest in detaining the countess' mother. We made a call on the Howlands who are staying at the Hotel de l'ecu. They were out but came to see us. Mr. H. has gone to Paris to see a physician. We arranged to go to Chamonix together. In the afternoon we took a drive a little out of the town and stopt at Pres Fleuris where Mary was born. Mrs. Wolf who then lived there has sold it. Geneva is a large city and in parts not very pleasant. The fortifications are converted into a promenade. We went to call on Madame Bouchés, a daughter of Mme. Wolf who remembered Uncle and Auntie well. And afterwards we drove out to Vandoeuvres a village a few miles from Geneva to see Dr. Malan who lives here now. The ride was charming past many pretty villas and country houses. Dr. Malan lives in a poor house, but is happy everywhere, in doing good. He has a beautiful face especially the eyes and long white hair. He talked with us upon the duty of Christians to believe themselves such without doubting; & told the story of a diamond in a brook which was rough, but only wanted polishing, and was still a diamond.

*Wednesday, Aug. 19th, St. Martin's.*

We left Geneva for our excursion to Chamonix in a vetturino all but Uncle who wished to accomplish some things in Geneva. Georgie and Eliza went in another carriage. We passed the Savoyard frontier and the scenery began to be interesting. At twelve we stopt at Bonneville to lunch. The cliffs began to be steep and rugged. In one was a grotto, where a woman fired cannons, and the echo was grand, rolling among the mountains like thunder. St. Martin's is in a valley, Salence is a small town near by. From a bridge over the Arve, which is here, there is, on a clear day, a splendid view of the mountains.

*Thursday, Aug. 20th, Chamonix, Savoy*

We left St. Martins' at half-past eight and had a delightful ride of four hours and a half. We had to leave our carriages and take smaller ones, as the road was very narrow. We wound about among hills and valleys, following the course of the Arve. The mist broke away and we had some superb views of the Alps the snow clad mountains. We stopt at a town called Chede to give the horses some bread, and saw there a Chamois. He was about the size of a goat, had little black horns and sharp horns, and kept jumping up upon a table, and down again. We saw some lovely waterfalls, coming from the cliffs, and they were almost lost in the great height, before reaching the ground. All around us were high crags which rose up ghost-like, partly shadowed in mist. As we advanced we came in sight of the Mt. Blanc range to the right, St. Gervais, to the left, the Aiguilles du Midi and stretching in two parts the Glacier du Bossons. Soon Chamonix became visible and the Mer de Glace and a waterfall from it which forms the Arveron. We see all this from the windows of our hotel, but rain has prevented our yet going out much except to some shops where carved objects are sold.

*Friday, Aug. 21st, Chamonix.*

I woke up early and O what a beautiful sight met my eyes, a clear sky and Mt. Blanc 15,760 ft. high, distinct as day itself, with its snowy peaks glittering in the first sunbeams. Peak after peak was lighted up, and then

*La Mer de Glace vue du Montanvert*

the sun itself, rose in grandeur, above the "needles," and filled the whole valley before cold and dark, with a flood of warm sunlight. We had a grand day for our excursion to Montanvert to see the glacier. We started at nine o'clock, each on a mule with Ranzani and accompanied by Georgie and Eliza. We were shown by our guides, of which we each had one, the very summit of Mt. Blanc, it looks round, and not so high as other peaks, because it is behind them. On one side is the Dome de Gouté below that the Aiguilles du Gouté and on the other side the Aiguilles du Midi and other singular pointed peaks. Below Mt. Blanc is the glacier du Bossons and the Grands Mulets are three or four pointed rocks at the top of the glacier. An excursion to these can be made in a day, but for Mt. Blanc they must start from there at midnight, so as to reach the top, and descend the next day. They can stay on the top but a short time on account of the cold and the rarefied air, no one has stayed I believe more than 3/4 of an hour. My guide was very inquisitive, he asked me all about where we were going and whence we came. The path was very steep, ascending rapidly for about two hours. The views of the valleys below were fine. We found a house on the top a poor affair, many other visitors came up after us. We sat on a flat terrace and looked down on the glacier below. I was a little disappointed in this, it looked dirty, but it was singular. Above rose the Aiguilles Verte and du Dru on the right, other snow mountains, needles like. The sight was impressive. The sky was clear with only a few fleecy clouds floating about the peaks.

After resting awhile we went down by a small foot path, leaning on Alpine stocks to see the glacier. We walked upon it a short distance but it was very cold. I sat by a fissure which was quite green, in color, stones were thrown in and made a loud noise. The Jardin is reached by crossing the glacier, and going round a point of rocks. We did not see much vegetation on the edge, only a few hare-bells. We climbed up to the hill again, took a lunch and then commenced the descent which we did not find difficult.

After our return we saw a splendid sun-setting. The snow became a delicate rose color and continued longest on Mt. Blanc, showing its greater height; long after the rose color had faded, a light seemed to rest upon the snow, whether sun or moon I could not tell. Two young Americans went up to the Grands Mulets with six guides tied two and two together, for fear of falling. Cannon were fired upon their return, and music played.

*Saturday, Aug. 22, Geneva.*

We left Chamonix at a little after seven and here parted from Georgie and Eliza who will return another way. I have enjoyed the excursion to Chamonix very much. We saw the first ray of sunlight in the morning, on Mt. Blanc. Then it poured down into the valley, and as we rode along rose again and again from the higher "needles." We rode all day till six in the evening. It was a fine day though warm. We found Uncle expecting us. The sunset from here was fine, we could see Mt. Blanc distinctly.

*Sunday, Aug. 23rd, Geneva.*

Mary and I went to the nine o'clock service at the Church of the Oratoire. We heard a French pastor. Merle d'Aubigne preaches here sometimes. In the afternoon to the Eglise du Temoinage where Dr. Malan preaches and heard him. He sold his home in town but keeps the church.

*Monday, Aug. 24th, Geneva.*

We went out shopping this morning. And afterwards to the cemetery and saw the spot where Calvin is supposed to be buried, only marked by a small stone. There was also a monument to Sir Humphrey Davy who died in 1828. In the cathedral is the sounding board which echoed with Calvin's voice. The building is plain, the arches partly round partly pointed. The house where Calvin lived has been replaced by a new one.

*Grand Quai a Genéve*

*Tuesday, Aug. 25th, Lausanne.*

We left Geneva in a vetturino, for Lausanne and rode along the shore of the lake. It is a beautiful drive all the way. We passed many fine country places. After an hour or so we stopt at Coppet and took an outside view of the chateau of M. Neckar and Mme. de Stael his daughter. It is a large quadrangular building, a little out of the town and still belongs to some connection of the family. We stopped for lunch at Rolle and Uncle, Mary and I walked on a mile or two. The roads here are most excellent, like a floor and the slopes quite gradual. We reached Lausanne in good season, and heard that Mr. Sheffield and his family were in the same hotel. After dispatching our letters and our tea we went to see them, and found them very cordial and pleasant. They have been every where, and are going every where, but almost envy us in returning home so soon.

*Wednesday, Aug. 26th, Bulle, Canton Friburg.*

The ride today has been very pleasant. The first hour and a half led us along the lake shore with beautiful views of the mountains at its east end. One had snow on its peak, and is called Dents du Midi. Vevay where we first stopt is a most beautifully situated spot. The hotel is right upon the lake, and seats are placed in the grounds to view the lake and the mountains. Mary and I took a carriage to visit the castle of Chillon about an hour's ride. It is celebrated by Byron in his *Prisoner of Chillon* and also historically. In 1532 Bonnivard was imprisoned there, who tried to reform Geneva and free it from the Savoyard yoke. In 1538 the Genevese and Bernese took the castle and rescued him, who returning to Geneva found it free and Protestant.

The castle is situated at the foot of a beautifully wooded hill, on a rock almost surrounded by water. It is in good preservation and used now for storing ammunition. We crossed over a bridge and went in. We were shown the old banquet room of the dukes of Savoy. The ceiling is of wooden panels, and the fireplace about ten feet long. The hall of justice is much the same, adjoining is a small room of torture and a staircase leading to the subterranean cells. The duke's bed chamber was in another part. The wall was red and formerly had silver crosses all over it. The oubliettes in a lower part of the castle were awful things. It was a square hole with three descending steps, the prisoner was made to believe there was a fourth, but instead, upon stepping down, he was precipitated thirty feet upon sharp lances. The subterranean dungeons were approached by a gloomy chapel like a crypt. Bonnivard's dungeon was cut out of the solid rock on a level with the water, and almost dark. We saw the ring to which he was fastened by a chain two or three feet long. Lord Byron's name is inscribed on one of the pillars. We saw the "potence" or gallows in the dim light, and the horrible thoughts connected with all these things, almost made me shudder. The duke's chapel is a small one, now used by the soldiers and people about the castle.

Villeneuve lay beyond us at the farther end of the lake. We returned to Vevay, took dinner and again entered our vetturino and began to ascend the hill to Bulle. Up, Up, we went, slowly winding around the hills. And beautiful views we had of the towns and mountains and the lovely lake below us. We saw today some little Swiss cottages very picturesque, like those we buy in miniature. We are in the Canton de Vaud now. We have had a charming ride, all the afternoon, with perfect weather. From the lake view we passed on to hills, wooded hills, and deep ravines, then to green meadows where they were haying. Bulle is in the middle of a plateau 2300 feet above the sea. It is a small town, our windows look out upon the meadows, behind which, the sun went down gloriously this evening.

*Thursday, Aug. 27th, Berne.*

Another bright clear day. We rode all day through a lovely country, part of the way along the river Saarine which flows in a deep gorge. At

*La Jungfrau dans la valée de Lauterbrunnen*

noon we stopt at Freyburg an old town with walls and towers still remaining. The view from the hotel was very picturesque. We looked down into a very deep valley in which were houses far below us. We could see the famous suspension bridge which crosses this valley. It was one of the first made, and is the largest, suspended on a single curve. It appeared very light and delicate. Over the gorge of Gotteron is another smaller one. The great object of interest in Freyburg, is the organ, which is one of the finest in the world. It was in the cathedral and we went there to see and hear it. The regular organist was away, and an inferior one played but even with his handling, it was very fine. It imitated voices, like a choir of boys accompanying the instrument, also a violin, bass instruments, and an operatic singer like Madame Grisi. Some of the notes were deliciously sweet.

We crossed the bridge and then went on our journey. The sun we found very hot. Our drive was charming. We came into Berne through the little picturesque cottages that are so attractive everywhere here. The women here wore their costumes, and they are almost the only ones in Switzerland who continue to do so, ordinarily. It was a black or dark colored skirt, black bodice and velvet embroidered collar, white chimisette and sleeves, and a silver chain passing from front to back, under the arms, also a straw hat, or a black cap with black lace border. We saw the chain of snowy Bernese Alps looking grandly. Berne itself is rather a large town

*Wengernalp vers la Jungfrau au Mönch et Eiger*

with irregularly built houses. In the environs are pretty country houses. Soon after arriving we rode up upon the Engle, a high promenade just outside the town, and saw the sun-set on the Alps. I never saw anything more glorious. Highest of all rose the Jungfrau, to the left of the Mönch, then Eigher then the Finster-Sarhorn, the Schreckhorn and Wetterhorn. To the right were the Blumlis Alps and the Niessen was a dark hill in front. All were of a bright rose color, it was perfectly lovely. Far below us was Berne and also the river Aar.

*Friday, Aug. 28th, Interlachen.*

This morning we went to some shops in Berne and then to visit the bears. These are the emblems of Berne, and are much valued, being kept in a castle, with a yard to walk about in. I saw six of them. Leaving Berne we drove two or three hours through a country still beautiful, here and there a pretty chaumiere and views of the snowy mountains. We came to Thun at last. The hotel is quite pretty with walks about it, and flowers, and an exquisite view of the Niessen, the lake of Thun with little cottages on the water's edge, and the Blumlis Alps in the distance.

We took a lunch here, and embarked on board of the steamer at three. It was crowded with passengers. The lake of Thun is small but very lovely. On one side is the bold Niessen, and the Stockhorn a conical mount, and snowy Alps behind them, on the other side are steep, but lower hills, coming to the water's edge. The sail was a little over an hour only. Interlachen is between this lake and that of Brienz. We drove a mile or two to reach the town. We have rooms looking down upon a piazza, and in a clear day should see the Jungfrau. In sight is a house with two towers, where Uncle and Auntie once spent a summer. Tomorrow we cross the Wengern Alp.

### Saturday, Aug. 29th, Grindelwald.

We left Interlachen at nine and stopt a moment at the house where Uncle and Auntie stayed. We found it was kept by the same woman and her husband, but is now a hotel. We went through a narrow gorge, following a stream formed by the melting snows. The road was most romantic, we saw some splendid views of the snow mountains. We reached Lauterbrunnen after a drive of an hour or two. Here we had a view of the Stanbach Falls. The side view is the best. It descends from a great height and the quantity of water being small, it is dashed into powder, as it would seem. It is very beautiful. The valley of Lauterbrunnen is quite narrow, but wild and romantic. Above rises the Jungfrau. Here we mounted our horses for the ascent of the mountain; and had also a chaise à porteur, so that M. and I could alternate with that and the horse, and

_Grindelwald vers le Wetterhorn et le glacier superieure._

*Wetter & Wellhorn & le Glacier Rosenlaui vus de la Haslischeideck*

be less fatigued. Auntie, Ranzani and Frances went, to meet us, at, Grindelwald by carriage. The ascent was quite abrupt. Up up we mounted stopping often to rest the men and horses. Strawberries were offered us on our way. We met a man with a horn of Uri and he blew it, there was an echo, and the effect was very fine, among the mountain peaks. In about three hours we reached a house on the top of the Wegernalp. Our views on the way up looking back way into Interlachen were fine. We found some flowers but the rhododendrons were all gone. Upon the summit the view was beyond description. A narrow gorge only separated us from the majestic Jungfrau rising far above us and white with the purest snow. On the right was the "white Monch" on the left the "black Monch" one covered with snow and the other of rock. All was so still it was very impressive.

The inn is quite tolerable, for such a place. Hamlets are to be seen here and there nearly up to where we were, and the Bernese chalet with its sloping roof, held down by stones, pretty in their very roughness. After taking a lunch at the inn, we walked on, before the horses were ready, and our attention was arrested by a noise like thunder, and conjecturing the cause we looked towards Jungfrau and saw, as it were, a white powder falling from the snow on its side. It was an avalanche and the powder was probably blocks of snow and ice large enough to destroy horses or trees if beneath them. Listening, we heard four or five others, though we saw no more. It was a beautiful day, the air on the summit was cool but very fine.

The descent did not begin till we had reached another house, on the Lesser Scheideck, and then in some places it was quite precipitous. From this spot we had a splendid view of the valley of Grindelwald far far below us; patches of grain looked in the distance like logs of wood. The Mettenberg and Wetterhorn lay on our right and the glacier of Grindelwald beneath them. Far off bounding the view was the Scheideck which we are to cross on Monday. We descended, and the valley as we neared it, grew more beautiful, the fields were of a sweet green and chalets dotted the landscape. On our way down we stopt at a chalet where two women played for us on a dulcimer and sang. They sang a Ranz de Vache which I had been longing to hear. Another was a yodeling song, which sound is very difficult to make, by any but the native Swiss. We left the chalet, and the women in gratitude for a piece of money from Uncle, stood together on the hill and sang after us as long as we could hear them. We noticed many cattle on the hills, each one had a bell attached to it and made a soft and pleasant tinkling. We reached Grindelwald about six after a most delightful day. The hotel is built like a Swiss house, with other buildings attached.

*Sunday, Aug. 30th, Grindelwald.*

To our surprise we found there was an English service in the pension of the hotel. About thirty attended both morning and afternoon. It was a bright beautiful day. The view of the sweet valley of Grindelwald, from our windows, was very lovely. In one direction the dark peaks of the Wetterhorn rose up and the great glacier, with its waterfall which we heard distinctly, next was the Mettenberg and between them the sun rose up and poured its rays into the valley. From another window we looked out upon the smaller glacier which seemed very near. Above it rose the snowy peaks of the Finsteraar horn and the Eigher. The village church was Reformed German. It was a sweet sight, the people flocking to church in their neat Bernese costumes. Some of the women wore their hair braided down their backs. Uncle attended this church in the morning, and he said that men and women sat on different sides, and the preacher wore a large ruff instead of band or collar.

*Monday, Aug. 31st, Reichenbach Hotel, Meyringhen.*

We left Grindelwald at half-past eight and made quite a cavalcade

*Maison de Paisan á Meyringen*

with six of us, besides five horses, two chairs, and eight men. We did not ascend a very precipitous path at first, but passed along near the large glacier and under the base of the Wetterhorn, from which avalanches sometimes fall, and make the path dangerous, but we were preserved. We heard a horn blown and the Wetterhorn echoed it softly and beautifully. We reached the top of the Sheideck, in three hours, a point 6480 feet above the sea. The descent was very pleasant through groves of evergreen and along delicious little brooks. We heard and saw more avalanches. On our right was the glacier of Swartzwald, and the Welhorn above it, so called from the number of streams flowing from it. Continuing, we came to where a part of the Rosenlaui glacier was visible between the Welhorn, and the Engelhorner, (angel horn). We left some of our party at a little inn, and went in the chairs, a half mile up a steep path to see the glacier. We came first to the Wiesbach Waterfall, a most lovely one though small.

We walked over the bridge, which crosses a chasm 250 feet deep, through which the stream rushes. It was fearful to look down. We passed on, facing a cold icy wind, until we stood on the edge of the rock, facing the glacier, where between us and it, rushed a tremendous, foaming, dashing roaring torrent. It passed under an arch of ice of a most exquisite blue color, and was a striking sight. The whole glacier was very blue and sloping much. A piece of ice broken off was as clear as glass and blue also, the guide seemed to distinguish the rose color, but we could not. We crossed the stream on a log bridge and stood on a rock touching the ice; here we looked into a hole where the ice was melting and the color very blue. Uncle climbed up some distance upon the ice to see another blue chasm, but we thought it safer to remain below. It was a perfect glacier, one of the most beautiful in Switzerland.

We stopped a while for lunch at the inn where were sold pretty carved articles and Alpine flowers. On our way down we had some rain. We followed the Reichenback Stream which flows in a deep ravine, covered with evergreens and, just as the valley of Meyringhen opened into view and the path became very steep and stony we turned off to see the falls of the Reichenback. The first one is very beautiful, snowy white, and passing over the rocks so gently. The next is more tremendous, a great rush of water, and broken by a rock at the bottom. The last one we saw from a small house, it comes through rocks and trees and is very lovely. The hotel where we are is but a short distance thence. Thus ends our eventful and most delightful day.

*Tuesday, Sept. 1st, Lucerne.*

We left Meyringhen this morning. At a little distance from us was the town of Meyringhen, we had stayed in the outskirts. We crossed the Aar joined by the Riechenbach and continued along the plain to the Brunig Pass. Auntie had a chair, the rest of us were on horseback. We went up a steep path, and had very fine views. We could see a little of the lake of Brienz beyond a craggy point. The valley was very flat except here and there great rocks covered with trees, which, once probably, fell from the mountains which form an amphitheatre about them. After ascending nearly to the summit we came upon a pretty plain, where were a few chalets. Mary's horse fell with her, but she was not hurt. It was so steep that I preferred to walk part of the way down. We came down into Lungern Canton Unterwald and there took a carriage for four hours, but saw little of the scenery for we were in a pouring rain and as the sides of the carriage were open we had to cover ourselves with umbrellas. We passed the little lake of Lungern and stopt at Alpnach where after waiting a while we took the steamboat to Lucerne. Our hotel is the Englishe Hof directly upon the lake of Lucerne.

*Wednesday, Sept. 2nd, Lucerne.*

A cloudy day but we embarked, at half-past eleven on the *St. Gothard* for a sail to the end of the "lake of the four cantons." This is a most beautiful lake, the mountains are very high all around it and are either covered with verdure, or else steep wild precipices. It is quite irregular in shape and at this end is a sort of transept, as it might be called, at one end

*Chapelle du Guillaume Tell*

of which is Alpnach, at the other Kussnacht. Rigi is in sight from here, with the houses upon it and also Mt. Pilatus, a dark gloomy mt., so called from a tradition that Pilate threw himself off from here. We passed through a narrow opening between the two noses as two green promontories are called. There were many towns along the shores, at some of which the boat stopped. Unterwald is the canton nearest Lucerne, and on the other side is Schwytz, and we looked down in another direction upon a part of the lake called the bay of Uri. The view was exquisite, a background of hills folding one over the other, the smooth green water and pretty boats gliding over it. Upon a green meadow on the right bank, just at the water's edge and at the foot of a precipice, the league was concerted in 1307 between Uri, Schwytz, and Unterwalden. They were to defend their country from the Austrian oppression, and not to injure the counts of Hapsburgh, the ruins of whose castle, we saw at a distance down the bay of Kussnacht. At some distance farther on, is Tell's Chapel, a small building close on the water's edge. Here, it is said, he leaped ashore when, he was unbound by Gessler, to steer his boat, and one story is, that he shot Gessler near by, when pursued by him. At Flüelen the end of the lake we remained about an hour and rain came on while there. The sail back was beautiful with the sunlight on the green slopes, and streaming in a silver line over the water. The rain obliged us to retreat again to the cabin before reaching Lucerne. The moon has come out this evening and its reflection in the lake is beautiful.

*Thursday, Sept. 3rd, Rigi-Kulm.*

We left Lucerne in our old vetture which had reached there at last having gone by mistake from Thun to Interlachen. We continued along the lake, upon the bay of Kussnacht for about two hours, and then we all mounted horses for our ascent of the Rigi. It was somewhat cloudy and we doubted whether we should have a view after reaching there. Our path led through fields and open ground until the ascent became very steep indeed and we toiled up for a long time. We saw many fine cattle on our way up, they were mostly black, white, or chocolate color. Our views of the lakes of Lucerne and Zug were fine, we reached the summit in about three hours. The hotel consists of two large buildings and internally, except that the wood is unpainted, it has all the comforts of a less elevated position. We had a private parlor, and two good bedrooms, by <u>telegraphing up</u>. Mary and I walked out on the summit, after our arrival to see the view. The mist then covered only a part of the distant mountains the rest was very fine. On one side was the lake of Zug, a very beautiful one just at the foot of the Rigi and the little town of Aarth. Turning towards the east, there was the mountain of Rossberg, just at the foot of which once stood Goldau, but it was overwhelmed in 1806 by a fearful avalanche, of mud and rocks, with a whirlwind, and over 400 per-

*Arth (au pied du Righi)*

sons were killed. We saw distinctly the course of the rocks, which will ever remain a monument of the catastrophe. A little lake near by, called Lowertz, was partly filled up by it. On the side which our windows overlooked were mountains without number, on one we saw the Pass of St. Gothard. Just below us, here and there we could see Lake Lucerne and other lakes of small size. It clouded over soon, and the view was shut off. The night was cold.

*Friday, Sept. 4th, Zurich.*

This morning if it had been clear we were to have been awakened by the sound of a horn, at half-past four to see the sunrise. But mist wrapped us round, and none was to be heard. The Rigi hotel is open from the middle of June to the middle of October, and during the winter two servants stay there to take care of the furniture. It must be dismal to remain so far away from other habitations, and in such severe cold. On the door of all the rooms there is this notice, "On avertit Mesdames les Etrangeres qu'il est defendu de prendre les couvertures (de laine) des lits de sortir avec elles au sommet." We were quite disappointed that the morning view was not better, but we had a glimpse of some of the mountains.

We left between eight and nine. Auntie had a chair and Mary and I one between us. I walked about half-way down perhaps four miles. We had Alpine stocks but found so steep a descent quite fatiguing. We heard a boy on the hills yodeling, it is a most singular sound. We were glad to reach Aarth on the border of the lake of Zug and refreshed ourselves before going our way in the vetture which here met us. Our road lay along the lake of Zug and through the town of that name, and also along the lake of Zurich. This is a long lake and pretty, there are many villages upon it, and it is a thrifty Protestant canton, that of Zurich. Our hotel is near the lake, of which we have a pleasant view.

*Saturday, Sept. 5th, Basle.*

Before leaving Zurich we went into the cathedral for a moment. It is an old building of 10th or 12th century and very plain. We went into the gallery. There are round arches and large square pillars and just below us was the wooden pulpit where Zwingle used to preach. We took the 10 o'clock train to Brugg and there met our vetturino and drove the rest of the way. Brugg is a very old town. Its walls and towers still remain. On a hill at some distance we saw the ruins of an old castle of the Hapsburgs. From this family Rudolph was called to the imperial throne. We came again to the Rhine, at noon we stopped at Stein, and arrived at Basle about seven.

*Grossmünster (or) Cathedrale a Zurich*

**Sunday, Sept. 6th, Basle.**

Went to hear the English service, in a little room in this hotel, fitted up as a chapel. The clergyman was earnest and interesting. In the afternoon there were only five persons present besides ourselves.

**Monday, Sept. 7th, Strasburgh.**

We went out this morning before leaving Basle to see the Hitz's and DeWettes and found only the latter at home, the others came to see us before we left. We came here in four hours and before going to the hotel visited the cathedral, and were just in time for they close it at six. We looked first at the celebrated clock which is at one end of the transept. Above it is a figure of the Saviour and at twelve o'clock the apostles pass in order before him, bowing their heads and a cock flaps his wings and crows. Beneath is a standing figure of Time and before it passes at certain times, Childhood, Youth, Manhood, and Old Age, the first, childhood, strikes the 1st quarter. Youth strikes the half-hour, Manhood the three quarters and Old Age the full hour. Beneath these, are three genii, one with a bell another with an hour glass. We were there at six o'clock. One genii struck the bell another turned the hour glass and old age struck the full hour. Connected with this clock, is an astronomical arrangement to predict the eclipses of the sun and moon and an ecclesiastical table for holy days. There are three aisles to the cathedral, at one end is a circular window with a diameter of 43 feet. The glass is stained and of various ages. The choir is raised above the rest of the church. The columns are mostly clustered & at a distance appear like a forest of trees. In one transept is a monumental statue to a count of the Hapsburg who founded the church in 1015. In another place is the tomb of a bishop who gave all his property for the building of the spire. This is 468 feet from the ground and will probably ever be the only one, though two were intended. It is a Gothic building and an impressive structure. The doors are ornamented with figures and the kings, Clovis, Dagobert, and Rudolph appear on horseback above them. In the same square is the Bishop's Palace, and there is a house of the 9th century and another of the fifteenth.

*Tuesday, Sept. 8th, Epernay.*

We took the train at twelve, which was the only one that would suit us, and passing through Nancy and many other places reached Epernay at half-past seven, where we stopped for the night. It was rather a poor lodging place.

*Wednesday, Sept. 9th, Paris.*

We left Epernay at half-past eight in the way train. We entered Paris on the Boulevards and passed the Porte St. Denis. We have good rooms in the Hotel Wagram on the first story at the corner of the Rue Rivoli and Rue Vingt Neuf Juillet, the same rooms that Uncle and Auntie had when she was so sick here twenty years ago. We ended the day by doing a little shopping.

*Thursday, Sept. 10th, Paris.*

Mary and I went in the morning to the Louvre for the first time. We drove into the Place de Carousel. The Tuilleries and Louvre are connected together by a very handsome line of buildings. The Louvre is an immense pile containing museums of all kinds. We went to see the paintings first to the Salon Carré where are the choicest ones of all. We saw there Raphael's *Michael and the Dragon*. The angel treads but lightly on the prostrate devil but seems to crush him to the ground. I do not in some respects like it as well as Guido's. The Marriage at Cana is by Paul Veronese. It is a large picture, the bride and bridegroom sit together at one end of the table. Murillo's *Immaculate Conception* cost more than 165,000 francs. The virgin is in the clouds, with her foot on the crescent and cherubs around her. Her drapery is blue and white, and her face is very sweet. La Belle Jardiniere is a lovely Madonna by Raphael. The virgin is seated with the Saviour at her knee and John is presenting a cross. Another was also beautiful the Saviour leaps from his cradle to his mother, and angel strews flowers over her and Elizabeth is teaching her son to adore him. A girl with mirrors held before and behind her, by Titian.

The rooms and halls are very splendid with vases and antiques about them; and, richly gilded. We also went through the eight or nine rooms which contain the French school of paintings. Saw a picture by Girodet of the hermit and Chactas, taking to burial the body of Itala. The hermit's face was admirable, and the despair of the lover who held her feet, was well depicted. There was a large scene representing Napoleon revisiting the battle field of Eylau; snow has fallen, and the dead and wounded are strewn about. A Roman scene in the Pontine Marshes by Leopold Robert *Going to the Field*. A young man leans on the yoke of two buffaloes and in the cart is a group of men and women; one man walks by the side holding a bundle of grain, another with a scythe is dancing, and another plays a bag pipe. *The Return From a Pilgrimage to Lal Madonna del Arc*, is by the same artist. A yoke of white oxen are drawing a cart dressed with flowers; and men, women and children are dancing and playing around it, decked out with flowers, and their gay Neapolitan dresses. There were many sea views by Joseph Vernet. Another room was full of pictures of dogs.

We then went into the Musèe des Souverains. The first room was the bedroom of Henry IV, and here was shown his armour and that of Francis I, Henry II and Charles VIII. In the next was the altar and other ornaments from the Chapel of the Holy Ghost founded by Henry III. The altar cloths and mantles were embroidered with little flames as symbolical representations. Continuing on to the next room we saw the baptismal font of St. Louis, Philip Augustus and the Count de Paris. A splendidly wrought gold box given by Richlieu to Anne of Austria. Charlemagne's prayer book, and his golden sword. Louis XVI's sword and a little one, that belonged to the poor young dauphin. A splendid little mirror set with cameos, emeralds and onyxes, given by Venice to Marie de Medici. The chaise `a porteur of Louis XV and a jewel wardrobe that once had belonged to Marie Antoinette. We saw also the arm chair of Dagobert. We walked through the marine museum where were models of ships and also through several rooms full of the drawings of old masters, but we had not time to examine them all.

*Friday, Sept. 11th, Paris.*
We went this morning to the Palais de Justice on the Isle de la Citee.

It was the ancient palace of the kings, of the first and third races of France. It is used now mostly for lawyers business. We had not a permit so we could not see the prison where Marie Antoinette was confined. Connected with this is the Sainte Chapelle, a beautiful little Gothic church. It was begun by Louis IX and is now in process of restoration to its original state. The government devotes annually 2,000,000 francs towards it. The interior is richly gilded and painted in the Byzantine style with little ibis and sphinxes all over it. There are also beautiful lancet windows and a fine rose window as wide as the chapel itself. The altar is gilded. There was a grated window where, they say Louis XI used to go to hear mass, being very much afraid of assassination. A recess in the side of the chapel was for St. Louis and his queen and one opposite for his mother Blanche of Castile.

We visited also Notre Dame which is on the island too. The western facade is fine. There are two square towers, and arches, pillars, and various ornaments. The interior has been restored lately by the emperor on the occasion of his marriage. There are three aisles and the pillars are alternately round and clustered. The capitals are gilded and the ceiling blue with gold stars. The walls and pillars are painted in various colors. The effect is quite gorgeous. We saw some splendid things in the sacristy. A reliquary or altar ornament with large rays formed by diamonds. There were all sorts of gold church ornaments and utensils, a splendid jeweled cross given by the present emperor, some priestly robes elegantly ornamented. The imperial mantle of Napoleon of crimson embroidered with gold. There were other mantles worn on different important occasions. In the choir are some bronze figures given by Napoleon I at his marriage. There are many side chapels in which are paintings, but of no great merit. The carriage had not come so Mary and I sat down in the church to wait and had been there some time when the verger came up and said it was not allowed to sit with our faces to the door, as we had been doing, but towards the altar.

*Saturday, Sept. 12th, Paris.*

Went first, this morning to the Quai des Fleurs to see the flower market. It was really a very pretty sight, all the little booths and each woman with her sweet wares before her. There were pots of oleanders, gladioli, heliotropes, forget-me-nots, geraniums, roses, etc. and also bouquets all made. The fruit is now in great perfection here we see carts full of grapes sold in the streets. We spent the rest of the morning at the Maison de Lille one of the finest dry goods stores.

In the afternoon we went to the Gobelin tapestry manufactory which is far away in the outskirts of the town. I was much interested in what I saw. There were many pieces finished. One a copy of a painting at the Louvre, Pyrrhus protecting Andromache and her son from Orestes. Peter the Great in a dreadful storm in a boat, holding the rudder, while his mast is broken etc. The colors are very rich, and the work so fine that even very near they appear like paintings. We saw how the work was done. They do it on the wrong side. The web is marked and when the thread is passed through, they push it down with an ivory stick. There are all varieties of shade and color, but the difficulty must be to select. They make most elegant carpets besides the tapestry work. A portrait of the emperor and empress was being made and also portraits of artists for the gallery of Apollo in the Louvre. It costs the government, who alone has what is made here 6,000 francs a day, to support the establishment.

We went afterwards to the Church of the Magdalen a beautiful building with Corinthian pillars supporting a pediment. In the interior are three small domes richly gilded, in the semicircles contained in the side arches are paintings and in each chapel, some fine pieces of sculpture. To the right on entering is the marriage chapel and here is a picture of the marriage of the virgin; to the left is the baptistry, and in it one representing the baptism of the Saviour. At the altar is a large group around the *Magdalen in Ecstasy* who is borne up by four angels. We went to hear music from a band on the Place Vendome but did not stay long, as there was quite a crowd and the policeman would not allow us to stay there in a carriage, and as we were alone we did not want to leave it.

*Sunday, Sept. 13th, Paris.*

We went to the Tailbout Chapel in the morning, and heard a good French sermon, we stayed through the intermission and attended the American service, which, while the American church is building, is held here. Mr. Porter who is tutor to cousin Edward's boys read the Episcopal service and then a Mr. Wall of the S.C. preached a sermon. We met there cousin Edward and his wife, the Wheelers, the Forbes, and Miss Tucker.

*Monday, Sept. 14th, Paris.*

We commenced a busy day by going with Auguste the valet to the Pantheon. It was built by Louis XV as a church of St. Genevieve and it is also a monument to several French heroes. The pediment, and front of the portico, are richly adorned with bas reliefs and a flight of steps leads to the entrance. All around the interior which is in the form of a Greek cross is a colonnade of Corinthian columns. The floor is of mosaic. On the dome, which is very high, is a fresco representing St. Genevieve in glory, with many of the kings of France. On the pendentives are four frescoes Death, La Patrie, La Justice and Glory embracing Napoleon.

We asked to see the vaults but were told there was not "assez de monde" to make it worth while, I suppose. So we went to the Palace of Luxembourg which is a most splendid palace, built around a square. We passed through one or two ante rooms to a saloon where is a statue of Napoleon I. The next hall is the most splendid imaginable. In the centre is a throne used by Napoleon when First Consul, it is gilt and crimson, and gilt caryatids support a canopy of the same. On the walls are numerous paintings. Napoleon III visiting the work on the Louvre when, president, the same elected emperor. Napoleon I when general and a young man. The ceilings and walls were most gorgeously decorated with gold. From the throne room we went through a corridor adorned with busts of the senators. Then into the library where books are arranged round the room, and from the windows of which is a beautiful view of the gardens which are quite extensive. The Senate Chamber is semicircular. Here was the president's seat, and there were galleries for spectators, though these are not now allowed to be present. Marie de Medeci the second wife of Henry IV occupied this palace and we saw one room called her bed-room, which was very elegant. Upon the ceiling was a painting of her, crowned, and around, portraits of members of her family by Rubens.

We walked a little in the garden which is a little stiff but has some pretty flower beds, and a grove of trees connected with it. We went again to the Pantheon and found it quite crowded and a little too much for our comfort. We, that is, priests, soldiers, men and women, an Englishman and his wife, Mary and I, all followed a guide with a cocked hat, down into the dark crypt. First we came to Rousseau's tomb, it is a sarcophagus and a hand holding a bone is protruding from the door. We saw many others, that of Marshal Lannes Sufflot, the architect of the Pantheon and Voltaire. This latter has a statue near by with a dreadful expression of countenance. In one part was a striking echo. The guide knocked the wall repeatedly and it sounded like the report of a cannon.

I was glad to see daylight again, after a short stay in the abode of the infidel dead, where darkness was made visible by the dim light of a lantern, and where our companions were not the most agreeable. Then, as this was the day for visiting it we went to the Hotel des Invalides. It was founded by Louis XIV and intended to afford 3,000 sleeping rooms for poor soldiers. The chief object of interest is the chapel where is the tomb of Napoleon. It is in shape much like the Pantheon. In a chapel is an altar containing his heart and body, and behind, upon a cushion are seen his hat and sword. In the middle of this chapel an opening is made, by which the crypt is made visible and in that is a porphyry sarcophagus prepared for the body which is not yet placed in it. Around this opening is a marble balustrade and angels are seen below upholding the floor above, their faces are sad and they all look towards the tomb. The altar is superb, it has twisted columns of black and white marble, the base is of that and serpentine and the gilding is very rich. Behind is the entrance to the crypt guarded by two severe figures of bronze and above is inscribed Napoleon's wish, that his ashes might repose in the midst of the people, he loved so much. On one side of the church is a monument to Turenne one of Louis XIV's generals, on the other one to Vauban. The soldier's chapel is behind, visible through a grating. In the afternoon we made calls on the Wheelers and Forbes.

*Tuesday, Sept. 15th, Paris.*

We have been this morning to the Tuilleries to see the state apartments which are the only ones shown. We passed through one or two anterooms ornamented with antique busts on high pedestals, then into the ball room. The walls and pillars are much gilded it is furnished with ottomans and is very showy. Next is a square room with a gallery around it, and called the Salon des Marechaux. It has paintings of Napoleon's marshals, all around the room, from a little balcony adjoining is a fine view of the gardens, the arch, and obelisk of Luxor. We looked down from one room, upon the chapel, the imperial seat is at one end richly covered with velvet. The "Salon Blanc" is now used as a card room, it is gilt and white in its ornaments. Then we came to the throne room. There were two seats upon the throne, and above a canopy, and behind on a crimson ground a gold eagle and the other imperial arms. Then following more rooms, of which one has the name of Salon de Louis XIV. The Salon de Mars is furnished in green. They were all very rich and constitute the suite of state apartments.

*Wednesday, Sept. 16th, Paris.*

We went this morning to the church of St. Denis six miles from here. The road was paved all the way and was not at all interesting. The abbey of St. Denis was first founded in the time of Dagobert. Pepin built a church which was finished by Charlemagne but the crypt is the only part of the most ancient building remaining, the rest is more modern. There is one square tower and the façade is ornamented with figures. St. Louis built the church as it is now, and it was used as a burial place for the kings until the Revolution, when the bones were taken away. Napoleon replaced them and repaired the church. All around the choir and nave are little chapels which are now being painted in the original style and look very gorgeous. The high altar is the one, brought from the gallery of the Louvre, at which Napoleon was married to Marie Louise. A gold cross at one of the other altars was given to the church by St. Louis. Dagobert was the first one buried there, his monument is on the left side. Farther on, is the mausoleum of Louis XII and his wife Anne of Brittany. A canopy of white marble covered the figures of the king and queen which are lying below, as on a couch. The twelve apostles are sculptured on the pedestal. Next is a monument of Henry II and Catherine de Medici, in the same general style. Near by is a porphyry pillar with a vase on the top to Francis II, husband of Mary Queen of Scots, who died at eighteen. A similar pillar is erected to Henry III who was assassinated at St. Cloud. Opposite is a fine monument to Francis I and Claude his queen. Above are kneeling figures of the two with the dauphin, the duke of Orleans and the Princess Charlotte, their children. In the choir was, as we were told, a statue of the queen of St. Louis and Jean his son. In the vestry room were paintings. Charlemagne at the consecration of the church, and sitting upon his throne, etc. In one chapel were the tombs of some of the constables of France.

In the crypt were old monuments. They are mostly in the form of a sarcophagus with an effigy. Those that we saw were the monuments of Clovis, Chilpheric, Childebert, Dagobert, Charles Martel, Carloman and Charlemagne. St. Louis and Charles of Anjou, Louis XVI and Marie Antoinette were two figures kneeling at the altars. To Louis XIII and Louis XIV there were quite handsome monuments. In the middle is a sort of catacomb where the ashes of Louis XVI and his wife and those of the other kinds taken away at the Revolution. In the Treasury we saw the crowns of Louis XIV and his queen and Louis XVIII they were of gold fleur de lys; also other valuable articles. A man sleeps there with weapons so as to defend them if necessary. In the evening we went to see the Howlands.

*Thursday, Sept. 17th, Paris.*

In the morning we went to the dress maker's and then I went to see Mrs. More and found her at home. This afternoon Uncle, Mary and I went out to St. Cloud. There is a fete held there now, on Sunday and Thursdays one of the principal ones near Paris. The palace is then freely opened. We went through the rooms which are shown. The billiard room is hung with Gobelin tapestry the history of Marie de Medici. The Salon de Mars is very elegant, the walls are covered with marbles and the floor is of wood mosaic. In the middle is a candelabra ornamented with artificial flowers and surrounded by an elegant tapestry divan. From this we went to the Salon d'Apollon a long hall used as a dining room on very grand occasions. Here are paintings and cabinets of brass and tortoise shell. From this opens the Salon de Diane and over the door is a portrait of *Philip Egalite* father of Louis Philippe and one of Louis XIV on horseback.

Returning, we passed from the Salon de Mars into a vestibule, where, I believe, Henry III was assassinated. From it leads the staircase d'homme, very rich the railing is gilded. On the wall is a painting representing Napoleon with Josephine by his side receiving his appointment as emperor; this scene took place in the orangerie at St. Cloud. A door on e stairway leads to the emperor's private apartments which were once the favorite ones of Marie Antoinette, Josephine and Marie Louise. The air of St. Cloud is very fine. From it Paris can be seen to good advantage. We could not see the private gardens but we went into the park which is very extensive. The fountain or rather artificial cataract was not playing. The walks were cool and shady.

The people whom the fete had assembled made a very gay scene. There was a theatre, a circus, learned dogs and monkeys, tumblers, cosmoramas, dancers, jugglers and wooden horses made to revolve, for children to ride upon, and all sorts and kinds of things. Drums beating, fiddlers playing, bells, lotteries and all sorts of games mostly of a low sort. Then there was one long avenue completely lined with stalls for the sale of different things. Leaving St. Cloud we drove on along the Seine we passed a place where they were dyeing, as the water just there, is considered particularly good for that purpose. To our left was a fortification called Mt. Valerian near which Mme. de Genlis is buried. We crossed the Seine at Neuilly and so returned through the Barrière de l'etoile to our hotel. On our way out to St. Cloud we passed through Passy where Franklin lived when in Paris. Anteuil we also rode through.

*Friday, Sept. 18th, Paris.*

We drove out to Versailles a ride of about two hours, passing through Sevres. The original palace at Versailles was built for a hunting seat by Louis XIII but Louis XIV made the palace what it is, spending upon the palace and garden 40,000,000 pounds. We went first to the Grand Trianon a small palace on the edge of the park. It consists of only one story, and contains long halls and suites of rooms. In one room were two elegant Sevres vases about five feet high. In another was a table made of one piece of oak, ten feet in diameter. In one hall were statues and copies of antiques. We saw the bed covered by a canopy, which Josephine used to use. A room fitted up for Queen Victoria, when she was expected on a visit to Louis Philippe furnished with crimson and gold. Napoleon's bed room, hung with a light blue hangings and furniture. In the carriage house was the state carriage of Charles X fitted up for the baptism of the present little prince. It was most gorgeous, wheels and all were of gilt and a crown on the top. Another less magnificent, was used by the emperor at his marriage.

We then drove down one of the long avenues which form everywhere charming vistas, to the Petit Trianon. This was a building of small size into which we did not go. Around it are pretty flower gardens. The particular associations of this place are with Marie Antoinette. Here she had her farm, and amused herself away from the tedious ceremonies of the court. We saw a little summer house, surrounded by grass, with chairs and table within and the walls covered with figures and arabesques, where she used to embroider with her ladies. There was a pond and little brooks, which we saw, walking through the woody paths. There was a rockery in imitation of an old castle and an artificial grotto all of her planning, I believe. Then we came upon her dairy where she made cheese, the floor is marble; then a mill for grinding corn, and a thatched house where she used to spend some time. All is kept up by the emperor in perfect order and sentinels guard the place. Then there was a pretty little ivy-grown house, with only one room of any size. It was a sweet place, the day was fine, the air cool and pure and the birds sang pleasantly. We sat down on a seat near by and ate our luncheon of bread and fruit, and enjoyed it very much. We passed a café house on the shore of a piece of water, in the form of a Grecian temple.

We then went on to Versailles proper. It is a large mass of buildings and is full of paintings, about 6,000 making eight miles of pictures. My memory could not contain all even if in three or four hours I could see them all so I will mention but a few. Several rooms were full of scenes in the Crusades, and the walls were emblazoned with the shields of the crusaders. There was a model of La Valettes tomb, and his portrait. St. Bernard, Peter the Hermit, the meeting of Richard Coeur de Lion and Philip Augustus. The siege of Jerusalem and thanksgiving after it. Baldwin made emperor. Then there was the whole race of French kings. We saw the bedroom of Louis XIV and in which he died, the canopy and coverlid are richly embroidered. It was from the balcony of this room, that Louis XVI addressed the mob which came to take him to Paris. The theatre is small, it was built by XV and the first play was acted at the marriage of Louis XVI then dauphin. Here a splendid supper was given to Victoria, when on her visit here.

The gardens are laid out in parterres, there are ponds, fountains, pyramids of box., trees, etc. Continuing to look at the paintings, we saw the marriage of Napoleon to Marie Louise, at Notre Dame a splendid scene. His coronation and that of Josephine. The battle of the Pyramids when he is in the act of saying, "Courage soldiers from the summit of those pyramids 40 centuries contemplate us." The bivouac before the battle of Austerlitz. St. Louis administering justice under an oak. The death of St. Louis. The siege of Yorktown, Gen. Washington and a French general stand talking together. Meeting of Henry VIII and Francis I on the field of the cloth of gold. Louis Philippe in the midst of the national guard in 1832, and many, many more. We reached our hotel again at about six and a half returning through St. Cloud and the Bois de Boulogne.

*Saturday, Sept. 19th, Paris.*

Mary and I went to Père la Chaise which is quite a long drive from here. It is named from Père la Chaise the confessor of Louis XIV who used to live upon the spot. The tombs are nearly all vaults, each family has one, and one is buried on the top of the other. We saw the tomb of Heloise and Ablelard, it is the oldest in the cemetery. It consists of a canopy, over a couch upon which their two figures lie. Abelard was a great scholar in the time of Louis VI; many persons used to flock to hear his lectures. Then we went to the Hotel Clugny, on the other side of the Seine. It is a specimen of a house of the 16th century and quite peculiar. It is used as a museum and contains all sorts and kinds of old things. Among these was the bed of Francis I when Count d'Angouleme, the posts are carved there is a coverlid and canopy of faded tapestry. One room is called the bed-room of "La Reine Blanche" as Mary sister of Henry VIII and wife of Louis XII was called. We saw the signature of Catherine de Medici, and a set of crystal chess-men given to Louis IX by an Arab chief. Adjoining, in the court were the old Roman ruins of the baths there is only one chamber with part of the roof remaining. We did some shopping, in the afternoon.

*Sunday, Sept. 20th, Paris.*

Went again to the French service in the morning, and the English, or I should say American in the afternoon, we saw Mr. and Mrs. Sidney Morse besides other friends we had met before.

*Monday, Sept. 21st, Paris.*

We have had an unusually quiet day. We made calls on the Wheelers and Mrs. Breeze but saw only the former. At five we all went to cousin

Edward Woolsey's rooms to dine. The Howlands were also there. We had a very pleasant time. In the evening when the gas was lighted on the Champs Elysées some of us went out escorted by Uncle, cousin Edward, and Charlie Woolsey to see the shows. We stopt at the whirligigs with wooden horses, upon which we were urged to mount to be turned round and round like a top. There are little booths also where gambling is carried on for candy and gingerbread. A board is whirled round and in the manner of a tetotum according as it stops, one has, for a sou, so much candy and gingerbread. Cousin Edward gave some sous to a boy, for him to try it, which he was most happy to do. Then we went to the Caffès Chantantes, where men and women in little houses, two sides glass, and one open to the air sing for three francs pay the whole evening. They sat there (the girls) in the cool evening air, with bare necks and arms. One girl sang quite well and was in no ways objectionable. If thought to have talent they are engaged for the opera. Mr. and Mrs. Wm. Aspenwall came in the evening, they live in the same house, as do also Mr. and Mrs. John A.

*Tuesday, Sept. 22nd, Paris.*

We went to the Blind Asylum this morning. It is vacation so there was not as much to see but still it was interesting. The boys are on one side and the girls on the other. In the boys department we saw the dining room, they have for dinner, soup, beef, and a desert, and four meals a day I believe. Many were playing on pianos of which they have sixty or seventy. They seem very fond of this. One, who played for us did remarkably well. Another was feeling of the raised notes, so as to learn the tune. Others were copying music, one boy would feel and tell each note, which the other by a piece of brass, cut into square holes, pricked into the paper. Their writing is quite elaborate, they have to make a number of marks for one letter, but they do it very fast indeed. The chapel is supplied with psalm books in their form; a monk takes charge of the service. They give concerts in the spring which are very fine, the orchestra are all blind. We then went into the girls' rooms and saw them making nets of twine and knitting, most seemed happy, some rather sad. The girls too played on the piano.

Then we went to the Louvre again, over some parts where we had been before and into the Musèe des Souverains, to a room filled with relics of Napoleon, his old grey cloth coat and cocked hat, a dress coat of green velvet and gold, one red and gold and one red silk. An elegant velvet cloak. His coronation crown said to be Charlemagne's. His gold filled dinner service; dishes, plates, knives, forks, and spoons, teapot etc. all in gold. Also a dressing, toilet set basin and pitcher, cups, and tooth brush, all of gold. There was his field table and arm chair, which did not match the rest of the articles and a field bureau. His watch and chain. Two Oriental saddles given to Napoleon by some Arabs. A gold rattle with coral handle, and whistle, which belonged to the young "king of Rome" Napoleon's son. A poignard given by Philip II of Spain to La Valette Grand Master of the Knights of Malta after the raising of the siege. It has a gold handle and sheath. This afternoon we have been to make calls. We found Mrs. Bruin and her daughter out and the Howlands also. Mr. and Mrs. Morse were at home. They are in the Hotel du Louvre a splendid house, able to contain a thousand persons. Mr. and Mrs. Wheeler called in the evening.

*Wednesday, Sept. 23rd, Paris.*
We went to the dressmaker's and packed our trunks. In the afternoon we went to cousin Edward's to bid good bye. Then to Dr. King's. But Mr. and Mrs. and Miss King were all out. Mrs. K. wears her Greek dress still and attracts a good deal of notice. Then Uncle, M. and I took a drive in the Bois de Boulogne to the Prè Catelan. There were some pretty flowers in the beds, and singing and dancing going on in one part.

*Thursday, Sept. 24th, Boulogne.*
Contrary to our expectations we are here for the night. We were to go at seven this morning but decided to wait until ten o'clock. We left Frances in Paris. We were seven hours in the cars and found on reaching here that the seven o'clock boat does not go tonight, almost the only night in the month when it does not go. This is a disappointment to us, as we can not now go, until two o'clock tomorrow, and this is a dull place to wait in.

*Friday, Sept. 25th, London.*
We took a walk in Boulogne in the morning it is a dreary kind of place, a half desert. At two we went on board the steamer and had a good passage over. We lay down most of the time, some persons were very sea-sick. The custom house officers are very strict in their search, they charged 13 or 14 dollars for three new bonnets and one dress. We took the train and in two and a half hours arrived in London at our old quarters in Thomas' Hotel.

*Saturday, Sept. 25th, London.*
London is quite deserted now. We spent a quiet day in the house mostly.

*Sunday, Sept. 27th, London.*
Went this morning to hear Dr. Cummings in Crown Court, Little

Russel Street, and had an excellent sermon on six verses of Psalm 139. The church was very crowded, but as we went early and gave a fee to the sexton so we had a very good seat. In the afternoon we wanted to go to the Bedford Chapel where Baptist Noel used to preach before he left the established church. It was not open until seven in the evening so we went into a Presbyterian chapel next, and heard a queer minister preach a queer sermon.

*Monday, Sept. 28th, London.*
Spent the day in some last business. We received our last letters, and also wrote some.

*Tuesday, Sept. 29th, London.*
Mary and I went out shopping. We drove far down into the city as far as Paternoster Row to some bookstores. There was a very thick mist and it was very disagreeable. We returned at two well tired.

*Wednesday, Sept. 30th, London.*
Mary and I went to Westminster Abbey again. On the way seeing something going on at the Parliament House we stopt to see it. It was the ceremony of swearing in the new lord mayor. There was a procession in carriages of sheriffs, aldermen and mayor in their robes. One carriage was most gorgeous and looked quite old fashioned. We went into the abbey but as the service was about to commence we could only look a few minutes at the "poets corner."

*Thursday, Oct. 1st, London.*
We had intended to go to Liverpool and have time to rest there but as some things from Paris had not arrived, and on other accounts we put it off until the next day. It was damp and I had a bad cold, so I stayed in all day.

*Friday, Oct. 2nd, Liverpool.*
Left old London for the last time. We were six hours in reaching Liverpool. The hotel was full and our accommodations poor.

*Monday, Oct. 12th, "The Asia"*
Having probably passed through half of our voyage I write a few of our sad experiences. We left Saturday morning in a little steamer, to go out into the river to the old *Asia*. It seemed very familiar. Saturday and Sunday were quite calm and we were not sick until Sunday evening and

then it began and Monday was a miserable day. O the horrors of the sea! We had an English poet on board, Mr. Mackay, and he having experienced them has been desired to pour fourth his melodies in verse upon that subject. We have had nearly the whole time a very rough sea. Friday night was the worst we have had. Few slept all night. It was hard to keep from falling out of our berths, the ship pitched so. The wind blew furiously that night and we were truly glad to see the break of day. The waves have washed over the deck so much, that we have been obliged to stay in the cabin nearly all the time. We have made a pleasant acquaintance with the Clarks of Brooklyn.

*Friday, Oct. 16th, The Asia*
Since I last wrote we have had better weather and have been up in the air more, for which we began to pine very much. When we were upon the banks of Newfoundland I saw the spout of a small whale. Today we were aroused quite early by the sudden stopping of the ship and getting up to see what was the matter, found that it was to take on board the pilot. He says we have been expected for two days and a half. He brought newspapers which told of many failures in business. There is some hope of our getting into dock tonight if the weather is good. If not we shall cruise about outside the Hook. I am truly thankful to be so near the end of our voyage, we have been most kindly protected all through our wanderings. It seems strange and most joyful to think of being home again tomorrow. So ends my journey to Europe, full of pleasure, and profit, and yet with some drawbacks.

# Index